AF470954

Complete this form to be in the draw to win a week's FREE B&B stay. Simply have the host sign after each stay. When you have obtained eight signatures mail the form to us, postage paid. Winner will be drawn on 7 January 2015.

Name: ____

Phone: ____

Email: ____

Date: _______________________________

B&B Name: _______________________________

Host Signature: _______________________________

Date: _______________________________

B&B Name: _______________________________

Host Signature: _______________________________

Date: _______________________________

B&B Name: _______________________________

Host Signature: _______________________________

Date: _______________________________

B&B Name: _______________________________

Host Signature: _______________________________

Date: _______________________________

B&B Name: _______________________________

Host Signature: _______________________________

Date: _______________________________

B&B Name: _______________________________

Host Signature: _______________________________

Date: _______________________________

B&B Name: _______________________________

Host Signature: _______________________________

Date: _______________________________

B&B Name: _______________________________

Host Signature: _______________________________

The New Zealand Bed & Breakfast Book 2014

www.bnb.co.nz

MOONSHINE
PRESS

Published by:

Moonshine Press
P.O. Box 6843
Wellington
New Zealand
Tel: +64 4 385-2615
Fax: +64 4 385-2694
Web: www.bnb.co.nz
Email: info@bnb.co.nz

Welcome to this edition of The Bed & Breakfast Book

The New Zealand Bed & Breakfast Book is not just an accommodation guide – it is an introduction to a uniquely New Zealand holiday experience. The best holidays are often remembered by the friends one makes. How many of us have loved a country because of one or two memorable individuals we encountered? For the traveller who wants to experience the real New Zealand and get to know its people, bed and breakfast offers an opportunity to do just that.

We recommend you don't try to travel too far in one day. Take time to enjoy the company of your hosts and other local people. You will find New Zealand hosts friendly and generous, and eager to share their local knowledge with you.

Bed & Breakfast in New Zealand means a warm welcome and a unique holiday experience. Most B&B accommodation is in private homes with a sprinkling of guesthouses and small hotels. Each listing in the guide has been written by the host themselves and you will discover their warmth and personality through their writing.

Carradale Manor

Inspection & Standards

Qualmark™ is New Zealand tourism's official mark of quality. All QualmarkTM licenced accommodation listed in this directory means they have been independently assessed as professional and trustworthy, so you can book and buy with confidence. They will meet your essential requirements of cleanliness, safety, security and comfort; and offer a range and quality of services appropriate to their star grade.

Bed & Breakfast Association of New Zealand logo represents the largest organisation of hosted accommodation providers in New Zealand. It assures you of a warm welcome from friendly, helpful hosts. Accommodations displaying this logo are regularly assessed every two years and have met the quality standards set by the Association.

Heritage Inns; A collection of luxury historic hosted character bed and breakfast lodges across NZ, are superior and often recommended by tourists. Our B&Bs have knowledgeable and friendly hosts. Our luxury accommodation ranges from the quiet honeymoon lodge in boutique romantic locations to central city accommodation - rivaling superior apartments, hotels or motels. Alternatively, enjoy the genuine NZ experience of an idyllic farmstay, lodge or luxury country B&B.

Finding your way around

We travel from north to south listing the towns as we come to them. In addition, we've divided New Zealand into geographical regions, a map of which is included at the start of each chapter. In some regions, such as Southland, our listings take a detour off the north to south route, and follow their nose – it will soon become obvious.

Hosts in *The New Zealand Bed & Breakfast Book* are committed to offering quality hospitality. If you receive hospitality which is less than you expected please discuss your concerns with your hosts at the time. If you are not satisfied you should contact the publishers who will take up the matter with the hosts. If you are still not satisfied the publishers will refund their assessment of a fair proportion of the tariff you paid.

10% Voucher

At the front of the book there are five 10% discount vouchers. Each voucher entitles you to a 10% discount off your stay. Redeem the voucher at a participating B&B displaying the logo.numbers.

Be in the draw to win a week's FREE B&B stay

Fill in th eform at the back of the book and go in the draw to win a week's FREE B&B stay. You need the signatures of 8 hosts, one for each place you have stayed. Mail the completed form to us. The postage is paid. The winner will be drawn on 7 January 2015.

Calling NZ numbers from outside the country

The New Zealand country code is **64**. Use your usual international dialling prefix then '64' and drop of the initial '0' from the listed telephone number. For example, if the B&B phone number is **(07) 123 4567**, you might dial **0011 64 7 123 4567**. This method also works for mobiles.

About Bed & Breakfast

Our B&Bs range from homely to luxurious, but you can always be assured of generous hospitality.

Types of accommodation

Traditional B&B Generally small owner-occupied home accommodation usually with private guest living and dining areas.

Homestay A homestay is a B&B where you share the family's living area.

Farmstay Country accommodation, usually on a working farm.

Self-contained Separate self-contained accommodation, with kitchen and living/dining room. Breakfast provisions usually provided at least for the first night.

Separate/suite Similar to self-contained but without kitchen facilities. Living/dining facilities may be limited.

Bathrooms

Ensuite and private bathrooms are for your use exclusively.

Guests share bathroom means you will be sharing with other guests.

Family share means you will be sharing with the family.

Tariff

The prices listed are in New Zealand dollars and include GST. Prices listed are subject to change, and any change to listed prices will be stated at time of booking. Some hosts offer a discount for children – this applies to age 12 or under unless otherwise stated. Most of our B&Bs will accept credit cards.

Reservations

We recommend you contact your hosts well in advance to be sure of confirming your accommodation. Most hosts require a deposit so make sure you understand their cancellation policy. Please let your hosts know if you have to cancel, they will have spent time preparing for you. You may also book accommodation through some travel agents or via specialised B&B reservation services.

Breakfast & Dinner

Breakfast is included in the tariff, with each host offering their own menu. You'll be surprised at the range of delicious breakfasts available, many using local produce. If you would like dinner most hosts require 24 hours notice.

Smoking

Most of our B&Bs are non-smoking, but smoking is permitted outside. Listings displaying the no smoking logo do not permit smoking anywhere on the property. B&Bs which have a smoking area inside mention this in their text.

Accessibility

Certified as being wheelchair accessible.

Schedule of Standards

General

- Friendly, warm greeting at door by host
- Local tourism and transport information available to guests
- Property appearance neat and tidy, internally and externally
- Absolute cleanliness of the home in all areas used by the guests
- Absolute cleanliness of kitchen, refrigerator and food storage areas
- Gate or roadside identification of property
- Protective clothing and footwear available for farmstay guests
- Hosts accept responsibility to comply with local body bylaws
- Host will be present to welcome and farewell guests
- Hosts' pets and young children mentioned in listing
- Smoke alarms in each guest bedroom and above each landing
- Evacuation advice card displayed in each bedroom (recommended)
- Working torch beside every bed
- Suitable fire extinguisher in kitchen and on landing of each upper floor (recommended)
- Fire blanket in kitchen (recommended)

Hosts accept responsibility to comply with applicable laws and regulations

- Fire safety laws and requirements
- Insurances
- Swimming and spa pool regulations
- Other laws impacting on operation of a B&B

Bedrooms

Each bedroom solely dedicated to guests with…

- Bed heating
- Heating
- Light controlled from the bed
- Wardrobe space with variety of hangers
- Drawers
- Good quality floor covering
- Mirror
- Power point near a mirror
- Waste paper basket
- Drinking glasses
- Clean pillows with additional available
- No Host family items stored in the room
- Night light for guidance to W.C. if not adjacent to bedroom
- Blinds/curtains on all windows where appropriate
- Good quality mattresses in sound condition on a sound base
- Clean bedding appropriate to the climate, with extra available

Bathroom & toilet facilities

At least one bathroom adequately ventilated and equipped with…

- Bath or shower
- Wash handbasin and mirror
- Covered wastebasket in bathroom
- Extra toilet roll
- Lock on bathroom and toilet doors
- Electric razor point if bedrooms are without a suitable power point
- Soap, towels, bathmat, facecloths, fresh for each new guest
- Towels changed or dried daily for guests staying more than one night
- Sufficient bathroom and toilet facilities to serve family and guests

New Zealand & Regions

North Island

South Island

North Island

Northland
Houhora
Coopers Beach
Kaitaia
Ahipara
Okaihau
Kerikeri
Paihia
Russell
Opua
Pakaraka
Bay of Islands
Whangarei
Taiharuru
Whangarei Heads
Ruakaka
Waipu
Waipu Cove
Matakohe
Te Hana
Wellsford
Sandspit
Warkworth
Snells Beach
Puhoi
Orewa
Kaukapakapa
Silverdale
Whangapa
Helensville
Albany
Auckland
0   Kilometres   45
0   Miles   27
1
10
1
12
12
14
1

Doubtless Bay Lodge   Coopers Beach

B&B
4 km N of Mangonui

33 Cable Bay Block Road, Coopers Beach, 420
(09) 406 1661 or 021 824 571
enquiries@doubtlessbaylodge.co.nz
www.doubtlessbaylodge.co.nz

Double: $105–$125
Single: $75–$85
Children: $25

4 Bedrooms: 3Q 1T
Bathrooms: 4 ensuite

Ian and Barbara Easterbrook

Friendly New Zealand hosts. Breakfast on the balcony or in the dining room with panoramic views over Doubtless Bay and surrounding countryside. Short walk to the golden sands of Coopers Beach and local shops. Each room has own ensuite, Sky TV, fridge, tea/coffee making facilities, Wi-Fi and own private entrance. Guest laundry and barbeque available. Cape Reinga tours, fishing trips and golf games can be arranged. Visit many historic places, beautiful isolated beaches and local wineries in the area. A great holiday destination.

- Own kitchenettes – no cooking
- Queens with table and chairs, set of bunks available for children, also a divan in one queen room
- Full breakfast
- Children welcome
- Internet available

Bush Walk B&B/Homestay   Kaitaia

B&B Homestay
15 km S of Kaitaia

42 Te Rore Road, RD 1, Kaitaia 0481
(09) 408 4959 or 021 182 7553
sandra21madhousefarm@xtra.co.nz
www.bnb.co.nz/BushWalkBB/Homestay.html

Double: $90
Single: $70
Children: 3–12 years half price, under 3 free

2 Bedrooms: 1Q 1S
Bathrooms: 1 family share

Sandra

Enjoy a relaxing sojourn in a peaceful bush setting and experience all Northland has to offer. A warm welcome awaits guests who come to stay at this unusual 'A' frame, timber interior home situated on six acres of garden and native bush. Wake up to birdsong and at the end of the day relax and watch the sun set behind the hills. BBQ facilities are available.

- Full breakfast
- Pet-free home
- Children welcome

Ahipara

Ahipara Beachfront

2 self-contained and serviced apartments
15 km SW of Kaitaia

14 Kotare Street, Ahipara
90 Mile Beach, Northland 0449
(09) 409 4007 or 021 227 3376
pauljenny@beachfront.net.nz
www.beachfront.net.nz

Double: $120–$350   Single: $120–$350
Children: $30 per extra person over the age of 2 yrs

4 Bedrooms   Bathrooms: 4 ensuite

Paul and Jenny Steele

- Breakfast: $15–$25
- Dinner: $60 pp by arrangement
- Breakfast by arrangement
- Children welcome
- Internet available

With the sand of 90 Mile Beach at your doorstep and unsurpassed surf views from every pillow this is the ultimate in prime oceanfront accommodation. You'll love it! Choose between an upstairs two double bedroom apartment with sundecks or at ground level the Studio with an additional adjoining double bedroom option. Wi-Fi. Cape Reinga Tour pickup from door – links golf course five minutes away. Torpedo fishing a specialty. Paul and Jenny are 5th generatiion New Zealanders with a cat called Sunshine who is not allowed in the apartments.

Kerikeri, Bay of Islands

Kerikeri Inlet View

B&B Homestay Farmstay
10 km N of Kerikeri Central

99C Furness Road, RD 3 Kerikeri, 293
(09) 407 7477 or 027 567 4477
Kerikeri_inlet_view@hotmail.com
www.bnb.co.nz/kerikeriinletview.html

Double: $85
Single: $50
Children: $15

3 Bedrooms: 2Q 2S
Bathrooms: 1 ensuite, 1 guest share, 1 private

Trish and Ryan Daniells

- Dinner: $20 by arrangement
- Full breakfast
- Pets welcome
- Children welcome
- Internet available

We welcome you to our spacious home on top of our 1100 acre beef and sheep farm. Enjoy the panoramic views from the Kerikeri Inlet to the Bay of Islands while you relax in our spa pool. Join us for breakfast consisting of seasonal fruit, homemade bread and butter, free-range chook eggs, and our own sausages, before exploring the many attractions around Kerikeri. We have avocado and olive orchards and free farm tours. Note: Please phone for detailed directions. We can speak some Japanese.

Glenfalloch

B&B Homestay
20 km N of Paihia

48 Landing Road, Kerikeri
(09) 407 5471
glenfall@ihug.co.nz
www.kerikeri-accommodation.co.nz

Double: $90–$115
Single: $80–$90
Children: $25

VISA MasterCard

4 Bedrooms: 1K 3Q 1S
Bathrooms: 3 ensuite, 1 private

Keith

Venture down Glenfalloch's driveway to our secluded bed and breakfast, nestled in a garden paradise. Enjoy the hospitality of Keith. Relax in the spa and swimming pool and on teh decks, or for the energetic there is lawn tennis. Glenfalloch is just 500 metres from Kerikeri's Stone Store and Kemp Mission House, and adjacent to the lovely Rainbow Falls walking track. Kerikeri is unique and offers some good golf courses within short distances, lovely shops and excellent restaurants.

- Dinner: $30pp by arrangement
- Full breakfast
- Children welcome

Landing Cottage Bed and Breakfast

Luxury B&B
3 km NE of Kerikeri

184 Landing Road, Kerikeri, Bay of Islands 0230
(09) 401 7974
elaine@landingcottage.co.nz
www.landingcottage.co.nz

Double: $170–$190   Single: $150–$170
Children: under 5 stay free. Children 12 and under
$45 per child

VISA MasterCard eftpos NEW ZEALAND LIMITED

3 Bedrooms: 1K 1Q 1T
Bathrooms: 1 private

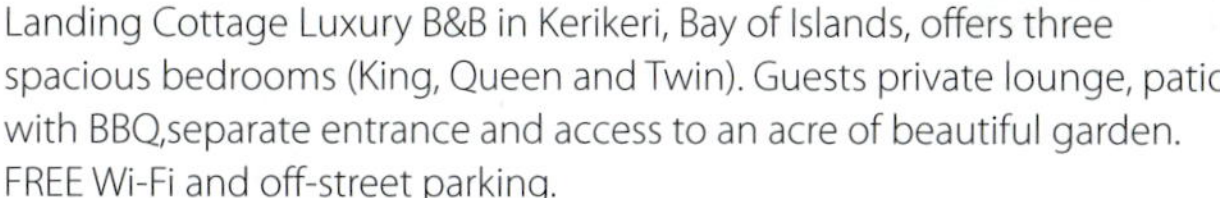

Elaine and Ian McGovern

Landing Cottage Luxury B&B in Kerikeri, Bay of Islands, offers three spacious bedrooms (King, Queen and Twin). Guests private lounge, patio with BBQ,separate entrance and access to an acre of beautiful garden. FREE Wi-Fi and off-street parking.

We are suitable for families or groups of up to six people (Children Welcome) and our single-party booking policy ensures your privacy.

Close to Kerikeri with all the Restaurants etc. but quiet and peaceful.

Watch our video for a good overview of what we offer.

- Extra adults $70 per night
- Dinner: free booking no card charges
- Full breakfast
- Children welcome
- No smoking on property
- Internet available

Kerikeri

The Carriage House – Bay of Islands

Farmstay&Cottage Apartment with Kitchen
2 km E of Kerikeri

175 Kerikeri Inlet Road, Bay of Islands, Kerikeri, 245
(09) 407 9854
sylvia@thecarriagehouse.co.nz
www. The-Carriage-House.co.nz

Double: $160–$250
Children: $50

VISA MasterCard

2 Bedrooms: 1K 1KT
Bathrooms: 2 ensuite

Adrian and Sylvia Garrett

- Laundry with washing machine, dryer, iron & board
- Accommodation only
- Pets welcome
- Children welcome
- No smoking on property
- Internet available

Self-contained cottage apartment on horse breeding farm overlooking Kerikeri Inlet. A Rate for two Guests and A Rate for four Guests. Two ensuite king bedrooms, large Living Room, Dining area, Fully equipped Kitchen and laundry. Two km to historic town and restaurants. Go to website for more Photos and driving Directions. Check availability and get instant confirmation. Kerikeri is three hours North of Auckland. A good central location to explore beaches and Mangonui to North, Waitangi and Russell to South and Paihia for boat trips. Kerikeri first settlement and StoneStore are just a short walk.

Paihia, Bay of Islands

Craicor Accommodation

Luxury B&B • Apartment with Kitchen
0.5 km SE of Wharf

49 Kings Road Paihia, P.O. Box 15 Paihia 0247, Paihia, Bay of Islands
(09) 402 7882
craicor@actrix.gen.nz
www.craicor-accom.co.nz

Double: $180   **Single:** $130

VISA MasterCard

2 Bedrooms: 2K 2S
Bathrooms: 2 ensuite

Garth Craig and Anne Corbett

- King size beds luxury 100% cotton linen, down comforters.
- Continental breakfast optional $10pp. Multi day special rates available.
- Breakfast by arrangement
- Not suitable for children
- Internet available

The perfect spot for those seeking a quiet, sunny and central location. Discover the Garden Suite and Tree House. Self-contained modern apartments nestled in a garden setting with trees that almost hug you, native birds and sea views. Each apartment has ensuite bathroom, fully equipped kitchen for self-catering, super king bed, TV, insect screens and is tastefully decorated to reflect the natural colours of the surroundings. Safe off-street parking, all within a five minute stroll to the waterfront, restaurants and town centre.

Chalet Romantica

Luxury B&B
0.2 km S of Wharf

6 Bedggood Close, Paihia/Bay of Islands, 200
(09) 402 8270 or 027 226 6400
info@chaletpaihia.co.nz
www.chaletromantica.co.nz

Double: $135–$299
Children: $45 sharing room with parents incl.
breakfast

VISA MasterCard **eftpos** NEW ZEALAND LIMITED

4 Bedrooms: 2KT **2**Q
Bathrooms: 3 ensuite, 1 private

Ed and Inge Amsler

- Self catering apartment $179–$279
- Full breakfast
- Internet available

Spoil yourself and experience the magic of Chalet Romantica. We are Inge and Eddie and have been part of Paihia's hospitality and tourism industry for many years. Our passion is our B&B and we love to take the time to help you tailor your visit, so your holiday to our part of the world will be truly memorable.

All our upstairs rooms have balconies with stunning seaviews, quality furnishings and fittings, free Wi-Fi, crisp linen and extra comfy beds. One B&B room has garden views and a private patio. We are in central town within a stroll to the 'Bay of Islands Dolphin Departure Pier' and fabulous restaurants/café's and beaches. Feel free to use our in-house heated swimming pool, spa, gym and laundry facilities. Beautiful Bay of Islands views are the backdrop for a delicious full gourmet breakfast sourced from fresh local produce and delicatessen. Our small hobby farm with pet animals form part of the landscape surrounding Chalet Romantica.

We'd love to welcome you to our home and to share our glorious location with you!

Paihia

B&B • Apartment with Kitchen
1 km S of Paihia Central

30 H Sullivans Road, Paihia, 200
(09) 402 8606 or (09) 402 8606
allviewlodge@xtra.co.nz
www.allviewlodge.co.nz

Double: $225–$295

VISA MasterCard

3 Bedrooms: 3Q 2S
Bathrooms: 1 ensuite, 1 private

Robyn and Peter Rhodes

- Prices are seasonal. Extra person $60 a 2 day min stay may apply during peak season.
- Bathrooms: island View Suite has large 2 person bath.
- Full breakfast
- No smoking on property
- Internet available
- Courtesy pickup from Kerikeri airport or bus depot
- Trip Advisor Certificate of Excellence Award

Showcasing Paihia's best private beachfront location, uninterrupted sea and island views. Architecturally designed for your pleasure and privacy. Stroll along the beach to restaurants, cafés and tourist pier, crusie 144 islands, hole in the rock tour or take a 10 min ferry ride to historic Russell. Our one bedroom suite has two queen beds, ensuite with a two person bath. Our two bedroom suite has one queen bed and two single beds, private bathroom. Both suites have large walk-in showers, toiletries, hairdriers, bathrobes. Spacious dining/lounge areas with kitchenette, TVs, garden and patio areas from which dolphins are often seen. Furnishings and fittings are to a high standard. Guests full laundry adjacent to both suites. Private access to both suites is by external stairway or internal lift. Comprehensive breakfast menu is included in tariff and served in our conservatory ding area. Local art and sculptures displayed throughour the Lodge. Friendly local hosts. Complimentary kayaks, start of the coastal walking track. Tariff for single, extra person, longer stays or off-peak are available on application. We have two friendly toy poodles, Cleo and King Louis.

Admiral's View Lodge

Separate Suite • Apartment with Kitchen
1 km N of Paihia

2 MacMurray Road, Paihia, 200
(09) 402 6236 or 0800 247 234
admiralsviewlodge@ihug.co.nz
www.admiralsviewlodge.co.nz

Double: $95–$195
Children: welcome in apartments and twin studios

11 Bedrooms: 4K 6Q 2D 6T 11S
Bathrooms: 11 ensuite

Penny and Craig Boles

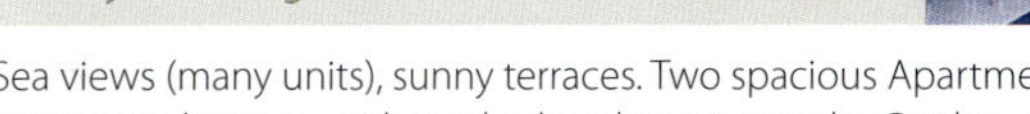

Sea views (many units), sunny terraces. Two spacious Apartments, seven Luxury studios, two with spa baths, plus our popular Garden studios.

Meander along to the beach, restaurants/cafés and activities, take the ferry to romantic Russell or soak up historic Waitangi. Meet our children – Guy and Anna – and our friendly cat, Eva.

Sky TV; airconditioning (most units); high speed internet; free internet kiosk, DVD players, activity booking service; free bikes and tennis; guest BBQs and laundry; filtered water.

- Apartments $175–$275
- Bathrooms: all of our rooms have showers and our two premium studios both have a luxurious double spa bath.
- Quiet location
- Breakfast by arrangement
- Children welcome
- Internet available

Morepork Riverside Lodge

B&B Homestay
8 km NW of Paihia

846 Puketona Road, Paihia, Bay of Islands
(09) 402 5577 or 021 986 687
enquiries@moreporklodge.co.nz
www.moreporklodge.co.nz

Double: $140–$195
Single: $125–$160
Children: May not suit, enquire before booking

3 Bedrooms: 2K 1KT 1S
Bathrooms: 3 ensuite

Paul and Barbara

Welcome to our B&B/Homestay set in four acres on the Waitangi River. Stroll through native bush and gardens, home to many NZ birds including Moreporks. Feed our alpacas, sheep and goat. Meet our timid, gentle cat. We provide full breakfast. We'll happily advise you on local attractions and restaurants. We offer evening meals and we're both 'Kiwi' born and bred. Our rooms have an ensuite (one with a large bath), TV/DVDs, Wi-Fi, tea/coffee/refrigerator and welcome pack. Two have private decks.

- Special packages for special occasions
- Gourmet or light evening meals by arrangement
- Full breakfast
- Internet available

Paihia, Bay of Islands — River Retreat

Luxury B&B
8 km SW of Paihia

838 Puketona Road, Paihia
(09) 402 7092
jan@riverretreat.co.nz
www.riverretreat.co.nz

Double: $170–$230

2 Bedrooms: 2Q
Bathrooms: 2 ensuite

Roger and Jan Turnbull

- 2 Queen sized
- Continental breakfast
- Pet-free home
- Not suitable for children
- No smoking on property
- Internet available

River Retreat is set amongst two acres of gardens and native plantings. It is strategically positioned to capture the best of the tranquil Waitangi river front setting. We offer luxury Bed and Breakfast accommodation in two purpose built queen sized rooms. Each room has its own entrance and private deck and are situated in a separate pavilion.

Enjoy a continental breakfast in this unique architect designed home.

Opua, Paihia, Bay of Islands — Rose Cottage

B&B • Separate Suite
5 km S of Paihia

37A Oromahoe Road, Opua 0200, Bay of Islands
(09) 402 8099 or 027 605 9560
pdjansen@xtra.co.nz
www.bnb.co.nz/rosecottageopua.html

Double: $120–$140
Single: $100
Children: Not suitable

2 Bedrooms: 1Q 1D
Bathrooms: 1 private

Pat and Don Jansen

- Continental breakfast
- Pet-free home
- Not suitable for children
- No smoking on property
- Internet available

Welcome to our peaceful hilltop home. Sunny guest rooms open onto a private deck overlooking panoramic upper harbour, bush and rural views. Guest wing has private entrance, tea/coffee and fridge facilities, also TV. and free Wi-Fi. Hosting one party at a time is ideal for 2,3 or four guests. Close to coastal and bush walks, also wineries. Pat is a retired nurse and Don a retired carpenter. Interests include hosting guests, local history, gardening, reading and fishing. We look forward to sharing this beautiful and historic area with you.

Seascape

B&B • Apartment with Kitchen • Self-contained Flat

5 km S of Paihia

17 English Bay Road, Opua, Bay of Islands
(09) 402 7650 or 027 475 6793
frankandvanessa@leadley.co.nz
www.bnb.co.nz/leadley.html

Double: $120–$140
Single: $100–$120

VISA MasterCard

1 Bedroom: 1Q
Bathrooms: 1 private

Vanessa and Frank Leadley

Seascape is on a tranquil bush-clad ridge. Enjoy spectacular water views and our beautifully landscaped garden, stroll the coastal walk-way, experience the many activities in the Bay, or relax on your private deck. Our interests include NZ and international travel, music, art, gardening and Rotary. Our fully self-contained flat has queen bed, TV, laundry, kitchen, BBQ, free Wi fi, own entrance and deck. Attractive continental breakfast provided daily in the flat, or self-cater for a reduced tariff. Two night minimum preferred.

- Self-contained flat $120–$140
- Continental provisions supplied
- Pet-free home
- No smoking on property
- Internet available

Please let others know how you enjoyed your B&B experience.
Add a comment to the listing on the internet.
www.bnb.co.nz.

Matauwhi Bay, Russell, Bay of Islands

Ounuwhao B&B

B&B • Separate Suite • Cottage with Kitchen • Seperate Suite

1 km E of Russell

16 Hope Avenue, Matauwhi Bay, Russell 0202
(09) 403 7310 or 027 414 1310
thenicklins@xtra.co.nz
www.bedandbreakfastbayofislands.co.nz

Double: $200–$350   Single: $160–$200
Children: under 12 $45

7 Bedrooms: 2K 4Q 3T 2S
Bathrooms: 5 ensuite, 2 private

Marilyn Nicklin

- 4 in guest lodge, 1 in garden suite, 4 in cottage
- Self-contained & garden suite double $280–$350 plus $25 child and extra adult sharing room in guest lodge=$50.00
- Full breakfast
- Children welcome
- No smoking on property
- Internet available
- Complimentary afternoon tea on arrival
- Laundry service available

Welcome to historic Russell, the Heart of the Bay of Islands and the first settled area of NZ. Take a step back into a bygone era and spend some time with us in our delightful, nostalgic, immaculately restored Victorian vill (circa 1894). Enjoy your own large guest lounge; tea/coffee and biscuits always available, with open fire in the cooler months, and wrap-around verandahs for you to relax and take in the warm sea breezes. Each of our four queen rooms have traditional wallpapers and paintwork, with hand-made patchwork quilts and fresh flowers to create a lovingly detailed, traditional romantic interior. Breakfast is served in our farmhouse kitchen around the large kauri dining table or alfresco on the verandah if you wish. It is an all home-made affair; from the freshly baked fruit and nut bread, to the yummy daily special and the jam conserves. Our self-contained cottage is set in park-like grounds for your privacy and enjoyment: with two double bedrooms, it is ideal for a family or two couples travelling together. It has a large lounge overlooking the reserve and out into the bay, a sunroom and fully self-contained kitchen.

Villa Russell

Russell, Bay of Islands

Luxury B&B
0.2 km N of Russell Central

2 Little Queen Street, Russell, Bay of Islands
(09) 403 8845 or 027 492 8912
info@villarussell.co.nz
www.villarussell.co.nz

Double: $185–$320
Children: Rollaway bed available, suitable for
children up to 6 years

3 Bedrooms: 2KT 1Q
Bathrooms: 3 ensuite

Sue and Steve Western

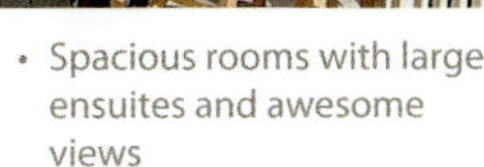

Enjoy a welcoming visit to Villa Russell, two minutes from the beach and
Russell's restaurants. Relax with magnificent views of the bay and wharf
from the deck of our beautifully restored 1910 Villa, or from one of two
spacious suites in the new guest cottage. A short walk takes you to a surf
beach or up the historic Flagstaff Hill. Off-street parking provided. Charters
on our 11.6 metre yacht Kingfisher may also be arranged to sail the Bay of
Islands.

- Spacious rooms with large
  ensuites and awesome
  views
- Full breakfast
- No smoking on property
- Internet available

Pipiroa Bay Homestay and Garden

Okiato, Russell, Bay of Islands

B&B • Apartment with Kitchen
9 km SW of Russell

348 Aucks Road, Russell, 272
(09) 403 8856 or 027 295 3640
gpfranklin@xtra.co.nz
www.bay-of-islands.co.nz/accomm/pipiroa.html

Double: $150–$150
Single: $100–$100
Children: $20 for each child

4 Bedrooms: 3Q 2S
Bathrooms: 2 ensuite, 1 guest share

Paula and Gary Franklin

Nestled in the hillside, overlooking historically significant Pipiroa Bay, at
Okiato Point, handy to Russell, Opua and Paihia, our warm north facing
purpose built homestay bed and breakfast will delight you. As kiwis, with
years of sailing experience in the Bay of Islands, we will ensure you enjoy
the best the Bay can offer. Choose from our self-contained apartment
and bed and breakfast suite and savour our delicious breakfast using
fresh produce from the garden. Other meals by arrangement. A shy silver
persian cat also lives with us.

- Off peak specials.
  Waterbased activities from
  $20 per person
- Dinner: $40 per person
  includes wine
- Full breakfast
- Pets welcome
- Children welcome
- Internet available

Russell, Bay of Islands   Lesleys BnB

B&B
1 km E of Russell

1 Pomare Rd. Russell,, 202
(09) 40 37 099 or 021 1080 369
three.gs@xtra.co.nz
www.lesleys.co.nz

Double: $130–$170
Single: $110–$130
Children: I have a great loft bedroom option for kids

VISA MasterCard

2 Bedrooms: 2Q **1**D **1**S
Bathrooms: 1 private

Lesley Coleman

- Bathrooms: antique clawfoot bath
- Dinner: Excellent dinner upon request.
- Special breakfast
- Children welcome
- No smoking on property
- Internet available

Lesleys B&B is one kilometre from Russell town, a ten minute walk past Matauwhi Bay to the wharf where boats leave daily to sail amongst the Bay of Islands.

Lesley is a known northland painter exhibiting in local galleries and in her home. Have an excellent cooked breakfast (she's also a chef).

The 'Fern room' has a fridge and tea/coffee making facilities andits own entrance. There is a guest conservatory with lots of books and comfy couch. Billy the terrior lives here too.

Our B&Bs range from homely to luxurious,
but you can always be sure of superior hospitality.

Bellrock Lodge

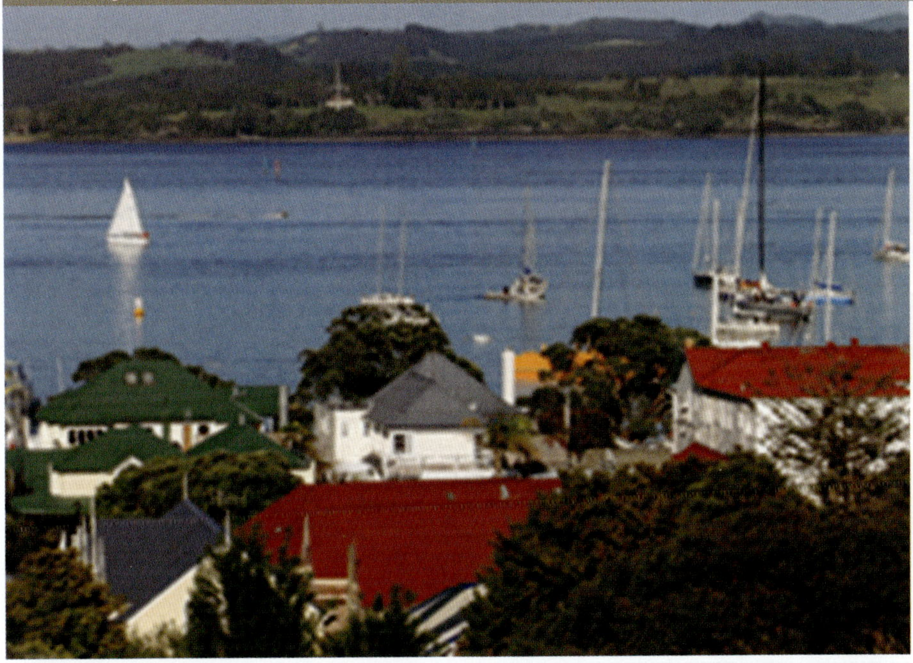

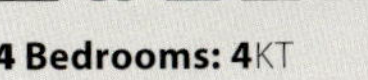

Luxury B&B • Luxury Lodge
0.4 km E of Russell Waterfront

22 Chapel Street, Russell, 202
(09) 403 7422 or 021 0263 7446
bellrockbandb@xtra.co.nz
www.russellbnb.co.nz

Double: $200–$280
Single: $175–$255
Children: No, but responsible teenagers welcome

4 Bedrooms: 4KT
Bathrooms: 4 ensuite

Peter and Lorraine Blignaut

- Beds can be made up in either Super King or 2 singles
- Breakfast continental ($15pp) or cooked ($30) available at extra charge.
- Dinner not provided
- Full breakfast
- Pet-free home
- Not suitable for children
- No smoking on property
- Internet available

For the best views in Russell, come to Bellrock. We are on the hill overlooking the lovely village of Russell and the bay. From your spacious ensuite room and private patio, you can see all the activity of the village. Bellrock is only a 5min stroll to the wharf and the waterfront with it's cafés, restaurants, bars and shops. Each room has its own private entrance, TV, DVD,Radio/CD/iPod dock, aircon, fully equipped kitchenette, two leather recliners, table and two chairs and patio furniture. Spacious bathrooms consist of shower, toilet, bidet, two hand basins, heater and heated towel rail. The wheelchair bathroom has only one basin and no bidet.

For the exclusive use of our guests, we have a guest lounge/dining room and bar on 1st floor. Here you can watch SKY TV ,DVD or listen to music. On the adjoining patio there is a gas barbeque, table and chairs. Off street parking is provided and Wi-Fi is available throughout the premises. A fully equipped laundry is available with washing machines, dryers, ironing board and iron.

We share our home with two cats, Tigger and Tomcat and with Shaka a black labrador.

Matakohe, Northland — The Old Post Office Guesthouse

B&B • Guest House
1 km E of Paparoa

Corner of State Highway 12 & Oakleigh Road, PO Box 79, Paparoa 0543
(09) 431 6444 or mob 021 1627 185
paparoadeb@xtra.co.nz
www.oldpostofficeguesthouse.co.nz

Double: $100–$110
Single: $55–$55

VISA MasterCard

6 Bedrooms: 2Q 1D 2T 4S
Bathrooms: 1 ensuite, 4 private

Deb and Kevin

- Dinner: $30–3 courses or by arrangement; vegetarian available
- Continental breakfast
- Pet-free home
- Children welcome
- Weddings and functions
- No smoking on property
- Internet available

From the moment you step inside you will succumb to the character and charm of this lovely old historic building (circa 1903), with delightful cottage garden and rural backdrop. Enjoy our true Kiwi hospitality, cuisine and homely atmosphere with separate guests lounges and free tea/coffee. Dinner by prior arrangement. Local restaurants Wednesay to Sunday. Spend a day at the world famous Matakohe Kauri Museum only 8 km away or if, like us, you enjoy the outdoors, visit Pahi Beach or our local bush reserve and walk around the local circa 1750's pa site and native bush reserve.

Whangarei — Lotus Lodge

B&B Farmstay • Self-contained Studio (double)
7 km N of Whangarei City

58 Great North Road, Springs Flat, Kamo, Whangarei
(09) 435 2294 or 021 207 5706
lotuslodge@clear.net.nz
www.bnb.co.nz/Lotus Lodge.html

Double: $120–$140
Single: $80–$90

3 Bedrooms: 2D 1T
Bathrooms: 1 guest share

Keith and Jill Clarke

- Studio – 1 Double
- Dinner by arrangement
- Continental breakfast

We invite you to share in our 200 acres of paradise. Two minutes from Kamo, five minutes to golf course. Experience moving cattle/sheep with farm dog Del, view native bush, find amazing limestone rocks, laze in the quietness of the garden, or read in the lounge. Make this your stop for seeing the north – beaches, fishing, diving, kauri forests, shopping, all in a days outing. Our interests: gardening, classic cars, travel, art and people.

Top Storey Bed & Breakfast — Whangarei

B&B Homestay
14 km E of Whangarei

73 Scott Road, Tamaterau, Parua Bay,
Whangarei, 174
(09) 436 2220 or 021 46 3330
info@whangareibandb.co.nz
www.whangareibandb.co.nz

Double: $80–$130
Children: under 2 free
VISA MasterCard

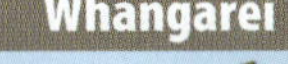

2 Bedrooms: 2Q **4**S
Bathrooms: 2 private

Jane and Ian Kippenberger

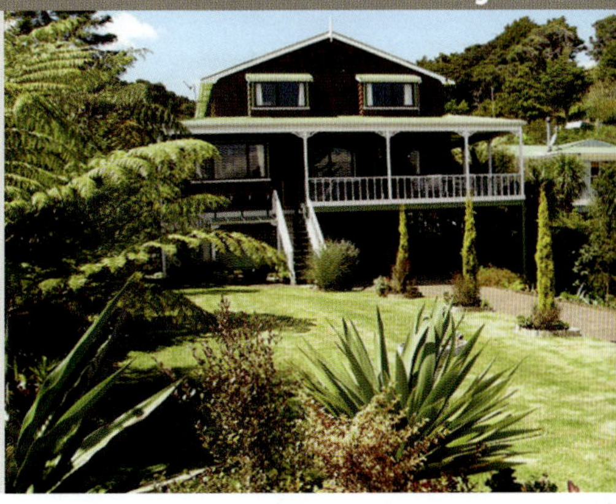

Start your Northland adventure with us as base. 2.5 hours North of Auckland 14 km east of Whangarei. Day trips easily made to Bay of Islands, West Coast, Waipoua Forest Kauri trees Matakohe Kauri Museum. Quiet and peaceful family friendly accommodation in spectacular Whangarei Heads Area. Spacious Top Storey two bedroom apartment sleeps 4/6 and an open plan Garden Unit – elderly friendly sleeps four. Both self-contained with own access and self catering kitchenette. Full breakfast included. Restaurants close by. Free Wi-Fi. Enjoy our hospitality.

- Garden unit open plan – 1 Queen bed, 2 King singles
- Extra persons $25 per night
- Full breakfast
- Pets welcome
- Children welcome
- No smoking on property
- Internet available

Whangarei Heads, Parua Bay B&B — Whangarei

B&B • Apartment with Kitchen

1407 Whangarei Heads Road, Whangarei
0800 4 PARUA or 027 20 555 30
stay@paruabay.co
www.paruabay.co

Double: $120–$120
Children: $20 per night
VISA MasterCard

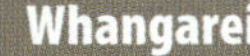

2 Bedrooms: 2KT **1**D
Bathrooms: 1 private

Trish Parkin and Leigh Crosbie

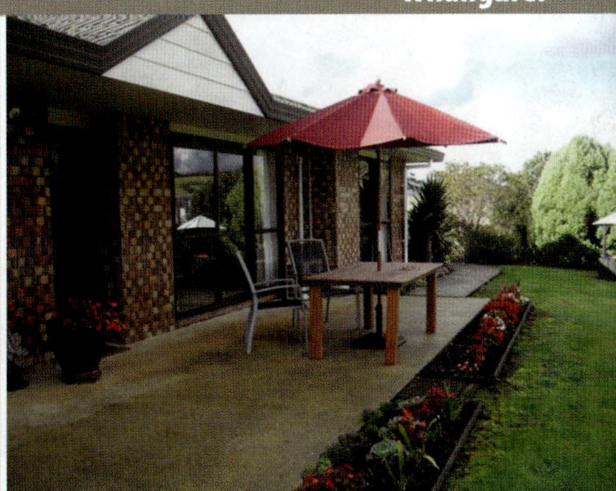

This place is ideally seated overlooking Parua Bay, short distance to McLeods Bay, Golf courses, Beaches, Boat facilities, Parua Bay Tavern and many more exciting things that Whangarei Heads has to offer. Covered Parking for boat, large section for the family, plenty of parking and friendly atmosphere. Between Smugglers Beach, Ocean Beach, Fishing, Diving. So much to choose from in this playground. Art is a hot topic in the area with many local talents and galleries.

- Full breakfast
- Pet-free home
- Children welcome
- No smoking on property

Northland

B&B

5 km SW of city centre

7 Tealmere Grove, Maunu Whangarei, 110
(09) 438 0347 or 021 045 7601
harryandanna@tealmeregrove-bnb.com
www.tealmeregrove-bnb.com

Double: $110–$120
Single: $80
Children: Extra Child from NZ$10

VISA MasterCard

3 Bedrooms: 1K **1**KT **1**Q **1**T **1**S
Bathrooms: 3 ensuite

Harry and Anna Evers

- Extra person in same room NZ$30
- Full breakfast
- Children welcome
- No smoking on property
- Internet available
- Free WI-FI
- Plenty of parking
- No traffic noise

Welcome to our beautiful home with private and peaceful garden, sunny decks adjacent to a nature reserve.

We are minutes from Whangarei city centre, town basin with lovely harbour, great shopping centre, golf course and Whangarei hospital.

We are walking distance to Barge Park Showgrounds and Funtion Centre with more than 400 km of tramping tracks and half an hour from many beaches. Refresments and home made baking are offered to guest when arriving. We speak English, Dutch and some German.

B&B

2 km N of Post Office

83 Hatea Drive, Whangarei
(09) 437 7115 or 21358055
stay@chelsea-house.co.nz
www.stay@chelsea-house.co.nz

Double: $135
Single: $120
Children: Under 5 years Free, 5–12 $35pn

VISA MasterCard eftpos

2 Bedrooms: 1KT **1**Q
Bathrooms: 2 ensuite

Di and Ray Houghton

- Cooked breakfast available at extra charge
- Continental breakfast
- Children welcome
- Non-smokers only
- Internet available

Our home is a 100yr old Villa with light airy decor and comfortable modern furnishings Four Restaurants are within a 15 minute easy walk. We are 25 minutes from white sandy beaches and beautiful bush walking tracks are on our doorstep. Paihia is just one hour away. We enjoy meeting people and chatting over a cuppa and Di's homemade baking. Ray is a retired Teaching Golf Pro, Di is a consultant for ENJO chemical free cleaning fibres.

Pentland House B&B

B&B

9 Pentland Road, Whangarei, 112
94302944 or 021 318898
roger@pentlandhouse.co.nz
www.pentlandhouse .co.nz

Double: $145–$155
Single: $130–$135

VISA MasterCard eftpos

3 Bedrooms: 1K 2KT 1Q
Bathrooms: 3 ensuite

Roger and Bardy Campbell

Roger and Bardy live here with their small dog a Jack Russell called Susie. We love our home so close to the city centre and the local marina.

Stylishly renovated 1920s bungalow with a private guest floor with separate entrance, three ensuite rooms, kitchenette, patio and Free Wi-Fi. Just four minutes walk to Whangarei city centre, Whangarei Town Basin cafés, shops, walkway and marina and Whangarei Aquatic Centre. Situated in a quiet cul de sac overlooking the picturesque Hatea River, Whangarei.

- Full breakfast
- Internet available

Edgewater B&B

B&B • Separate Suite
25 km S of Whangarei

225 One Tree Point Road, Ruakaka, 118
(09) 432 7174 or 021 1150 918
penez@xtra.co.nz
www.edgewaterbnb.co.nz

Double: $115–$115
Single: $90–$90

1 Bedroom: 1D
Bathrooms: 1 ensuite

Penny Britton

A warm and friendly welcome awaits you at my near new beachfront retreat. Enjoy beach walks and magnificent uninterrupted views of Whangarei harbour and Mount Manaia. The unit is private and self-contained with a double bed and ensuite. The living area consists of a sleeper/sofa with microwave oven, fridge and Sky TV, plus tea and coffee making facilities. A full continental breakfast is provided within the tariff. Surfing beaches, fishing, golf and restaurants are all within a few minutes drive. Pets on site.

- Double sleeper sofa available
- $20 extra person
- Continental provisions supplied
- Not suitable for children

Waipu Cove

labonte@xtra.co.nz

Homestay Farmstay • Apartment with Kitchen
10 km S of Waipu

PO Box 60, Waipu, Northland
(09) 432 0645
labonte@xtra.co.nz
www.bnb.co.nz/labonte.html

Double: $120
Single: $75

VISA MasterCard

3 Bedrooms: 1K 1Q 2D 2S
Bathrooms: 2 private

Andre and Robin La Bonte

- Dinner: $25 by arrangement
- Continental breakfast

Sleep to the sound of the ocean in a separate studio apartment or in guest bedrooms on our 36 acre seaside property. Explore our limestone rock formations or just sit and relax under the mature trees that grace our shoreline. The beach at Waipu Cove is a 10 minute walk along the sea. We are a licensed fish farm, graze cattle, have flea-free cats and an outside dog. We are ocean and coastal engineers who enjoy hosting guests from around the world. American spoken.

Please let your hosts know if you have to cancel.
They will have spent time preparing for you.

Auckland
Waipu
Waipu Cove
Langs Beach
Paparoa
Kaiwaka
Mangawhai
1
Omaha Beach
Warkworth
1
Puhoi
Waiwera
Orewa
See Auckland City next page
Hobsonville
Devonport
Auckland central
Waimauku
Maratai
Beachlands
Swanson
Mangere
Drury
2
1
0 Kilometres 20
0 Miles 12

1
Whangaparaoa
Dairy Flat
Auckland City
Waiheke Island
Coatesville
28
1
18
16
Albany
Rangitoto Island
Bayswater
Birkenhead
Milford
Beach Haven
Devonport
Ponsonby
Mission Bay
St Heliers
Auckland Central
Orakei
Mt Eden
Epsom
Howick
Botany Downs
Titirangi
Mangere
1
Manukau City
Auckland International Airport
Manurewa
0
Kilometres
5
Miles
0
3

Omaha Orchards Self-contained B and B

B&B • Cottage with Kitchen • B&B Self-contained unit

13 km E of Warkworth

Omaha Orchards, 282 Point Wells Road, RD6
Warkworth 0986
(09) 422 7415 or 027 659 1385
jmaltby@clear.net.nz
www.bnb.co.nz/maltby.html

Double: $90–$110   Single: $80–$100
Children: Extra guest $15

1 Bedroom: 1Q 1D
Bathrooms: 1 ensuite

Barbara and John Maltby

Our home and self-contained unit is nestled beside the Whangateau Harbour. Relax in the extensive gardens and swim in the beautifully appointed pool. Only five minutes by car to the popular 'Boutique' village of Matakana with its movie theatres, shops, eateries etc. Nearby is Omaha Beach, golf, tennis, vineyards, restaurants, art and craft studios, pottery works, and Kawau Island. This is some of the prettiest coastline in New Zealand. John and Barbara look forward to sharing their little slice of paradise with you.

- Bathrooms: modern bathroom with shower, basin, and toilet.
- Dinner: $20–$30 by arrangement
- Full breakfast provisions
- Children welcome
- No smoking on property
- Internet available

Melody Lodge

B&B Homestay • Apartment with Kitchen

1 km SW of Warkworth Township

15 Blue Gum Drive, Warkworth, 910
(09) 422 2581
melody@melodylodge.co.nz
www.melodylodge.co.nz

Double: $130–$140
Single: $120

2 Bedrooms: 1KT 1Q
Bathrooms: 2 ensuite

Melody Gard

Melody Lodge, formerly in Waipu Cove, is now relocated in Warkworth and we extend a warm welcome to our new B&B offering peace, privacy and birdsong. The Lodge is handy to all local attractions yet only one km from this historic riverside town. Enjoy refreshments in the picturesque gazebo. Small Art Gallery adjacent portraying the beauty of nature, plus exclusive greeting cards and postcards.

A handy stop enroute to the north, or a last holiday night before the airport.

- 1 separate apartment, queen bed, ensuite, lounge, kitchen, own entrance
- Continental breakfast
- Not suitable for children
- No smoking on property
- Internet available

Puhoi

Hungry Creek Bed and Breakfast

Luxury B&B
11 km N of Orewa

5, Hungry Creek Road, Puhoi, P.O. Box 404009, Puhoi, 0951, Auckland
(09) 422 0183 or 027 813 7464
hungrycreek@clear.net.nz
www.hungrycreekbandb.co.nz

Double: $115–$150   Single: $75–$85
Children: Facilitys for babys

VISA MasterCard Diners Club **eftpos**

3 Bedrooms: 2Q 2S
Bathrooms: 1 ensuite, 1 family share

Phil and Sue Tisdall

- Bathrooms: in floor Spa Bath in Luxury Suite
- Dinner: Light meals on request
- Full breakfast
- Pets welcome
- Children welcome
- No smoking on property
- Internet available

Hungry Creek Bed and Breakfast is located in a Tuscan villa set on 1/12 acres of gardens bordering the Puhoi River.

We have three rooms to choose from including a large luxury suite with large private in-floor-spa, walk-in-shower, ensuite and its own private access. Each room is north facing and opens onto a shared private courtyard overlooking the grounds.

Relax and enjoy a glass of wine alfresco style while you take in the spectacular country scenery surrounding Hungry Creek Bed and Breakfast.

Rai Valley

Opouri B and B and homestay.

B&B
60 km N of Nelson

Opouri valley, Rai valley, 7194
(03) 571 6136
stuart.mcmurray@yahoo.co.nz
www.opouribandb

Double: $110
Single: $55

eftpos

2 Bedrooms: 1K 2S
Bathrooms: 1 guest share

Glennis and Stuart

- Dinner extra $20 per person
- Full breakfast
- Not suitable for children
- No smoking on property
- Internet available

Glennis and Stuart welcome you to Opouri B and B. We live on a lifestyle block halfway between Nelson and Blenheim. Our B and B is a popular stopover for travellers and cyclists who have come from the Picton ferry on their way to Nelson. Homemade biscuits and tea or coffee on your arrival. We love sharing a BBQ meal with our guests if they request a meal when booking and offer a glass of good Marlborough wine. Internet available. Quiet and.

Villa Orewa

Luxury B&B

35 km N of Auckland Central

264 Hibiscus Coast Highway, Orewa, Auckland
(09) 426 3073 or 021 626 760 (Ian)
rooms@villaorewa.co.nz
www.villaorewa.co.nz

Double: $175–$250

VISA MasterCard

3 Bedrooms: 1KT 2Q
Bathrooms: 3 ensuite

Sandra and Ian Burrow

Welcome to our beautifully appointed Mediterranean style home, with white-washed walls and blue vaulted roofs. A taste of the Greek Isles on beautiful Orewa Beach. Stay in one of our self-contained rooms, each with private balcony, and enjoy the panoramic beach and sea views, or socialise with us in our spacious living areas. Orewa offers a great range of activities and amenities; with cafés, restaurants, and shopping all within a short level walk. We are sure your stay will be enjoyable and memorable.

- Greek-style rooms with white vaulted roofs
- Full breakfast
- No smoking on property
- Internet available

Hibiscus House B& B

B&B

5 km S of Orewa

13A Marellen Drive, Red Beach, Whangaparaoa
– Hibiscus Coast, Auckland 0932
(09) 427 6303 or 0274 472056
jb.marsden@clear.net.nz
http://www.hibiscushousebandb.co.nz/

Double: $120
Single: $95
Children: Only children 12 years or over

3 Bedrooms: 2Q 2T
Bathrooms: 2 ensuite, 1 private

Judy and Brian Marsden

We offer quality bed and breakfast, opposite a beach for the relaxing break you deserve, on route to Northland. Judy and Brian give friendly, personal hospitality in a very convenient location. Handy to shops, markets, cinema, beaches, golf courses and a leisure centre complex with heated swimming pool. Easy walks to surf, tennis and squash clubs. RSA five minutes away. Gulf Harbour Marina for ferries, fishing and sailing. Restaurants/bars/cafés for all tastes and occasions 5–15 minutes away. Sorry no pets. Children over 12 welcome.

- Dinner by prior arrangement or negotiation
- Continental breakfast
- Pet-free home
- Not suitable for children
- No smoking on property
- Internet available

Red Beach — Hadley Park B&B

B&B • Apartment with Kitchen
4 km S of Orewa

85 Whangaparaoa Rd, Red Beach, 932
09–5540810 or 021–1340345
info@hadleypark.co.nz
www.hadleypark.co.nz

Double: $140–$140
Single: $120–$120

VISA MasterCard

3 Bedrooms: 3Q
Bathrooms: 3 ensuite, 1 private

Max Miller and Noel Marley

- 2 bedrooms in B&B and 1 bedroom in apartment
- Visa/Mastercard, cash or bank account direct deposit acceptable
- Continental breakfast
- Pets welcome
- Not suitable for children
- Internet available

In a two acre lifestyle on the Weiti River estuary, Hadley Park is very private and quiet yet is on the Whangaparaoa Peninsula surrounded by 12 beautiful beaches, three golf courses and is just off the motorway and only minutes from Orewa and Silverdale. Our rooms all have their own ensuites, queen beds with quality cotton linen, LCD TVs and free wi-fi. Noel has spent years in the hotel industry and he and Max will do their utmost to make your stay enjoyable.

Whangaparaoa — Duncansby by the Sea

B&B
4 km E of Orewa

72 Duncansby Road, Whale Cove, Stanmore Bay, Whangaparaoa
(09) 424 0025 or 027 200 9688
duncansby@xtra.co.nz
www.duncansbybnb.co.nz

Double: $125
Single: $95

VISA MasterCard

2 Bedrooms: 2Q
Bathrooms: 1 ensuite, 1 private

Kathy and Ken Grieve

- Full breakfast

Duncansby, our new home, offers relaxing panoramic sea views of the Hibiscus Coast. Located at Whale Cove between Red Beach and Stanmore Bay, our modern sunny well appointed rooms have own entrances, TV, decks, white linen, tea/coffee facilities. Paradise for golfers with three local courses including International Gulf Harbour Course with its boating marina. Bird watchers visit Tiritiri Island Bird Sanctuary, walk Shakespeare Park. Enjoy petanque, nine superb beaches, excellent local restaurants and cafés. Only 35 minutes north of Auckland City, we welcome you.

Hillside B&B — **Woodhill**

B&B Farmstay
35 km N of Auckland

74 Tarrant Road RD2, Woodhill, 875
(09) 420 8586 or 0210 222 8658
stay@hillsidebandb.co.nz
http://hillsidebandb.co.nz/

Double: $120–$120
Single: $80–$80
Children: Foldout bed for child or extra guest $25

1 Bedroom: 1Q
Bathrooms: 1 ensuite

Wendy and Buzz Dunning

Hillside B&B is a family-run bed and breakfast on a quiet, rural smallholding in Woodhill, overlooking the Kaipara River valley, northwest of Auckland. Close to many award-winning wineries, Woodhill Sands Equestrian Centre, West Coast surfing, the Twin Coast Discovery Highway, Woodhill Mountain Bike Park, Tree Adventures, Parakai thermal pools, historic Helensville and the Kaipara Harbour. Whether you are touring the region, wanting a weekend retreat or a base for a longer holiday, Hillside B&B is your home away from home.

- $200 Weekend rate – two people Friday and Saturday night
- Continental provisions supplied
- Children welcome
- No smoking on property
- Internet available

Panorama Heights — **Swanson, Waitakere Ranges**

B&B • Self contained available on request
4 km SW of Swanson

42 Kitewaho Road, Swanson, Waitakere City, Auckland.0614
(09) 832 4777
nzbnb4u@clear.net.nz
www.panoramaheights.co.nz

Double: $185   Single: $175

VISA MasterCard

4 Bedrooms: 2Q 1D 1T
Bathrooms: 3 ensuite, 1 private

Allison and Paul Ingram

Paul and Allison invite you to visit and share our extremely special location high in the Waitakere Ranges with tranquility, privacy and magnificent panoramic views across Native Rainforest to Auckland City and Rangitoto Island beyond. Explore 250 km walking/hiking trails in surrounding Regional Park, West Coast beaches (Piha, Karekare, Bethells, Muriwai) Wineries, two Scenic Golf courses. Train to City is nearby. Excellent quality accommodation for you to Enjoy. Your hosts, who reside nextdoor encourage relaxation while we spoil you. Please Phone/Email for Bookings/Directions.

- Dinner: Available on request with reasonable notice.
- Full breakfast
- Children welcome
- Weddings and functions
- No smoking on property
- Internet available

Titirangi, Auckland — Kaurigrove

B&B
15 km SW of Auckland Central

120 Konini Road, Titirangi, Waitakere 0642, Auckland
(09) 817 5608 or 027 275 0574
kaurigrove@yahoo.co.nz
www.bnb.co.nz/kaurigrove.html

Double: $130–$130
Single: $65–$70

VISA MasterCard

2 Bedrooms: 1Q 1S
Bathrooms: 1 private

Gaby and Peter Wunderlich

- Continental breakfast
- Children welcome

Welcome to our home! Kaurigrove offers a tranquil location amidst kauri trees in a park-like setting yet close to shops, cafés and restaurants. Situated at Titirangi, we are near Auckland's historic west coast with its magnificent beaches and vast native bush with a wonder-world of walking tracks. Gaby and Peter, your hosts of German background, are keen travellers themselves and are happy to introduce you to the highlights of Auckland and its surrounding areas. Non-smoking inside residence.

Albany, Coatesville — Camperdown

B&B Farmstay • Cottage with Kitchen
7 km N of Albany

455 Coatesville/Riverhead Highway, RD 3, Albany, Auckland
(09) 415 9009
chris@camperdown.co.nz
www.camperdown.co.nz

Double: $160–$170   **Single: $110**
Children: $50

6 Bedrooms: 1K 1KT 3Q 3S
Bathrooms: 1 ensuite, 2 private

Chris and David Hempleman

- Dinner: $50
- Full breakfast
- Children welcome
- Weddings and functions
- Internet available

We are only 20 minutes from Auckland City, relax in secluded tranquillity. Our home opens into beautiful gardens, native bush and stream offering the best of hospitality in a friendly relaxed atmosphere. On the farm we have sheep, cattle and pet lambs Our spacious guest areas consist of the entire upstairs, and the studio above the garage.

Guests can relax and stroll in the secret garden by the stream, or head to the tennis court via the swing bridge.

Ponderosa Lodge

B&B
2 km SW of Browns Bay

5, Margaret Henry Crescent, 632
021 079 4429 or (09) 476 7896
info@ponderosalodge.co.nz
www.ponderosalodge.co.nz

Double: $125–$135
Single: $90–$125

3 Bedrooms: 2Q 2S
Bathrooms: 1 ensuite, 1 family share, 1 private

Andie Moore

Ponderosa Lodge is just three minutes each way from bustling Browns Bay Beachfront and Sunday market and Albany's Westfield Shopping Centre. Park n ride to CBD closeby. A warm welcome awaits you at our modern comfortable home. Our rooms are serviced daily and have tea and coffee making facilities in each one. Wi-Fi, own key and seperate guest TV lounge. A delicious Continental breakfast served to start your day. We give great value accommodation in a relaxing informal enviroment.

- Payment online banking or deposit and cash balance on arrival
- Continental breakfast
- Pets welcome
- Not suitable for children
- No smoking on property
- Internet available

Crown Hill B&B

Milford, Auckland

B&B • Very private (separate entrance), modern and stylish ensuite bat

212 East Coast Rd, Milford, North Shore, Auckland 0620
(09) 449 0567 or 027 291 1466
crownhill_bb@yahoo.co.nz
www.bnb.co.nz/4814.html

Double: $100–$140   Single: $80–$100
Children: cot available on request

VISA   MasterCard   eftpos

1 Bedroom: 1KT
Bathrooms: 1 ensuite

Zorana and Alex Vucic

Crown Hill B&B offers all the comfort, charm and warmth that you could imagine. Friendly and welcoming European hosts who are now proud to call New Zealand home are ready to make every effort to ensure your stay is the highlight of your visit to New Zealand. Your bedroom is bright, immaculate and very private (separate lockable entrance). You have a choice between two king single beds or one super king size bed (very comfortable). Cot available upon request.

- Bathrooms: very modern and stylish bathroom (shower)
- Dinner: $35 per person (three course meal, aperitif, glass of wine/beer)
- Full breakfast
- Non-smokers only
- Internet available

Auckland – Bayswater | Beresford B&B

B&B Homestay
4.5 km N of Devonport

46A Beresford Street, Bayswater, North Shore, Auckland 0622
(09) 445 3959
info@beresfordbandb.co.nz
www.beresfordbandb.co.nz

Double: $130–$165   Single: $90–$100
Children: 15 years and under $25 per night

2 Bedrooms: 1Q 1T
Bathrooms: 1 private

Lesley Brown and Gordon Storey   **10%**

- Each extra adult $45 per night
- Cooked breakfast available at extra cost
- Continental breakfast
- Children welcome
- Internet available

A very warm welcome to our comfortable, modern home and B&B in peaceful Bayswater. Relax, feel at home, but be within easy reach of all Auckland has to offer. Walk to ferry – downtown Auckland 10 minute trip away. Short drive to motorway, Devonport, Takapuna, restaurants, shopping. Two spacious bedrooms with private bathroom and your own TV/sitting room – accommodating 1–4 guests. Generous continental breakfast included. Free wi-fi, parking, laundry, ferry pick-up. We look forward to welcoming you!

Devonport | The Jasmine Cottage

B&B • Cottage with kitchenette
0.25 km E of Devonport Township

20 Buchanan Street, Devonport, Auckland
(09) 445 8825
joanjohnlewis@xtra.co.nz
www.jasmineroom.co.nz

Double: $120

1 Bedroom: 1Q
Bathrooms: 1 ensuite

John Lewis

- Washing machine avaliable
- Continental breakfast
- No smoking on property

Welcome to our cosy smoke-free quiet and private guest cottage. We are right in the heart of historic Devonport village with all its attractions, cafés, beaches, golf course and scenic walks. The ferry to Auckland city and the Hauraki Gulf is three minutes walk away. Kitchenette with tea, coffee, cereal and milk. Fridge and Toaster.

Mahoe

B&B • Apartment with Kitchen
0.5 km N of Devonport

15B King Edward Parade, Devonport, 624
(09) 445 1515 or 027 291 3727
info@mahoe.co.nz
www.mahoe.co.nz

Double: $170–$200
Children: By arrangement

VISA MasterCard

3 Bedrooms: 3Q
Bathrooms: 1 ensuite, 1 private

Judith Bern

Mahoe is an old school house transported from Huntly in 1985. Situated on the Devonport waterfront up a driveway in a peaceful setting. The upstairs B&B has two queen rooms one with a deck and large lounge. The bathroom is separate. Our B&B is suitable for one couple or three or four people who are family or friends. We can accommodate three couples by including the apartment, which has a separate entrance and is fully self catering.

We do have a small dog, Hazel, which is a friend to all.

- Bathrooms: ensuite with shower in the apartment plus extra toilet downstairs.
- 1 bathroom with shower and toilet and 1 extra toilet in the B&B
- Breakfast by arrangement
- No smoking on property
- Internet available

Auckland Birdwood House B&B

B&B
8 km N of Auckland City Centre

12a Moore Street, Hillcrest, Auckland 0627
(09) 418 1612 or 0274 7777 22
barbie@birdwood.co.nz
www.birdwood.co.nz

Double: $150–$170
Single: $130–$150
Children: Not suitable under 16

VISA MasterCard eftpos

3 Bedrooms: 2Q **1**D
Bathrooms: 2 ensuite, 1 private

Barbie Bell and David Scott

Our restored farmhouse-style villa has wrap-around verandahs surrounded by native bush, birds and an Italian-style courtyard. Three beautifully appointed rooms with quality linen and wool duvets. The modern bathrooms are tiled, with under-floor heating. We serve a delicious two course breakfast. We are between the suburbs of Takapuna and Birkenhead with its many popular restaurants and shops. A regular bus service is close by. 15 minutes to CBD. More than 15 restaurants 5 minutes away – map provided.

- Full breakfast
- Pet-free home
- Not suitable for children
- No smoking on property
- Internet available

B&B Hotel

1 km SW of Auckland Central

30 Ponsonby Terrace, Ponsonby, Auckland 1011
(09) 376 5989 or 0800 766 792
info@greatpons.co.nz
www.greatpons.co.nz

Double: $220–$400
Single: $185–$350

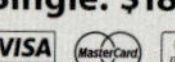

10 Bedrooms: 6KT **4**Q
Bathrooms: 10 ensuite

Sally James and Gerard Hill

- Full breakfast
- Pets welcome
- Children welcome
- Internet available

Come and stay at the Great Ponsonby, providing bed and breakfast in Auckland. Just two minutes stroll to Ponsonby's vibrant cafés, fashion, galleries and just five minutes by taxi to the harbour or city centre.

Our breakfasts are legendary—friendships have been forged in the dining room, egg benedict lingered over on the verandah.

Eleven rooms of varying size and price. All rooms have everything you could need. All have modern and Pacific artworks. Courtyard studios are much bigger than the villas. The spacious suites and penthouse are twice as large again.

Our sitting room is a place to read, listen to our extensive CD collection or have a drink with friends. There is no TV. The TVs are in the bedrooms.

Ponsonby, an urban village, is one of the earliest areas of Auckland and luckily many of the historic buildings still remain. It is the trendiest part of town, a place to come to eat, drink coffee and to have fun. It is very close to the city centre. The Great Ponsonby, set in a large, beautiful garden is in the perfect place from which to explore Auckland.

Great Ponsonby has an Enviro Gold award and Sally and Gerry are committed to sustainability.

Hemi and Tom are the resident dog and cat.

Bays Luxury B&B & Homestay

Luxury B&B Homestay

54A Sprott Road, Kohimarama, 1071
(09) 528 9274 or 0274 741029
bayshomestay@xtra.co.nz
www.bnb.co.nz/8378.html

Double: $220

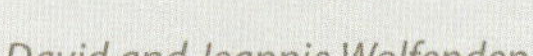

1 Bedroom: 1D
Bathrooms: 1 private

David and Jeannie Wolfenden

Bays Luxury B&B and Homestay offers high quality private accommodation in a luxury townhouse with garaged parking in one of Auckland's most desirable areas. Beautiful sea views of Rangitoto from your private TV lounge. Your rooms are located in a separate wing of the house.

Only a short walk to Kohimarama Beach, cafés, restaurants, shops and a large park. We have bikes available for hire and it is a wonderful flat ride along Tamaki Drive to the city.

- Dinner: $45 per person. Evening meals with hosts by arrangement
- Full breakfast
- Pet-free home
- No smoking on property
- Internet available

Nautical Nook/Free Sailing

B&B Homestay
4.8 km E of Auckland Central

23B Watene Crescent, Orakei, Auckland
(09) 521 2544 or 0800 360 544
info@nauticalnook.com
www.nauticalnook.com

Double: $151–$162
Single: $108

2 Bedrooms: 2KT
Bathrooms: 2 ensuite

Trish and Keith Janes

Friendly, relaxed beachside hospitality overlooking park/harbour, 4.8 km from downtown. 100 metres from Okahu Bay. Gourmet breakfast. Stroll along picturesque promenade to Kelly Tarlton's Underwater World and Mission Bay beach. Bus at door to downtown, ferry terminal, museums and Eden Park (Rugby). Unwind for 2–3 day stopover. Complimentary sailing on the harbour on our 34' yacht. We have a wealth of local knowledge and international travel experience and can assist with sightseeing, travel planning. Welcome! Pay cash and deduct 7.5% off listed rates. Excellent website! Free Wireless Internet.

- Full breakfast
- Children welcome

St Heliers, Auckland — McPherson B&B

B&B
10 km SE of Auckland

102 Maskell Street, St Heliers, Auckland
(09) 575 9738
ronjillmcpherson@xtra.co.nz
www.bnb.co.nz/mcpherson.html

Double: $140
Single: $90

2 Bedrooms: 1Q 1T
Bathrooms: 1 private

Jill and Ron McPherson

- Continental breakfast

Welcome to our modern home with off-street parking in a smoke-free environment. One group of guests is accommodated at a time. Having travelled extensively ourselves we are fully aware of tourists' needs. Eight minutes walk to St Heliers Bay beach, shops, restaurants, cafés, banks and post office. Picturesque 12 minutes drive along the Auckland waterfront past Kelly Tarlton's Antarctic and Underwater Encounter to downtown Auckland. Interests including all sports, gardening and Jill is a keen cross-stitch embroiderer. Not suitable for children/pets.

St Heliers, Auckland — Pippi's B&B

B&B
10 km E of Auckland CBD

15 Tuhimata St, St Heliers, 1071
(09) 575 6057 or 021 989 643
pippisbnb@gmail.com
pippis.co.nz

Double: $190–$220
Single: $140–$160

VISA MasterCard

3 Bedrooms: 2Q 1S
Bathrooms: 1 ensuite, 1 private

Pippi and Philip Wells

- Full breakfast
- Pets welcome
- Children welcome
- No smoking on property
- Internet available

Pippi's Bed and Breakfast provides luxurious, comfortable and homely accommodation in St Heliers in Auckland's eastern suburbs. It is a charming 1930s English style home with a tranquil sunny back garden set in a pretty tree lined street. We are in a quiet location yet only a short stroll from the beautiful harbour beach, shops and many cafés of St Heliers village.

Your hosts are Pippi and Philip, Oscar our little Cavoodle, Jillie (my mother's terrier cross), and Bobby and Peggy our gorgeous cats.

Airport Bed & Breakfast

B&B • Guest House
4 km NE of Airport

1 Westney Road, Corner of Kirkbride Road,
Mangere, Manukau
Freephone 0800 247 262 or Landline (09) 275 0533
airportbnb@xtra.co.nz
www.airportbnb.co.nz
Double: $98–$135   Single: $85–$110
Children: neg

10 Bedrooms: 1K 2Q 5D 2T 9S
Bathrooms: 4 ensuite, 6 guest share

Laurel Blakey

Just five minutes drive from Auckland Airport a friendly welcome and great value accommodation awaits. 10 smart rooms, four ensuites, central heating, large dining room air-conditioned and TV lounge. Internet kiosk,, FREE WI-FI, two hrs or 200MB. Two minutes walk to city bus stop – see Auckland by bus and ferry on the $16 day pass. Restaurants/takeaways nearby. Car, cycle and luggage storage. Rental cars and NZ wide sightseeing tours booked. Courtesy airport transfer 5.00am – 9.00pm. Buffet breakfast, complimentary tea/coffee.

- Triple $135–$160
- Bathrooms: standard rooms have share bathroom facilities; all rooms have vanity units
- Continental breakfast
- Pets welcome
- Children welcome
- Internet available

Hillpark Homestay

B&B Homestay
2 km S of Manukau City Centre

16 Collie Street, Manurewa, Auckland 2102
(09) 267 6847 or 021 207 2559
stay@hillpark.co.nz
www.hillpark.co.nz

Double: $120–$120
Single: $80–$80
Children: $25

3 Bedrooms: 1Q 4S
Bathrooms: 1 ensuite, 1 guest share

Katrine and Graham Paton

Welcome to our sunny, spacious home and meet our friendly tonkinese cat. We are 15 minutes from Auckland Airport, 20 minutes from Auckland City centre, on the route south and the Pacific Coast Highway. Nearby are restaurants, Auckland Regional Botanic Gardens, Vodophone Events Centre, Tipapa Events Centre, Manukau City Shopping Centre, Manukau Superclinic and Surgery Centre. Our interests include teaching, classical music, painting, gardening, photography, Christian activities, reading and travel. We are a smoke-free home. Directions: please phone or visit our website.

- All beds have fleecy wool underlays and electric blankets
- Dinner: $25 by arrangement
- Full breakfast
- Children welcome
- No smoking on property
- Internet available

Drury — The Drury Homestead

B&B

3 km E of Drury

349 Drury Hills Road, Drury, South Auckland
(09) 294 9030 or 021 157 6531
druryhomestead@gmail.com
www.bnb.co.nz/thedruryhomestead.html

Double: $140
Single: $90
Children: negotiable

4 Bedrooms: 3Q 1T
Bathrooms: 3 ensuite, 1 private

Carolyn and Ron Booker

- Full breakfast
- Children welcome

The Drury Homestead is a wonderful old colonial house, built in the 1860s and lovingly restored by your hosts Carolyn and Ron.

With four beautifully decorated rooms to choose from where would you like to sleep? Upstairs looking out over the creek and bush is The River Room with queen-size bed and ensuite.

Dunedin has magnificent views across the countryside, a queen bed and ensuite.

Cape Reinga has twin king-single beds and it's own bathroom with shower, toilet, vanity and claw-foot bath and oh what views from the bath!

Downstairs is The Lily Room, a self-contained studio with kitchen facilities, a queen size bed and ensuite and own entrance and verandah. Ideal for a longer stay.

We also have a cot and pull-out beds available for children. We offer a discount for those staying three nights or more.

We are situated on a rural block, minutes from the motorway, 35 minutes from Auckland CBD and 20 minutes from the airport. Set amidst paddocks with surrounding bush and a stream, the only noise you will hear are the birds and the sound of the tumbling stream.

We love our lifestyle here and would like to make your stay in New Zealand a truely memorable one.

Regis Park B&B

Luxury B&B
2–3 km N of Pukekohe township

91 Beatty Road, Pukekohe, 2120
(09) 238 7193 or 021 936 017
eview@slingshot.co.nz
www.regispark.com

Double: $140–$180
Single: $120–$160

6 Bedrooms: 3K 2KT 1Q
Bathrooms: 3 ensuite, 1 family share

Evie and Warren Wordswort

Regis Park offers luxury B&B accommodation just minutes away from Pukekohe township. We have 6 beautifully presented bedrooms, one being part of a self contained until. Each bedroom is large with their own sitting and lounge type areas and most have their own fridge and tea/coffee making facilities as well as their own big screen T.V's. Enjoy all your home comforts with a touch of elegance. This property is semi-rural even though being so close to the township, and it very quiet and peaceful. An ideal place to either commence or finish your stay in N.Z. as we are only 25–30 minutes from Auckland International Airport.

- All bathrooms with toilet, shower and large vanity
- Continental breakfast
- Pet-free home
- Non-smokers only
- Internet available

All our B&Bs are non-smoking.

Waikato,
King Country
Kopu
2
Mangatarata
27
1
Hamilton
Raglan
23
Tamahere
Cambridge
1
Ohaupo
Pirongia
Te Awamutu
31
3
Waitomo
0 Kilometres 20
0 Miles 12
Te Kuiti
Piopio
3
30

Oak Lane Lodge — Morrinsville

Luxury B&B
3 km NE of Morrinsville

78a Horrell Road, Morrinsville, 3374
(07) 889 1045
info@oaklanelodge.co.nz
www.oaklanelodge.co.nz

Double: $220–$290
Single: $200–$220

VISA MasterCard eftpos

3 Bedrooms: 1K 1KT 1Q
Bathrooms: 3 ensuite

Alan and Cath

Oak Lane Lodge offers boutique Bed and Breakfast accommodation in one of Morrinsville's Grand Historic Homesteads.

Accommodation at The Lodge is Qualmark four star plus and consists of three well appointed Guest Rooms, each with their own private ensuite.

The Lodge is situated in amongst magnificent grounds, gardens and 100 year old oak, copper beech, black popular, flowering rhododendrons and camellia trees.

- Bathrooms: every room has its own ensuite
- Dinner: From $35 per person
- Full breakfast
- Pet-free home
- Children welcome
- Weddings and functions
- Internet available

Matawha — Raglan

Farmstay
20 km S of Raglan

61 Matawha Road, RD 2, Raglan
(07) 825 6709
jennyt@wave.co.nz
www.bnb.co.nz/matawha.html

Double: $120
Single: $60

3 Bedrooms: 1K 1D 4S
Bathrooms: 1 family share, 1 guest share, 1 private

Jenny and Peter Thomson

We live on the west coast and our family has farmed this land for 100 years. Come and enjoy our private beach, expansive garden, home-grown vegetables, spa, one cat and the peace of no other buildings or people for miles. Take bush or mountain walks, a scenic drive, go surfing or fishing, or maybe find the hot-water beach! Auckland 2.5 hours, Hamilton one hour, Raglan 30 minutes. We are the only B&B on the West Coast.

- Cash or cheque only please
- Dinner: $20pp
- Full breakfast
- Not suitable for children

Raglan

Raglan Farmhouse

B&B Farmstay
1 km E of Raglan Township

39 main Rd, Raglan, 3225
78258747 or 021 034 7132
hello@raglanfarmstay.com
www.raglanfarmhouse.com

Double: $80–$140   Single: $40–$100
Children: We are Not suitable for Toddlers & Pre Schoolers aged 1–4 yrs

VISA MasterCard eftpos

6 Bedrooms: 5Q 2T 5S
Bathrooms: 1 ensuite, 1 guest share, 2 private

Christopher David

- Dinner: you are welcome to cook for yourselves or together with us
- Full breakfast
- Pets welcome
- Children welcome
- Weddings and functions
- No smoking on property
- Internet available

Raglan Farmhouse offers unique quality bed and breakfast accommodation in the relaxed natural environment of Te Whare Farm, located on two acres at the edge of Raglan township, directly in front of the 50 km sign, and only a 10 min walk into town.

Share in our amazing rural and harbor views, where the massive sun soaked deck gives you a picture perfect view of the sun setting across the estuary and behind Mount Karioi, while soaking in our eight person spa pool.

Ohaupo, Hamilton

Green Gables of Rukuhia

B&B
4 km SW of Hamilton

35 Rukuhia Road, RD 2, Ohaupo 3882
(07) 843 8511 or 021 583 462
judi.earl@clear.net.nz
www.bnb.co.nz/greengablesofrukuhia.html

Double: $100–$130
Single: $65–$80

VISA MasterCard

3 Bedrooms: 2D 1T
Bathrooms: 1 guest share

Earl and Judi McWhirter

- Bathrooms: two rooms (1 double and 1 twin) have own hand basins
- Dinner by arrangement
- Continental breakfast
- Children welcome
- Non-smokers only
- Internet available

Warm, comfortable smoke-free family home in a quiet rural setting, close to Hamilton, Airport and field days (Mystery Creek). Free pick-up/delivery airport, bus, train terminal all part of the friendly service. 5 km to Vilagrad Winery; two minutes walk to Gostiona Restaurant. Two storeyed house with guest bedrooms and lounge/kitchenette downstairs; dining and hosts upstairs. Continental breakfast with fresh home-baked bread. Judi lectures statistics, University of Waikato. Earl is a school teacher.

Uliveto Countrystay

B&B Homestay • Countrystay B&B
12 km SW of Hamilton

164 Finlayson Road, RD 10, Ngahinapouri,
Hamilton
(07) 825 2116 or 027 755 8289 (Daphne) or 027 200
uliveto@xtra.co.nz
www.uliveto.co.nz

Double: $170–$170   Single: $140–$170

2 Bedrooms: 2Q
Bathrooms: 2 ensuite

Peter and Daphne Searle

Come and enjoy the peace and tranquility of the beautiful countryside.
Wander in our olive grove and gardens or relax on your private deck.
Hamilton City, the airport and National Fieldays are 20 minutes away.
Nearby attractions include – Waitomo Caves, lavender farm, golf course,
horse treks/tramping tracks on Mount Pirongia, Bridal Veil Falls, Raglan
beaches and cafés. To complete your day, share dinner and wine with us
or relax in the guest lounge or our therapeutic spa.

- Dinner by prior arrangement; 2 or 3 courses available
- Full breakfast
- Pet-free home
- Not suitable for children
- Weddings and functions
- No smoking on property
- Internet available

Home Hospitality

B&B Homestay
0.2 km N of Hamilton CBD

7A Hamilton Parade, Hamilton, 3204
(07) 838 1538 or 021 170 3210 text only
frediana@ihug.co.nz
www.hamiltonhomehospitality.co.nz

Double: $130
Single: $70
Children: Not suitable

2 Bedrooms: 1Q 2T
Bathrooms: 1 guest share

Diana and Fred Houtman

Comfortable self-contained accommodation in a quiet riverside
cul-de-sac in the centre of Hamilton. Private sitting room for guests, with
tea/coffee making facilities. Leave your car in our secure off-road parking
area and walk to restaurants, shops, theatres, sports venues, conference
centres – no parking hassles. A handy point from which to explore a
large area of central NZ. Hosts are well travelled and enjoy meeting new
people. Dutch spoken. Credit cards NOT accepted.

- Dinner: $30 – advance notice required
- Full breakfast
- Pet-free home
- Not suitable for children
- No smoking on property
- Internet available

Matangi, Hamilton

Kowhai Lodge

B&B Homestay
10 km SE of Hamilton

81 Butcher Road, RD4 Hamilton, 3284
(07) 8296 014
kowhai.lodge@yahoo.co.nz
www.bnb.co.nz/KowhaiLodge.html

Double: $0–$120
Single: $0–$95

3 Bedrooms: 2Q 1T
Bathrooms: 3 ensuite

Sheila and John

- Dinner by arrangment
- Full breakfast
- Pet-free home
- No smoking on property

Sheila and John would like to welcome you to Kowhai Lodge, a new pet free home built in Matangi. Located 90 minutes from Auckland Airport and just 15 minutes from Hamilton city centre. A few minutes drive from State Highway 1 and 1B, Matangi is centrally situated for Hamilton airport, Mystery Creek Event Centre and day trips to Rotorua, Tauranga or Waitomo Caves. Matangi is ideal for couples looking for the tranquility of the countryside in comfortable surroundings; rooms have tea/coffee making facilities and ensuites.

Hamilton

Braid Road Bed & Breakfast

B&B
4 km N of Hamilton Central

43b Braid Road, Hamilton, 3200
(07) 850 1624 or 0274 744605 Sue 027 248 1161 Dave
suez.dave@xtra.co.nz
www.bnb.co.nz/4541.html

Double: $125–$135
Single: $125–$135

VISA MasterCard

1 Bedroom: 1Q
Bathrooms: 1 private

Sue and Dave Douglas

- 1 double
- Full breakfast
- Non-smokers only
- Internet available

Come and enjoy our quiet secluded setting, a short drive to Hamilton City centre and Waikato Stadium. Easy stroll to lovely river walks and St Andrews' golf course. Excellant local café. A short car trip or handy city bus will take you into the city centre and restaurants, theatres, museum etc. Covered deck allows for outside breakfast if you choose. Laundry, internet off street parking available. Bedroom has TV and tea/coffee facilities. Courtesy pick up. Shy puss in residence.

Glenelg

B&B Homestay
2 km S of Cambridge

6 Curnow Place, Cambridge
(07) 823 0084
glenelgbnb@ihug.co.nz
www.cambridge.co.nz

Double: $130
Single: $85
Children: $25

4 Bedrooms: 3Q 1T
Bathrooms: 3 ensuite, 1 private

Shirley and Ken Geary

Glenelg welcomes you to your home away from home. We offer spacious, quality accommodation, that is warm, quiet and private, overlooking Waikato farmland. There is plenty of off-street parking. Beds have electric blankets and woolrests. There are 200 rose bushes in the garden. Five minutes to Lake Karapiro. Mystery Creek, where NZ National Field Days and many other functions are held, is only 15 minutes away. Laundry facilities available. Homemade Kiwi dinners are available by arrangement.

- Dinner: $25 by arrangement
- Full breakfast
- Pets welcome
- Children welcome

Whitehall Cottage

Farmstay • Cottage with Kitchen
12 km S of Cambridge

178 Whitehall Rd, Cambridge, 3496
(07) 834 0382 or 021 255 6003
louise@whitehallcottage.co.nz
www.whitehallcottge.co.nz

Double: $110–$150
Single: $110–$150
Children: $20 per extra person per night

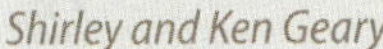

3 Bedrooms: 1Q 1D 3S
Bathrooms: 1 guest share

Steve and Louise Howse

Come and enjoy stunning views as you look out from this fully self-contained cottage. With three bedrooms, the cottage sleeps up to seven. The full kitchen and laundry make this an ideal place to stay and unwind or use as a base to explore from. Only six minutes drive to Lake Karapiro and eight minutes into Cambridge, Whitehall Cottage is well located in the heart of the Waikato.

Perfect for families – feel free enquire about our family rates. Longer stays available at discounted rates.

- 1 queen bed, 2 single beds, 1 set of double/single bunks
- Long stay rates available on request
- Breakfast by arrangement
- Pet-free home
- Children welcome
- Internet available

Waikato

Karapiro, Cambridge — Gully Retreat Karapiro

B&B
12 km S of Cambridge

36 Fergusson Gully Road, Rd2 Cambridge, 3494
(07) 827 5646 or 021 136 5780
john.kay@clear.net.nz
gullyretreatkarapiro.co.nz

Double: $110–$140
Single: $100–$130
Children: By arrangement

3 Bedrooms: 1Q 2D
Bathrooms: 1 ensuite, 1 guest share

John and Kay Rennie

- Queen with ensuite and 2 rooms with double beds guest share bathroom
- Dinner by arrangement
- Continental breakfast
- Pets welcome
- Children welcome
- Internet available

John and Kay offer quality accommodation in the central Waikato. Surrounded by native bush, it is the perfect place to rest and unwind. 10 minutes south of Cambridge we are close to many attractions; Mystery Creek Events Centre, Hobbiton, Rotorua, Taupo, Waitomo Caves and of course just minutes from Lake Karapiro Domain. We can provide detailed information about unique attractions that are off the tourist trail.

Cambridge — Blairgowrie House

Luxury B&B • Guest House
15 km S of Hamilton

75 Peake Road, RDI Cambridge, 3493
021 659073 or (07) 827 5158
akmcwha@xtra.co.nz
www.blairgowriehouse.co.nz

Double: $169–$210

3 Bedrooms: 1K 1Q 1T
Bathrooms: 2 ensuite, 1 private

Annette and Kelvin McWha

- Dinner: $40 per person by arrangement
- Continental breakfast
- Pets welcome
- Not suitable for children
- No smoking on property
- Internet available

Retreat relax and recharge in our lovingly restored 1916 bungalow. Blairgowrie House sits on five acres of land surrounded by extensive gardens. The house has been tastefully restored and while retaining the charm and romance of the Edwardian era now has every modern comfort for the most discerning guest. All suites have tea/coffee facilities, fridge, TV, heat/air con pump. Guest laundry, private guest entrance, free car park. Five min from Cambridge. A vintage machinery collection is on site and may be viewed by arrangment.

Penny Lodge B&B

B&B Homestay
10 km SW of Te Awamutu

90 Penny Rd, Pirongia, 3876
(07) 871 9139 or 027 315 6509
jillyfraser@windowslive.com
http://pennylodge.co.nz/index.html

Double: $130
Single: $95

VISA MasterCard

3 Bedrooms: 2Q 2S
Bathrooms: 1 guest share

Jill Fraser

Nestled in the peaceful village of Pirongia, Penny Lodge Bed and Breakfast is the perfect place to stay to escape the bustle of city life and explore the outdoors. This spacious new home offers rural views over adjacent farmland and Pirongia Mountain. Located on a no-exit country road, here you can embrace peace and quiet.

Within walking distance of the local village, Penny Lodge B&B is in the perfect location to enjoy the Waikato - whether you are cycling or tramping in the native parks, or enjoying the local cafe scene.

- Bathrooms: all B&B rooms are serviced by one large guest bathroom
- Dinner: By prior arrangement
- Full breakfast
- Children welcome
- No smoking on property
- Internet available

Waitomo Caves Guest Lodge

B&B • Studio units each with own entrance
15 km SW of Otorohanga

7 Te Anga Road, Waitomo Caves Village
(07) 878 7641 or Freephone 0800 465 762
waitomocavesguest lodge@xtra.co.nz
www.waitomocavesguest lodge.co.nz

Double: $110–$140   Single: $90
Children: 3–14 years, $15. Not suitable under 3 years old

VISA MasterCard eftpos

8 Bedrooms: 7Q 8S
Bathrooms: 7 ensuite, 1 private

Janet and Colin Beeston

Right in Waitomo Caves Village, opposite award-winning Huhu Cafe, next to Waitomo Store and a short walk to Waitomo Glowworm Caves. Each ensuite studio unit has a private entrance and beautiful views of the cottage garden and surrounding hills.

Free Wi-Fi access and a laptop computer available for use by guests.

Expect a warm welcome from Gypsy, the family dog, as well as Colin and Janet, who can give you knowledgeable advice, make bookings for local activities and help with your itinerary.

- A variety of double, twin and family rooms
- Extra adult, $25
- Bathrooms: there is a bath in the private bathroom
- Continental breakfast
- Children welcome
- Internet available

Pio Pio, Waitomo District

Carmel Farm

B&B Homestay Farmstay
19 km S of Te Kuiti

1832 SH3, PO Box 93, Pio Pio
(07) 877 8130 or 0800 877 8130
Carmelfarms@xtra.co.nz
www.bnb.co.nz/carmelfarm.html

Double: $150
Single: $100
Children: $75

4 Bedrooms: 2KT **4**S
Bathrooms: 1 ensuite, 1 guest share

Barbara and Leo Anselmi

- Dinner: $35pp
- Continental breakfast
- Pets welcome
- Children welcome
- No smoking on property

Barbara and Leo Anselmi operate a 2000 acre sheep, beef and dairy farm. You will be welcomed into an established homestead set in a picturesque limestone valley. You will be treated to delicious home-cooked meals and the warmth of our friendship.

Whether mustering mobs of cattle and sheep, viewing the milking of 550 Friesian cows, driving around the rolling hills on the four wheeled farm-bike, basking in the sun by the pool or enjoying the gardens, you will feel relaxed and rejuvenated. Whether you seek excitement or tranquility, Carmel Farm is the perfect retreat.

We are ideally located for you to explore many other attractions. We are adjacent to a beautiful 18 hole golf course which welcomes visitors. The property is a short distance from black water rafting and canoeing activities, The Lost World Cavern, and the famous Waitomo Caves. Nearby are bush walks, waterfalls, and the home of the rare kokako bird. The Mangaotaki stream is a mecca for the trout enthusiast. We can help to arrange activities for people of all ages and interests; from garden visits to horse riding. (P.S. In the TV lounge there is Sky for those all-important rugby matches.) Please let us know your preference.

We are 140 km from Rotorua/Taupo.

Coromandel
Peninsula

Waiheke Island
Coromandel
Kuaotunu
Opito Bay
Whitianga
Hahei
Hot Water Beach
Beachlands
Whitford
Clevedon
Papakura
rury
Kaiaua
Te Puru
Tairua
Bombay
Thames
25
Whangamata
Mercer
2
Waihi
Waihi Beach
Kilometres
0
20
0
Miles
12

Thames

Mountain Top B&B

Homestay
6.4 km E of Thames

452 Kauaeranga Valley Road, RD 2, Thames
(07) 868 9662
elderberry@slingshot.co.nz
www.bnb.co.nz/mountaintopbb.html

Double: $130–$140
Single: $90
Children: half price

VISA · MasterCard · Diners Club International · AMERICAN EXPRESS

2 Bedrooms: 1Q 2T
Bathrooms: 1 guest share

Elizabeth McCracken and Allan Berry

- Dinner: $35–$40
- Full breakfast
- Pets welcome
- Children welcome

Allan and I grow mandarins, native trees and raise coloured sheep on a small organic farm. Our private, peaceful, guest wing with lounge, TV and extensive library has bedrooms and decks with superb views overlooking river, forest swimming pools and mountains. Nearby Forest Park has wonderful walking tracks. We have a productive, rambly garden, Jack Russell Roly, cat Priscilla. No cell phone coverage – best to phone mornings or evenings. We love entertaining and cooking for people, mostly from farm produce. Let's look after you.

Thames

Puriri B&B

B&B • Separate Suite
11 km S of Thames

8836 State Highway 26, Thames, 3578
(07) 868 1073 or 021 521 714
jamfitness@xtra.co.nz
www.puriribnb.co.nz

Double: $100–$120
Single: $80–$100

VISA · MasterCard

1 Bedroom: 1Q 1T
Bathrooms: 1 ensuite

Monique

- One queen bed and one king single twin share
- $35 extra person
- Continental breakfast
- Children welcome
- No smoking on property
- Internet available

We offer a beautifully appointed separate self-contained unit on our 1.5 hectare lifestyle block just 10 minutes south of Thames. Enjoy our heated swimming pool between November and March. Our comprehensive continental breakfast is extensive with home made blueberry muffins sure to hit the spot. Walking distance to a small country pub. Your room comes compete with a TV, DVD and CD player, Microwave, Fridge/Freezer. Tea and Coffee makings and Wi-Fi for your convenience. A little slice of rural New Zealand – enjoy!

Miranda Homestead

B&B

18 km SW of Thames

397 Front Miranda Road, RD 6, Thames 3576
(07) 867 3377 or 021 866 332
ellie.vette@hotmail.com
www.thamesaccommodation.co.nz

Double: $150
Single: $100

2 Bedrooms: 1K 1Q
Bathrooms: 1 private

Ellie Vette

Large, comfortable homestead with spacious bedrooms, in a rural setting one hour from Auckland. Explore abundant birdlife, Miranda Seabird Centre, and the migration of godwits on the Seabird Coast. Relax in the famous Miranda Hot Mineral Pools 2 km away. Savour famous Kaiaua fish and chips, walk the regional parks. Golf, horse riding and fishing nearby. Discover the beautiful Coromandel Peninsula. Guests are assured of a hospitable welcome from Ellie who is a registered nurse and was an international flight attendant.

- Dinner by arrangement
- Full breakfast
- Pet-free home
- Pets welcome
- Not suitable for children
- Weddings and functions
- No smoking on property
- Internet available

Te Puru Coast Bed & Breakfast

Te Puru, Thames Coast

B&B • Cottage with Kitchen • Cottage with 1 double bedroom 140.00 NZ dollars

12 km N of Thames

2A Tatahi Street, Te Puru, Thames Coast, Thames
(07) 868 2866 or 027 656 6058
tepurucoastbnb@xtra.co.nz
www.tepurucoastbnb.co.nz

Double: $120–$140   Single: $100–$100
Children: $25 under 12 years of age

3 Bedrooms: 1Q 1D 1T 2S
Bathrooms: 1 ensuite, 2 private

Bill and Paula Olsen

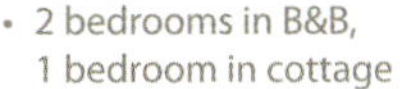

Welcome to the beautiful Thames Coast. Our modern comfortable home is 80 metres off the main coast road. Guest lounge has fridge, TV, books and tea and coffee facilities. You may choose a continental or cooked breakfast and evening meals are on request ($35pp) with complimentary New Zealand wine or beer. Our large deck is yours to enjoy or take a two minute walk to the beach. A warm welcome greets you on arrival with tea or coffee and homemade cookies.

- 2 bedrooms in B&B, 1 bedroom in cottage
- Cottage NZ$140 dollars (2 people)
- Dinner: $35pp, includes New Zealand wine or beer
- Full breakfast
- Pet-free home
- Children welcome

Coromandel — AJ's Homestay

B&B Homestay
10 km S of Coromandel

24 Kowhai Drive, Te Kouma, RD, Coromandel
(07) 866 7057 or 027 458 1624
rm.aj.hintz@actrix.co.nz
www.bnb.co.nz/ajshomestay.html

Double: $125–$145
Single: $125–$145

VISA MasterCard

1 Bedroom: 1Q
Bathrooms: 1 ensuite

Annette and Ray Hintz

- 1 bedroom
- Dinner: $40–$45
- Full breakfast
- Internet available

AJ's Homestay with panoramic sea views overlooking the Coromandel Harbour, spectacular sunsets. A 5 minute walk to a safe swimming beach. Our games room has a billiard and table tennis table. Wireless internet available. Dinner by arrangement. Directions: Thames coast main road (SH25) approximately 50 minutes. At the bottom of the last hill overlooking the Coromandel Harbour. Turn sharp left, at the Te Kouma Road sign. Travel past the boat ramp, next turn left. Kowhai Drive, we are number 24.

Coromandel — Jacaranda Lodge

B&B • Country home
3 km S of Coromandel

3195 Tiki Road, Coromandel, RD 1
(07) 866 8002 or 021 252 6892
info@jacarandalodge.co.nz
www.jacarandalodge.co.nz

Double: $135–$172.5
Single: $80–$167.5
Children: over 8 years only

VISA MasterCard

6 Bedrooms: 1K **3**Q **1**T **1**S
Bathrooms: 2 ensuite, 1 guest share, 1 private

Robin Munch

10%

- Bathrooms: shared bathroom is upstairs; private bathroom may be downstairs – most bedrooms are upstairs
- Special breakfast
- Pet-free home
- Not suitable for children
- Internet available

Robin invites you to share her spacious home set on six acres of tranquil country paradise. Located 3 km south of Coromandel Town, Jacaranda Lodge provides the perfect escape: relax in one of the guest lounges; stroll around the delightful gardens; experience Coromandel's walks, unique attractions and spectacular coastline. Delicious continental breakfasts include fresh organic produce from Jacaranda's orchard. Large, comfortable bedrooms. Free Wi-Fi. Guest kitchen (additional charge may apply). Special dietary needs can be catered for, including kosher. Sleep, eat, enjoy.

Te Kouma B&B — Te Kouma, Coromandel

B&B • Separate Suite • Apartment with Kitchen
8 km S of Coromandel

50 Puriri Road, Te Kouma, Coromandel
(07) 866 7971 or 021 263 5533
ko_jm_muller@xtra.co.nz
www.bnb.co.nz/*.html

Double: $130–$150
Single: $120–$120
Children: welcome

3 Bedrooms: 2Q **2**T
Bathrooms: 2 ensuite, 1 family share

Kurt and Jo Muller

Our well appointed home has the best views in the area. Kurt speaks German and makes delicious wholemeal breads, served for your breakfast with home preserved fruits and jams. Jo collects pacific seashells and old china. We live in a very tranquil place, abounding with bellbirds, tuis and pigeons, over looking Coromandel Harbour. Coromandel town 10 minutes North. Thames 45 minutes South.

- Queens have ensuites.; twins share bathroom
- Dinner: lots of options in Coromandel
- Continental breakfast
- Pet-free home
- Children welcome

Kaeppeli's — Kuaotunu

Cottage • Coastal Country B&B
17 km NE of Whitianga

40 Gray Ave, Kuaotunu, Whitianga, 3592
(07) 866 2445 or 027 656 3442
paradise@kaeppelis.co.nz
www.kaeppelis.co.nz

Double: $140–$210
Single: $95–$140
Children: negotiable

VISA MasterCard eftpos

4 Bedrooms: 2K **4**S
Bathrooms: 4 ensuite

Jill Kaeppeli

A unique, peaceful, secluded, eco-friendly haven with a rustic touch nestled on the hill above Kuaotunu beach. Stunning sea, bush and rural views. Relax, unwind, be yourself, enjoy the natural beauty that surrounds you. Comfortable sunny rooms with private decks and entrances. Dinner by arrangement. Panoramic gazebo dining room. Kitchen and BBQ for guest's use. Clean, safe, sandy beaches, kayaking, tennis, horsetrekking, fishing, golf, arts and crafts. Ideal for exploring Coromandel. Swiss/German spoken. Children welcome. Pets to pamper. Our view? Simply the best.

- Bathrooms: bath and shower, two with ocean views
- Dinner: $40 by arrangement
- Full breakfast
- Pets welcome
- Children welcome
- Internet available

Whitianga — Cosy Cat Cottage

B&B • Cottage with Kitchen
1 km S of Whitianga

41 South Highway (town end), Whitianga
(07) 866 4488
cosycat@xtra.co.nz
www.cosycat.co.nz

Double: $95–$125
Single: $80–$90

VISA MasterCard

3 Bedrooms: 2Q 1D 1S
Bathrooms: 2 ensuite, 1 private

Gordon Pearce

- 2 queen rooms and 1 single room with caty decor
- Cottage $90–$180
- Full breakfast
- Children welcome
- Internet available

Welcome to our picturesque two storied cottage filled with feline memorabilia! Relax with complimentary tea or coffee served on the veranda or in the guest lounge. Enjoy a good nights rest in comfortable beds and choose a variety of treats from our breakfast blackboard menu. You will probably like to meet Honey the cat or perhaps visit the cat hotel in the garden. A separate cottage is available with queen beds, bathrooms and kitchen. Friendly helpful service is assured – hope to see you soon!

Coroglen, Whitianga — Coroglen Lodge

B&B Farmstay • Separate Suite
14 km S of Whitianga

2221 Tairua-Whitianga Rd, RD 1, Whitianga 3591
(07) 866 3225
info@coroglenlodge.co.nz
www.coroglenlodge.co.nz

Double: $120
Single: $80

VISA MasterCard

3 Bedrooms: 2Q 2S
Bathrooms: 2 guest share

Wendy and Nigel Davidson

- Continental breakfast
- Children welcome

Coroglen Lodge is situated on 17 acres of farmland with cattle and alpacas. Nestled in the hills with views of the Coromandel Ranges, this is rural tranquillity. Halfway between Whitianga township and Hot Water Beach there is easy access to both areas and all attractions. Guest area is separate, relaxed, and spacious with a large sunny lounge area for your comfort. Wendy spins, knits and weaves with wool from her alpacas. Nigel has a collection of vintage tractors, and two classic cars.

We have two cats which do not enter the accommodation area.

Andrea's Bed & Breakfast

B&B
150 km SE of Auckland

244 Cook Drive, Whitianga, 3510
(07) 866 0568
welcome@andreasbnb.co.nz
www.andreasbnb.co.nz
Double: $135–$165

VISA MasterCard eftpos

2 Bedrooms: 2Q
Bathrooms: 2 ensuite

10%

Keith and Andrea Foster

We have two lovely, modern comfortable units in a quiet cul-de-sac just two minutes walk from Buffalo Beach. We are just 1.5 km from Whitianga's great selection of café's and restaurants and bars in the town centre. Whitianga is a hub for exploring the wonders of the Coromandel Peninsula's east coast; Mercury Bay, world famous Hot Water Beach and Cathedral Cove, Hahei, Cooks Beach, Kuaotunu, Matarangi or the beautiful unspoiled wonder of New Chum Beach. The breathtaking coastline, beautiful beaches and many other attractions and activities Mercury Bay has to offer will make your visit enjoyable and memorable.

- Full breakfast
- Not suitable for children
- No smoking on property
- Internet available

The Church

Guest House • Cottage with Kitchen • Studios and Separate Cottages
38 km S of Whitianga

87 Beach Road, Hahei, RD 1, Whitianga 3591
(07) 866 3533 or 0274 596 877
info@thechurchhahei.co.nz
www.thechurchhahei.co.nz

Double: $115–$245   Single: $115–$245
Children: $10–$15

VISA MasterCard eftpos

14 Bedrooms: 13Q 12T 13S
Bathrooms: 11 ensuite, 1 family share

Richard Agnew and Karen Blair

The Church, Hahei's unique accommodation and dining experience. The Church building provides a character licensed restaurant for delicious evening meals. 11 cosy, simple wooden cottages and house scattered through delightful bush and gardens offer a range of accommodation and tariffs. Ensuites, microwave, toaster, fridge, tea and coffee facilities. Some cottages and house fully self-contained with woodstoves for winter. Breakfast tray by arrangement. Conference facilities. Enjoy nearby wonders of Cathedral Cove, Hot Water Beach, and the Coromandel Peninsula. Seasonal rates. Winter specials.

- A selection of bedroom types
- Extra adult $20
- Dinner: fine dining
- Breakfast by arrangement
- Pets welcome
- Children welcome
- Weddings and functions
- Internet available

Whangamata

Kotuku

B&B Homestay
2 km S of Town Centre

422 Otahu Road, Whangamata, 3620
(07) 865 6128 or 027 358 1227
bookings@kotukuhomestay.co.nz
www.kotukuhomestay.co.nz

Double: $110–$150
Single: $90–$110

3 Bedrooms: 1KT **2**Q
Bathrooms: 3 ensuite

Linda and Peter Bigge

10%

- Full breakfast
- Not suitable for children
- No smoking on property
- Internet available

Comfortable homestay accommodation in a purpose built home. Rosie, our friendly dog, will give you a warm welcome too! Relax in the spacious lounge or private patio. Kotuku is situated at the quieter end of Whangamata, just a short stroll to the lovely Otahu Estuary Reserve; ideal for walking, swimming, kayaking and paddle boarding. Golf courses (two), shops, cafés a short drive and the surf beach an easy ten minute walk. Do use our kayaks to explore the estuary or visit the unique doughnut island. Wireless internet is available to you.

Whangamata

Pacific View B&B

Luxury B&B • Boutique
2 km SE of Whangamata

125 Pacific View Drive, Whangamata, 3620
(07) 865 8285 or 021 575 191
kofficer@xtra.co.nz
www.whangamatabandb.co.nz

Double: $195–$250
Single: $195–$250
Children: Unfortunately our home is unsuitable

3 Bedrooms: 1KT **2**Q
Bathrooms: 2 ensuite, 1 private

Kathryn Officer and Peter Brignall

- Advance bookings taken for dinner @ $50 pp
- Full breakfast
- Pet-free home
- Not suitable for children
- No smoking on property
- Internet available

Stunning Pacific Ocean views and great hospitality is what Pacific View is all about. This lovely contemporary home has three luxuriously appointed rooms. Start your day with a delicious full breakfast and finish by dining with your hosts Kathryn and Peter where you can be assured of a most enjoyable gourmet dining experience. Whangamata is a favourite Kiwi holiday destination with lots of day trip choices throughout the Coromandel Peninsula within an easy drive. Location is an easy two hour drive from Auckland and to Rotorua.

104onMoore Bed & Breakfast

B&B Homestay
2 km E of Whangamata Post Office

104 Moore Place, Whangamata, 3620
(07) 865 9795 or 027 245 5131
104onmoorenz@gmail.com
bedandbreakfastwhangamata.co.nz

Double: $120–$140

2 Bedrooms: 1K 1Q
Bathrooms: 1 guest share

Kevan and Yvonne Neems

104onMoore bed and breakfast offers you the comforts of home, in peaceful, private surroundings in our special part of the Coromandel.

Start your day with a stroll on the Otahu Estuary, and return to a delicious continental breakfast of homemade muesli, fresh local fruit, natural yoghurts, preserves, freshly squeezed orange juice, a selection of teas, and espresso coffee. You will not be disappointed!

Arrive as strangers, leave as friends.

- Continental breakfast
- Not suitable for children
- No smoking on property
- Internet available

West Wind Gardens

B&B Homestay
1 km S of Waihi

58 Adams Street, Waihi 3610
(07) 863 7208
westwindgarden@xtra.co.nz
www.athomenz.org.nz

Double: $90–$120
Single: $50–$65
Children: $20

VISA MasterCard

2 Bedrooms: 1D 2S
Bathrooms: 1 guest share

Josie and Merv Scott

We offer a friendly restful smoke-free stay in our modern home and garden. Waihi is the gate way to both the Coromandel and the Bay of Plenty with its beautiful beaches. Waihi is a historic town with a vintage railway and a working gold mine discovered 1878 closed 1952. Reopened in 1989 as a open-cast mine. Beach 10 minutes away, beautiful walks, golf courses, trout fishing. Enjoy a home-cooked meal or sample our restaurants. Our interests are gardening, dancing and travel.

- Dinner: $20
- Continental breakfast
- Children welcome

Coromandel

Waihi — Chez Nous

B&B Homestay
0.5 km SW of Waihi

41 Seddon Avenue, Waihi, 3610
(07) 863 7538 or 022 314 3188
sarap@slingshot.co.nz
www.bnb.co.nz/cheznous.html

Double: $85
Single: $65
Children: $20

2 Bedrooms: 1Q 1T
Bathrooms: 1 guest share

Sara Parish

- Dinner: $25pp by arrangement
- Continental breakfast
- Pet-free home
- Children welcome
- No smoking on property
- Internet available

Enjoy a relaxed and friendly atmosphere in a spacious, modern home in an attractive garden setting. Shops and restaurants are within easy walking distance. Discover past and present gold mining activities (tours available), sandy surf beaches, bush walks, 18 hole golf course, art, craft and wine trails. Waihi is an ideal stopover for the traveller who wants to explore the Coromandel Peninsula, Bay of Plenty and Waikato.

Waihi — Casa Mabati

B&B
1.5 km SW of Waihi

9135 State Highway 2, Waihi, 3682
(07) 863 3212
casamabati@orcon.net.nz
www.bnb.co.nz/8423.html

Double: $200
Single: $120

VISA MasterCard

2 Bedrooms: 2Q 1S
Bathrooms: 2 ensuite

Tony Belcher and Cathie Bullock

- 1 room with queen, other room has queen with king single in curtained alcove
- Price includes GST
- Full breakfast
- Not suitable for children
- Internet available

Small, certified organic orchard growing blueberries, feijoas and chestnuts. We also have sheep, poultry, guineafowl and an elderly Jack Russell terrier. The house is set amongst mature chestnut trees, our style is relaxed and rustic. Comfortable, spacious rooms with rural views, balconies, tea and coffee facilities, frig, TV. Ensuites have full-sized bath with shower over, toilet separate. Close to cycle trail, walking tracks, trout fishing. Paeroa side of Waihi, opposite Waihi Hire Centre. SH2 can be noisy, as can the roosters and guineafowl!

The Candy's B&B
Waihi Beach

B&B · Cottage with Kitchen
12 km N of Katikati

43 Athenree Road, Athenree, Waihi Beach
(07) 863 1159
neil.candy@vodafone.co.nz
www.bnb.co.nz/athenree.html

Double: $130–$135
Single: $80–$100

3 Bedrooms: 2K 2T
Bathrooms: 1 ensuite, 1 guest share, 1 private

Gloria and Neil Candy

Take time out: relax. Our modern home is on three acres, with beautiful harbour views: each room has a private patio. Walk to Athenree Hotpools, drive three minutes to Waihi Surf Beach, 10 minutes south to Katikati, two Local Golf Courses, Morton Estate Winery,. 10 minutes north to Waihi Goldmine, walks and excellent restaurants. Neil loves fishing, and Gloria loves crafts. Meals on request. This is paradise and our city pets agree. New one bedroom cottage self-contained no meals supplied.

- 1 Bedroom Cottage self-contained, 2 at main house
- Bathrooms: bath available at the B&B
- Dinner: $32pp
- Continental breakfast

Seagulls Bed & Breakfast
Waihi Beach

Luxury B&B
1.5 km N of Waihi Beach Village

8 West Street (off Pacific Road), Waihi Beach, 3611
(07) 863 4633 or 021 619 586
seagullswaihibeach@yahoo.co.nz
www.seagullsbandb.co.nz

Double: $160–$180
Single: $140–$160

2 Bedrooms: 2Q 1S
Bathrooms: 2 private

Peter and Jane Hughes

Relax and unwind at beautiful Waihi Beach – gateway to Coromandel Peninsula, historic Karangahake Gorge, Orokawa/Homunga walkways and Bay of Plenty. Enjoy spectacular panoramic views of main beach (3minutes walk) and Mayor Island. Watch the sunrise, listen to tui birds sing in the sub tropical setting. Seagulls is modern three level luxury home with guests TV lounge, tea/coffee facilities, fridge, bedrooms all with sea views. Excellent outdoor area, cafés/restaurants RSA closeby, swimming, surfing, fishing, beach and bush walks. Breakfasts include fresh seasonal fruits, homemade preserves, free range eggs.

- Bathrooms: large modern, one with bath and shower and one with shower only
- Full breakfast
- Pet-free home
- Children welcome
- Non-smokers only
- Internet available

Bay of Plenty
Kilometres
0
40
Miles
0
24
Katikati
2
Omokoroa
Mt. Maunganui
Papamoa
Tauranga
Te Puke
Matata
Whakatane
Ohope
35
Ngongotaha
Kawerau
Opotiki
Lake
Rotoiti
Rotorua
1
30
5
2
Taupo
1
Tuangir
Waihau Bay
Whatatutu
Waipaoa
Ormond
Gisborne
Waikaremoana
Mahanga
Beach
Wairoa
Waihi
Whangamata
Coroglen
Tairua
25
Hahei
aotunu

B&B Homestay

18 km S of Tauranga

147 Belk Road South, RD 3, Pyes Pa, Tauranga, 3173
(07) 543 5335 or 021 258 8270
millershaven@kinect.co.nz
www.millershaven.co.nz

Double: $120–$150
Single: $100

VISA MasterCard

2 Bedrooms: 1KT **1**Q
Bathrooms: 2 ensuite

Simon and Renu Miller

- One room with a queen bed, and the other room with two king singles
- Guest Lounge – TV, tea/coffee facilities, microwave
- Dinner $30 pp by prior arrangement
- Full breakfast
- Pet-free home
- Children welcome
- No smoking on property
- Internet available

Welcome to our Rural Homestay, conveniently situated between Tauranga and Rotorua, so really the best of both worlds, day trips to Rotorua, or head over to the coast for the beaches.

Central heating, Freeview TV, Free Wi-Fi, Private Guest Lounge. We provide the best in comfort, a real home away from home.

The homestay boasts real country tranquillity, nestled close to an untouched piece of NZ bush, with abundant bird life. Millers Haven is a truly wonderful place to unwind and relax from a busy city life!

Your hosts Simon and Renu would love to spend time with you, and help organize any trips using their local knowledge.

With a lifetime spent as dairy farmers we have a deep love for this country, and we are passionate about giving our guests the best possible time whilst at our homestay. Feel free to wander over our eight acre lifestyle farm, and gardens.

Te Puna Tauranga

Ngahuia Lodge B&B

Luxury B&B Homestay
13 km N of Tauranga City

191 Crawford Road, Tauranga, 3171
(07) 552 4811 or 21741005
debysowter@me.com
Ngahuialodge.com

Double: $180–$240
Single: $140–$160
Children: all ages catered for rates negotiable

VISA MasterCard eftpos

3 Bedrooms: 2K 1Q
Bathrooms: 1 ensuite, 1 guest share, 1 private

Deby Sowter

- Dinner: meal catered by prior arrangement $45 per person
- Full breakfast
- Children welcome
- Weddings and functions
- No smoking on property
- Internet available

Guests will enjoy the spacious and roomy home with magnificent views. A large open fire place or expansive decks to enjoy the sun

Sunset vista's with a cool drink before dinner. A hearty breakfast sends you out into the days discovering and enjoying all there is in the local area.or neighbouring Rotorua, Waikato or Coromandel.

Catering for a variety of needs we are happy to assist you to may your stay comfortable and memorable.

Mt Maunganui

Pembroke House

B&B
9 km S of Mount Maunganui

12 Santa Fe Key, Royal Palm Beach, Papamoa/Mt Maunganui
(07) 572 1000
PembrokeHouse@xtra.co.nz
www.pembrokehouse.co.nz

Double: $110–$120   Single: $80–$100
Children: $40

VISA MasterCard

3 Bedrooms: 2Q 1T
Bathrooms: 2 ensuite, 1 private

Cathy and Graham Burgess

- All bedrooms have own ensuite or private bathroom
- Full breakfast
- Internet available

A modern home. Cross the road to the Ocean Beach, where you can enjoy swimming, surfing and beach walks. Enjoy stunning sea views while dining at breakfast. Near Fashion Island and Palm Beach Shopping Plaza, restaurants and golf courses. Visit nearby attractions at Mount Maunganui, Tauranga, Rotorua and Whakatane. Separate guest lounge with TV and tea making facilities. Cathy, a schoolteacher, and Graham, semi-retired are widely travelled and enjoy meeting people. We share our home with Sheba – our Tonkinese cat. Unsuitable for pre-schoolers.

Wedge 'n' Wood

B&B
4 km SE of Mount Maunganui

10 Fairway Avenue, Mount Maunganui
(07) 574 6641 or 021 030 9393
wedgenwood@xtra.co.nz
www.wedgenwoodbnb.co.nz

Double: $120–$150
Single: $90–$110

2 Bedrooms: 2KT
Bathrooms: 2 ensuite

Peter and Alison

Our home is ideally situated for golfers, or anyone coming to enjoy what Mount Maunganui and the bay and beaches has to offer. We have two ground floor luxury rooms with super king/twin beds, own ensuite, fridge, TV, complimentary tea/coffee facilites. Two minutes walk to Mount Maunganui golf course, or an easy 10 minute drive to Mount and Tauranga shops. Courtesy pick up from public transport. Breakfast for a king in our sunroom, where our aquarium filled with tropical fish swim lazily about.

- Full breakfast
- Not suitable for children

Fothergills on Mimiha Bed & Breakfast
Pikowai, Matata

B&B • Separate Suite • S/C Suite with kitchen, 2 bedrooms
5 km NW of Matata

84 Mimiha Road, Pikowai, Matata, Whakatane 3194
(07) 322 2224 or 0274 605958
bev@fothergills.co.nz
www.fothergills.co.nz

Double: $150–$150   Single: $125–$130
Children: $30 under 13, $40 teens and extra adults, in B&B

VISA MasterCard

2 Bedrooms: 2KT **2**Q **1**T
Bathrooms: 1 private

Bev and Hilton Fothergill

Come here for rural accommodation with style – and a smile! Our comfortable, quiet, private, two-bedroom self-contained B&B suite is separated from the main house by a covered carport. The small kitchenette lets you prepare your own meal if you want to, and you can use our BBQ. You'll enjoy the peacefulness and lack of road noise or light pollution. With the blinds drawn you'll forget to wake up! Breakfast is hosted in our house or garden, home-grown, home-made, garden fresh, and you can choose the time you want it, or have it delivered.

- 3rd+ nights 10% discount = $135p.n.
- Dinner: $50 each, with wine, by arrangement
- Special breakfast
- Pets welcome
- Children welcome
- Weddings and functions
- Internet available

Whakatane

Whakatane Homestay – Leaburn Farm

Homestay Farmstay • Homestay on a dairy farm
7 km NW of Whakatane

237 Thornton Road, RD 4, Whakatane 3194
(07) 308 7487 or 021 21 21 196
info@whakatanehomestay.co.nz
www.whakatanehomestay.co.nz

Double: $100–$110
Single: $85–$100
Children: negotiable

2 Bedrooms: 1Q 2S
Bathrooms: 1 guest share

Kathleen and Jim Law

- Dinner: $25–$35 negotiable
- Full breakfast
- Pet-free home
- Pets welcome
- No smoking on property
- Internet available

Looking for peace and quiet, or do you want to explore this sunshine coast? If stimulating conversation or a browse in an extensive library is something you enjoy, you are welcome here. Other guests comments over the nearly 30 years we have been home-hosting, include: 'For us it is like coming home' John and Liz Australia. We are handy to the golf course not far from town and a café-gift shop (the Red Barn) on the premises. Be as busy as you like or enjoy restful country atmosphere.

Whakatane

Baker's

B&B Homestay • Cottage with Kitchen
10 km S of Whakatane

40 Butler Road, RD 2, Whakatane
(07) 307 0368 or 027 284 6996
bakers@world-net.co.nz
www.bakershomestay.co.nz

Double: $120–$140   Single: $90–$110
Children: $20

VISA MasterCard

4 Bedrooms: 1KT 2Q 2S
Bathrooms: 2 ensuite, 1 private

Lynne and Bruce Baker

- Bathrooms: fully tiled private ensuites
- Dinner: $50 by arrangement (wine included)
- Continental breakfast
- Pets welcome
- Children welcome
- Internet available

friendly welcome to our lovely country home nestled amongst mature gardens croquet lawn and Avocado orchard. Enjoy our Swimming or spa pool Choose between our delightful fully self-contained two bedroom cottage or be pampered with bed and our special breakfast in our warm spacious home. Sky TV in our comfortable guest lounge Lynne and Bruce are keen outdoor hosts enjoying fishing, surfing, gardening and travel White Island tours, dolphin watching, fishing and diving activities can be arranged for your memorable stay.

Devand

B&B Farmstay

8 km S of Whakatane

108 Te Rahu Road, Whakatane, 3193
(07) 308 0571 or 027 473 6575
gayle@devand.co.nz
www.devand.co.nz

Double: $90–$130
Single: $75–$110
Children: by arrangement

VISA MasterCard

3 Bedrooms: 1K 1D 1T
Bathrooms: 3 ensuite

John and Gayle Couch

- Comfortable rooms, all with ensuites, heating, quality linens and electric blankets.
- Bathrooms: king and twin rooms with showers, double with bath/shower.
- Dinner: two/three course by prior arrangement complimentary wine/beer
- Continental breakfast
- No smoking on property
- Internet available

Enjoy quality, quiet, comfortable accommodation with friendly hosts on a small Red Devon beef cattle stud farm. Relax in the lounge, on the decks, or take an interest in the farm. We have a large, attractive garden with a pond and also grow olives and blueberries; we have a shy pet cat. We have a wide range of interests, have travelled widely and enjoy meeting people.

We offer two and three course evenings meals made with our own, local and free range produce (whenever possible) served with complimentary New Zealand wine and/or beer, by prior arrangement. Special diets can be catered for with notice. Generous continental breakfast with the usual and more.

Comfortable bedrooms with quality linens, toiletries, heating and ensuites.

Kawerau, Whakatane

Kawerau Garden Views Homestay Bed & Breakfast

B&B Homestay • Separate Suite
28 km SW of Whakatane

16 Shepherd Road, Kawerau, Whakatane, 3127
(07) 323 7722 or 0272 295 688
tackenberg@xtra.co.nz
www.kawerauhomestay.co.nz

Double: $95–$120
Single: $80–$95
Children: from $35

VISA MasterCard eftpos

3 Bedrooms: 2K 1Q
Bathrooms: 1 ensuite, 1 family share, 1 private

Willy and Sue Tackenberg

- Continental Breakfast included in nightly rates.
- Dinner supplied if necessary, approximately $25.
- Continental provisions supplied
- Children welcome
- No smoking on property
- Internet available

We offer a peaceful setting with a sunny outlook. The Queen Bedroom with Ensuite is very comfortable and the Superking Bedroom is quite pleasant. Guests share a very nice lounge and diningroom with Sky TV and Wi Fi, There is Fridge/Freezer and other necessary utensils.

Continental Breakfast is included in the nightly charge.

Our new Studio Unit is self-contained and can be booked overnight or weekly. There is off road parking and our friendly G.S.D's are added security at night.

Our B&Bs range from homely to luxurious,
but you can always be sure of superior hospitality.

The Rafters

Apartment with Kitchen
8 km SE of Whakatane

261A Pohutukawa Avenue, Ohope Beach
(07) 312 4856
The_Rafters_Ohope@xtra.co.nz
www.wave.co.nz/pages/macaulay/The_Rafters.htm

Double: $100
Single: $85
Children: $10

2 Bedrooms: 1K 1S
Bathrooms: 1 ensuite

Pat Rafter

- Extra adult $20, limit 1
- Accommodation only
- Pets welcome
- Children welcome

Breakfast is not supplied, Unit is self-contained. Minimum two night stay. Maximum three guests. Sea views: White, Whale islands, East Coast. Safe swimming. Many interesting walks. Golf, tennis, bowls, all within minutes. Licensed Chartered Club Restaurant opposite. Trips to volcanic White Island, fishing, jet boating, diving, swimming with dolphins arranged. Full cooking facilities; private entrance, sunken garden, BBQ. Complimentary: tea, coffee, biscuits, fruit, newspaper, personal laundry service. Pat's interests are: philosophy, theology, history, English literature, the making of grape wines and all spirits, golf, bowls, music and tramping. Courtesy car available. House trained animals welcomed. Four restaurants and oyster farm within five minutes drive. I look forward to your company and assure you unique hospitality. Directions: on reaching Ohope Beach turn right, proceed 2 km to 261A (beach-side) name 'Rafters' on a brick letterbox with illuminated B&B sign.

Ohope | Moanarua Beach Cottage

Luxury • Cottage with Kitchen
10 km E of Whakatane

2 Hoterini Street, Ohope
(07) 312 5924 or 021 255 6192
info@moanarua.co.nz
www.moanarua.co.nz

Double: $135–$160
Single: $115–$140
Children: 1 baby or small child

VISA MasterCard

1 Bedroom: 1K 1S
Bathrooms: 1 ensuite

Miria and Taroi Black

- Dinner: BBQ hangi or 3 course meal by arrangement
- Continental provisions supplied
- Pets welcome
- Internet available

Naumai, haere mai Miria and Taroi welcome you to a unique cultural experience in a romantic hideaway, a restful retreat nestled between the ocean and the harbour in sunny Ohope. Feel free to use BBQ, luxury spa and expansive decks with views of ocean and harbour. Chat with us about local history and Maori art works that adorn our home, cottage and garden. Kick back, relax in your private fully self-contained cottage or enjoy many local activities. Boat tours and kayaks available for hire.

Rotorua | Hunts Farm

Farmstay
4 km SW of Rotorua City Centre

363 Pukehangi Road, Rotorua
(07) 348 1352
sonyahunt@xtra.co.nz
www.bnb.co.nz/hunt.html

Double: $125
Single: $80
Children: $30

2 Bedrooms: 2KT 1Q 2S
Bathrooms: 2 ensuite

Maureen and John Hunt

- Room 1: One queen bed plus one single bed
- Room 2: Two king single beds plus one single bed
- Full breakfast
- Children welcome
- No smoking on property

Come and relax in our spacious modern single story ranch style home as we help you plan your itinerary and book your local tours. Explore our 150 acre scenic farm running beef and deer. Views of farm, lake, forest and city are uninterrupted panoramic and magical. The Guest area has a private entrance, guest lounge with tea/coffee facilities, TV and fridge. There are two triple rooms each with an ensuite and private terrace. One Queen bed with additional single bed and ensuite; two King single beds with additional single bed and ensuite.

Serendipity Homestay

B&B Homestay
4 km S of Rotorua City

3 Kerswell Tce., Tihi-o-Tonga, Rotorua 3015
(07) 347 9385 or 027 609 3268
b.gore@clear.net.nz
www.serendipityhomestay.co.nz

Double: $150–$160
Single: $100–$100
Children: under 12 $40

2 Bedrooms: 1Q 2S
Bathrooms: 1 private

Kate and Brian Gore

Marvel at unsurpassed views of geysers, city, lakes and beyond from our home. Relax on the sunny deck, conservatory or in the privacy of our garden. Indulge in home-cooked cuisine with friendly hosts who have enjoyed hosting for many years. Our interests are, golf, walking, travel, the environment, and meeting people. Use our extensive local knowledge to help you plan activities and places of interest while in Rotorua. We are familiar with other highlights to visit as you travel through our beautiful country. Welcome! GPS Co-Ordinates 38°10′16″S 176°14′32″E

- Bathrooms: spa bath plus shower
- Dinner: $35 by arrangement
- Full breakfast
- Pet-free home
- Children welcome
- Non-smokers only
- Internet available

Walker Homestay & B&B

B&B • Cottage with Kitchen
5 km SE of Rotorua

13 Glenfield Road, Owhata, Rotorua 3010
(07) 345 3882 or 021 050 9633
colleen.walker@clear.net.nz
www.bnb.co.nz/walkerhomestay.html

Double: $120–$150
Single: $80–$100

2 Bedrooms: 1Q 1T
Bathrooms: 1 private

Colleen and Isaac Walker

A warm welcome awaits you in two – bedroom cottage in own garden area or guest room in a modest home with separate entrance. Have complete privacy or become part of family. Colleen is a retired business tutor and active in Lions. Isaac (Ike), a NZ Maori, is a coach driver, with a background in farming and paper industry, keen fisherman and golfer. Both enjoy motohome travel. 24 hours notice for Dinner. Off-road parking. Let them help you plan your time in this beautiful place.

- 2 single beds 1 queen sized bed
- Extra guest $20
- Dinner: $25–$45; 24 hours notice required
- Full breakfast
- Pet-free home
- Children welcome
- Internet available

Rotorua — Aroden B&B Homestay

B&B Homestay
4 km E of Rotorua

2 Hilton Road, Lynmore, Rotorua, 3010
(07) 345 6303 or 027 696 4211
aroden@xtra.co.nz
www.aroden.co.nz

Double: $140–$155
Single: $95–$110
Children: negotiable

VISA MasterCard

2 Bedrooms: 2Q
Bathrooms: 1 ensuite, 1 private

Leonie and Paul Kibblewhite

- Full breakfast
- Internet available

A great central location with character, style and comfort! Thermal and lakes nearby, Whakarewarewa Forest adjacent (glow-worms), city five minutes drive. Enjoy two lounge areas, well-appointed rooms with comfortable beds and fine linen, kitchen, central heating/open fire, patio, spa, a private and luxuriant garden. Paul, scientist, and Leonie, teacher, are fifth generation Kiwi with real knowledge of this remarkable area. And meet Enzo, Paul's delightful guide dog. Breakfast is definitely special – this couple enjoys food! Leonie parle francais. Internet, laundry available.

Rotorua — Lake Okareka B&B

B&B • Each room is self-contained, kitchenette, ensuite, terrace with l
10 km NE of Rotorua centre

10 Okareka Loop Road, R.D 5, Rotorua
(07) 362 8245
patricia.scott@xtra.co.nz
www.lakeokarekabnb.co.nz

Double: $140–$160
Single: $100–$120

VISA MasterCard

3 Bedrooms: 3Q
Bathrooms: 3 ensuite

Patricia and Ken Scott

- Special breakfast
- Children welcome
- No smoking on property
- Internet available

A very warm welcome awaits you at tranquil Lake Okareka, one of the most beautiful Lakes in the area. Our modern home captures magnificent Lake views. Stroll along the waters edge, enjoy the native bush, ferns and birdlife. Use our local knowledge on all nearby hot pools, fishing, scenic, thermal, adventure and cultural activities. Excellent swimming, complimentary kayaks available. Our environment is quiet and peaceful yet only ten minutes from Rotorua, the perfect retreat. Each room is self-contained with enclosed kitchenette, indoor and outdoor furniture, private entrance.

Lakestay Rotoiti

B&B
20 km NE of Rotorua

173 Tumoana Road, Lake Rotoiti, RD 4 Rotorua
(07) 345 4089 or 027 418 8404
lakestayrotoiti@xtra.co.nz
www.bnb.co.nz/user299.html

Double: $135–$160

VISA MasterCard

2 Bedrooms: 2Q
Bathrooms: 2 ensuite

Graeme and Raewyn Natusch

Lakestay Rotoiti, a very special destination for the discerning couple or individual travellers both summer and winter with friendly informative hosts and siamese cat. One of just three lakefront properties in a beautiful secluded sandy bay surrounded by native bush, forest and stunning lake views from all living and guest bedrooms. Excellent swimming, trout fishing, walking tracks and natural rejuvinating hot bath is nearby. Guests enjoy complimentary use of kyaks, dingy, windsurfer and bicycles. Wonderful evening dinner by arrangement. Directions are essential. A truely unique experience.

- Dinner: $35
- Full breakfast

The difference between a B&B and a hotel
is that you don't hug the hotel staff when you leave.

Rotorua

Rotorua's Legend on the Lake Homestay

B&B Homestay • Apartment with Kitchen
2 km N of Rotorua centre

33 Haumoana Street, Koutu, Rotorua
(07) 347 1123 or 027 492 7122
muzzandheb@kol.co.nz
www.troutnz.co.nz

Double: $150   Single: $150
Children: $20

VISA MasterCard

3 Bedrooms: 2Q 1D 1S
Bathrooms: 1 ensuite, 1 private

Murray and Heather Watson

- Additional Adults $30/night per person
- Bathrooms: yes available with the private facility.
- Dinner: $45per person. By arrangement
- Full breakfast
- Pet-free home

On arrival you will be greeted with our magnificent, quiet and secluded lakes-edge view and a genuine Kiwi welcome. Please join us beside the lake for refreshments as we would love to help you plan your stay by sharing our local knowledge of the area and its many attractions. Hearing the tranquil lapping of the lake you will find it hard to believe you are only three minutes drive from the city centre. You will find your self-contained apartment to have all the comforts of home (washing machine, TV, DVD, video, stereo, oven, microwave and dishwasher). Separate bedroom (queen) and living area/kitchen with ensuite access from both rooms. Free email access. Our smoke-free apartment ensures a freshness you will enjoy.

Breakfast includes fruit, yoghurt, cereal, juice and tea/coffee followed by a cooked breakfast – all this and you can choose the time you would like to have it served. Breakfast is a great time to get to know us and for us to help you make best use of your time in this volcanic thermal paradise. We are more than happy to assist with local bookings and recommend you sample some of the strong local Maori culture. Murray operates a trout fishing charter business on Lake Rotorua from our Lakeside jetty. Special rates apply. We have both travelled extensively, internationally and throughout New Zealand and enjoy meeting people from.

Lakeview Heights Farm Stay

B&B Farmstay
19 km N of Rotorua

269 Te Waerenga Road, Rotorua, 3096
022 049 5492 or 022 048 9964
lakeviewheightsnz@gmail.com
www.lakeviewheightsnz.co.nz

Double: $185–$200
Single: $170–$175
Children: welcome

VISA MasterCard eftpos

4 Bedrooms: 2Q 1T 4S
Bathrooms: 3 ensuite, 1 private

10%

Alan and Georgina Judd

Our country home has three guest rooms with superb views across the lake to the city and the volcanic Mount Tarawera in the distance. We are bordered by a Scenic Reserve with native trees, ferns Tuis and Bell birds. George and Alan are well travelled worldwide and would be delighted to give you a tour of the gardens and fields, with the sheep and chickens. Tui the dog will make you most welcome. Trout fishing, golf course and Rotorua's arttractions all nearby.

- Free Wi-Fi
- Dinner by arrangement 3 courses including drinks – $45
- Full breakfast
- Children welcome
- No smoking on property
- Internet available

Mokoia Downs Estate B&B

B&B Farmstay · Boutique
11 km N of Rotorua

64 Mokoia Road, Rotorua, 3097
(07) 332 2930 or 0210 451 760
mokoiadowns@yahoo.co.nz
mokoiadowns.com

Double: $160–$225
Single: $150–$185
Children: (under 12) $80 per child

VISA MasterCard Diners Club American Express eftpos

4 Bedrooms: 1K 3Q 1D 1T
Bathrooms: 1 ensuite, 1 family share, 1 private

Mick and Teresa O'Mahony

Mokia Downs Estate is a boutique Rotorua B&B offering a farmstay experience on five acres of beautiful, park-like grounds with small scenic lake. Situated in a secluded, enchantingly peaceful and sulphur-free setting, Mokoia Downs is just a short drive from central Rotorua and close to all main attractions. Wake up to the sound of native birdsong, smell the home-baked bread and freshly brewed coffee, and then perhaps take a swim or stroll before enjoying a memorable breakfast that will set you up for the whole day.

- Full breakfast
- Children welcome
- No smoking on property
- Internet available

Acacia Bay, Taupo

Leece's Homestay

Homestay
6 km SW of Taupo

98 Wakeman Road, Acacia Bay, Taupo 3330
(07) 378 6099 or 027 378 6099
www.bnb.co.nz/leeceshomestay.html

Double: $110–$120
Single: $80

2 Bedrooms: 1K 1Q 2S
Bathrooms: 1 ensuite, 1 guest share

Marlene Leece

- Continental breakfast

Your host Marlene and Jaspa (my Birman cat) extend a warm welcome to our large wood interior home with woodfire for winter and north facing sunny deck from guest bedroom. Also magnificent view of Lake Taupo from lounge and front deck. There are bush walks and steps down to lake to swim in summer with an extended new piece of road. Easy walking and different view. Awaiting your arrival with anticipation of making friends. Please phone for directions.

Rangatira Park – Huka Falls

Rive Gauche B&B Lodge

Luxury Homestay • B&B rooms plus self-contained studio unit with B&B option
2 km N of Taupo

128 Ferndale Way, Rangatira Park, Taupo 3384
(07) 377 6167 or 021 050 6735
info@rivegauchetaupo.co.nz
www.rivegauchetaupo.co.nz

Double: $195–$245   Single: $175–$200
Children: negotiable. Rollaway bed available for studio

3 Bedrooms: 1K 1KT 1Q 1S
Bathrooms: 3 ensuite

Lynne Fauchelle and Jim Veitch

- Dinner: Many restaurants in Taupo. Dinner by prior arrangement only.
- Full breakfast
- Pet-free home
- Children welcome
- No smoking on property
- Internet available

Set on a stunning one hectare site on the left bank of the Waikato River, Rive Gauche was purpose-built to offer quality lodge-style B&B accommodation. Our rooms offer single/double and twin/double/triple options, B&B or self-contained in the studio. Guests have access to a kitchenette with fridge, crockery and tea/coffee facilities, satellite TV, free Wi-Fi and barbecue. Independent access with off street parking adjacent. Warm hospitality is our priority and fluent French is spoken.

B&B Homestay
2.5 km S of Taupo

10 Coprosma Crescent, Taupo, 3330
(07) 378 6823 or 021 237 2405
stay@bnbnumberten.co.nz
www.bnbnumberten.co.nz

Double: $175–$195
Single: $130–$150

VISA MasterCard

2 Bedrooms: 1K 1KT
Bathrooms: 2 ensuite

Ann and John Page

'Are you looking for a Bed and Breakfast in Taupo that offers fun and a relaxed atmosphere? If so, then B&B @ Number Ten is the place for you. We have fabulous views of Lake Taupo, from our quiet, well furnished, modern home. Both groundfloor guest rooms are warm and sunny each with ensuite. We are happy to help you make the most of your time in Taupo and we love to hear of your travel adventures. Children can be accommodated by prior arrangement.'

- 1 King Bedroom, 1 Super King/Twin
- Full breakfast
- Pet-free home
- Children welcome
- No smoking on property
- Internet available

B&B Homestay
13 km N of Taupo

159 Palmer Mill Rd, RD 4 Taupo, 3384
(07) 378 8837 or 0274 785 606 (Heather)
info@kinara.co.nz
www.kinara.co.nz

Double: $185–$210
Children: 0 to 3 yrs free; 4 to10 $25 night

VISA MasterCard

3 Bedrooms: 2Q 1T
Bathrooms: 2 ensuite, 1 private

Heather and Graeme

Welcome to Kinara Country Homestay; where you will be welcomed as a friend into our comfortable, cosy home. We are situated in the countryside; close to the Wairakei Tourist Park amenities; Huka Falls, Aratiatia Rapids and the Lava Glass Gallery to name but a few. Wake up to birdsong and the aroma of freshly brewed coffee, bacon and eggs etc. We have lovely a private garden, lovely views and peace and quiet. Do come and be a part of our family for a while, you will be most welcome!

- Bathrooms: showers only
- Dinner: At time of booking or upon request (breakfast time)
- Full breakfast
- Children welcome
- No smoking on property

Bay of Plenty

Turangi — Brown Trout House

B&B Homestay
1 km SW of Turangi Information Centre

11 Kokopu Street, Turangi, 3334
(07) 386 0308 or 027 253 3415
kohinoor@xtra.co.nz
www.browntrouthouse.co.nz

Double: $130
Single: $90
Children: Negotiable

VISA MasterCard

3 Bedrooms: 1KT **1**Q **2**T
Bathrooms: 1 guest share, 1 private

Bruce and Nita Wilde

- Dinner: Lunches and Dinner By Prior Arrangement
- Full breakfast
- Internet available

Welcome to Brown Trout house overlooking the Tongariro River in Turangi, halfway between Auckland and Wellington. Your bedroom opens on to the spacious deck. Have refreshments or step out our gate on to the Tongariro River Walkway or in to world famous fishing pools. Bruce is a keen fisherman willing to share his knowledge. Shuttle pickup for the Tongariro Crossing arranged. Choose walks, golf, skiing or a hot swim five mins drive away. Friendly experienced hosts willing to give genuine kiwi hospitality.

Turangi — Omori Lake House

Luxury • Lodge
15 km SW of Turangi

31 Omori Road, Omori
(07) 386 0420 or 021 667 092
stay@omorilakehouse.co.nz
www.omorilakehouse.co.nz

Double: $175
Single: $165

VISA MasterCard

2 Bedrooms: 2K
Bathrooms: 2 ensuite

Niel and Raewyn Groombridge

- Dinner by arrangement
- Special breakfast
- Pet-free home
- Not suitable for children

Our new boutique accommodation high above Omori has stunning views across to Taupo. There are two ensuite guest rooms with king beds, tea/coffee facilities and private deck. Raewyn loves to cook and eating well is part of the experience. Enjoy barbeques or meals with kiwi classics Omori on the menu. We are close to a variety of activities including fly-fishing, The Tongariro Alpine crossing, bush walks, thermal pools and ski slopes.

Founders@Turangi

B&B

3 km SW of Tongariro National Park

253 Taupahi Road, Turangi, 3334
(07) 386 8539
chris@founders.co.nz
www.founders.co.nz

Double: $180
Single: $120

VISA MasterCard eftpos NEW ZEALAND LIMITED

4 Bedrooms: 2KT 3Q
Bathrooms: 4 ensuite

Peter and Chris Stewart

Welcome to Turangi and to our home where four ensuite guest bedrooms open onto the veranda. A myriad of outdoor activities are available at this place for all seasons, with the Tongariro River, the volcanoes of Tongariro National Park and magnificent Lake Taupo on our doorstep. Breakfast each morning, in our sunny dining room.

We happily cook early breakfasts for Tongariro Alpine Crossing adventurers!

Enjoy the views at lakeside restaurants or walk to dinner in town.

- Full breakfast
- Pet-free home
- Not suitable for children
- No smoking on property
- Internet available

The Birches

B&B Homestay

52 km S of Taupo

13 Koura Street, Turangi
(07) 386 5140 or 021 136 4264
tineke.peter@xtra.co.nz
www.thebirches.net.nz

Double: $170
Single: $150

VISA MasterCard

1 Bedroom: 1Q
Bathrooms: 1 ensuite

Tineke and Peter Baldwin

Close to the world renowned Tongariro River we welcome you to our charming residence set in park-like surroundings on a quiet street. This unique location is ideally suited for many outdoor pursuits such as tramping, fly fishing, skiing, rafting and golf. We offer superior and spacious ensuite accommodation with TV and coffee/tea making facilities in a separate part of the house. Your Dutch/Canadian hosts have lived in several countries and can speak Dutch and French. Dinner by arrangement.

- Dinner by arrangement
- Full breakfast
- Pet-free home
- Not suitable for children
- Non-smokers only
- Internet available

Turangi

Tui Lodge

B&B

1 km SW of Turangi

196 Taupahi Road, Turangi
(07) 386 0840
tui-lodge@xtra.co.nz
www.tui-lodge.com

Double: $270–$335
Single: $225

4 Bedrooms:
Bathrooms: 4 ensuite

Ian and Frances Jenkins

- 4 super/king
- Full breakfast
- Internet available

Tui Lodge is a purpose built B&B set in parklike grounds.

Peaceful accommodation with Kiwi hospitality. Underfloor heating, with four spacious bedrooms, separate guest lounge with tea/coffee making facilities.

Close to Restrauants, Tongariro Alpine Crossing, trout fishing, rafting, horse trekking, thermal area and hot pools.

Free Internet available.

If you need any information ask your hosts
they are your own personal travel agent and guide.

Whitewater Lodge

Luxury • Luxury Lodge B&B option or solely occupy lodge and self cater.

35 km S of Taupo

50 Herekiekie Street, Turangi
021 518 033 or (09) 420 4633
thecatos@xtra.co.nz
www.bnb.co.nz/8541.html
Children: Age dependant

5 Bedrooms: 2K **2**Q **1**D
Bathrooms: 1 ensuite, 2 guest share, 2 private

Heather Cato

- Beautiful top range Sealy beds Super Kings and Queens.
- Couples $160 per night. Singles $!30 per night
- Dinner by arrangement
- Breakfast by arrangement
- Pets welcome
- Children welcome
- No smoking on property
- Internet available

Only one person, Susan our lodge manager, will reside in Whitewater Lodge during your stay if you choose to have her there. Otherwise, you may choose to solely occupy the lodge and Susan will return each morning to provide breakfast and bed making etc if required. She is thoroughly familiar with Turangi, Taupo, Ruapehu and can direct you in your pursuit of the many local tourist activities. Or you may wish to completely relax at the lodge, read a book by the river, use the spa, enjoy the gardens, sit by the roaring open fire.

The lodge is very well configured to allow lots of privacy and quiet time away from other guests if there are any at all, as we like to keep numbers small or be exclusively booked by families or groups of friends etc.

The lodge is absolute riverfront and is down a long right of away therefore offering privacy and peace. It is set on over an acre of sunny gardens and expansive lawns. The lodge has just been redecorated throughout with luxurious beds, brand new appliances and quality floor coverings. It's a heavenly holiday retreat.

Gisborne
Waihau Bay
Te Kaha
Maraenui
35
Tolaga Bay
2
Gisborne
2
0 Kilometres 20
0 Miles 12

Papatahi

Homestay • Separate Suite
3 km N of Tolaga Bay

427 Waiapu Rd, Tolaga Bay
(06) 862 6623 or 021 283 7178
nickibrucej@xtra.co.nz
www.suffolks.co.nz

Double: $130
Single: $90
Children: half price

3 Bedrooms: 1Q 1D 2S
Bathrooms: 1 ensuite, 1 guest share

Nicki and Bruce Jefferd

Papatahi Homestay… easy to find being just 3 km north of the Tolaga Bay township, on the Pacific Coast Highway. We have a comfortable, modern, sunny home set in a wonderful garden. Papatahi offers separate accommodation with ensuite. A golf course, fishing charters, the Tolaga Bay Cashmere Co. and several magnificent beaches are all just minutes away. Daily farm activities are often of interest to our guests. Friendly farm pets add to the experience! Great country meals and good wine are a speciality. Inspection will impress!

- Dinner: $35pp
- Full breakfast
- Children welcome

Fairlight

B&B Farmstay
14 km S of Gisborne

52 Saddler Road, R D 2, Gisborne 4072
(06) 862 8499 or 027 440 9556
orchiston@clear.net.nz
www.bnb.co.nz/Fairlight.html

Double: $130
Single: $100
Children: By arrangement

4 Bedrooms: 1K 1Q 1D 3S
Bathrooms: 2 private

Kay and Don Orchiston

Our home is situated on a hill with expansive views of the sea, city and rural wine region. We are 14 kms south of the city. Gisborne has beautiful beaches, scenic walks, restaurants and excellent sport facilities. We have two friendly sheep dogs and two elusive bengal cats. Visitors welcome to experience handling sheep and cattle.

We now have a lovely swimming pool. Gisborne gets really hot during the summer months.

Trout fishing and deep sea fishing by prior arrangement.

- Bathrooms: 1 shower as well
- Dinner: We are happy to do dinner by arrangement
- Full breakfast
- Pets welcome
- Children welcome
- Internet available

Gisborne

Te Kura

B&B

14 Cheeseman Road, Gisborne, 4010
(06) 863 3497 or 027 303 0727
Paul@tekura.co.nz
www.bnb.co.nz/8373.html

Double: $140–$140
Single: $100–$100

VISA MasterCard

1 Bedroom: 1Q
Bathrooms: 1 ensuite

Paul and Bronwyn

- Full breakfast
- Not suitable for children
- No smoking on property
- Internet available
- Tea/coffee facilities in room
- Separate guest lounge
  with TV
- Swimming pool

A grand residence in the Arts and Crafts style; this is one of Gisborne's finest residential landmark properties! Located in a peaceful riverside setting in 3/4acre mature gardens yet with a convenient 10 mins riverside stroll to harbour/city restaurants and amenities. Relax in the guest lounge or by the pool overlooking the river. An ideal base from which to explore Gisborne and it's surrounds.

Free Wi-Fi. Full breakfast included. Recommended by Lonely Planet, The Rough Guide and Frommers Travel Guides.

Just as we have variety of B&Bs
you will also be offered a variety of breakfasts,
and they will always be generous.

Taranaki, Wanganui, Ruapehu, Rangitikei
Te Awamutu
Otorohanga
Waitomo
Te Kuiti
Piopio
30
3
4
Taumarunui
43
Owhango
47
Tura
New Plymouth
43
Egmont
National Park
Stratford
3
Ohakune
4
Taihape
3
Whanganui
Fielding
Colyton
Newbury
Woodville
Oroua Downs
Palmerston
North
Tokomaru
Foxton
Pahiat
Eketahuna
Ku
Levin
Otaki
0   Kilometres   40
0   Miles   24

New Plymouth

Timata Ora

Luxury B&B • Luxury B&B 5 min walk from CBD
0.01 km N of New Plymouth City

55 Gover Street, New Plymouth, Taranaki
(06) 757 9917 or 0274 523 885
carol_rodney@iconz.co.nz
www.timataora.com

Double: $145–$160
Single: $135–$150

VISA MasterCard eftpos

5 Bedrooms: 4Q 1T
Bathrooms: 4 ensuite

Carol and Rodney Hall

- $250 family suite when both bedrooms used
- Bathrooms: all suites each have own bathroom
- Full breakfast
- No smoking on property
- Internet available

We warmly welcome guests to our fully refurbished double glazed central city 1920's heritage home. Timata Ora offers four luxurious queen suites (one with four Poster) each with own bathroom, TV, fridge, hair drier, iron/ironing board, heated towel rails, complimentary beverages and in room treats. The family suite has an additional twin bedroom along with the queen bedroom. Breakfast in your suite, Dining Room, in the conservatory or on the terrace then enjoy the wonderful hospitality and sights New Plymouth and Taranaki offer.

Bell Block, New Plymouth

K & J's Bed and Breakfast

B&B
7 km SE of New Plymouth

94 Parklands Avenue, Bell Block, 4312
(06) 755 4199 or 027 294 9682
kjhosking@xtra.co.nz
www.bnb.co.nz/KKBedandBreakfast.html

Double: $120
Single: $90

2 Bedrooms: 2Q
Bathrooms: 1 ensuite, 1 private

Keith and Joy Hosking

- 1 down stairs and 1 upstairs
- Continental breakfast
- Pet-free home
- Not suitable for children
- No smoking on property
- Internet available

Lovely sea and mountain views very close to airport. 10 minutes to central New Plymouth. Restaurant, Bank and shopping facilities in walking distance. Able to walk to the beach. Situated in quiet street. 2007 winner of 'Supreme House of the Year' award. Broadband and Wireless available. Very close to Golf Course. We have bikes available to use on our beautifulwalkway. Lovely vibrant city with lots of cafés and parks easy to get around. No efpos cash or cheques accepted.

Hosking House — New Plymouth

Luxury B&B
1 km E of Isite

1 Victoria Road, New Plymouth, 4310
+64 21 307 603 or 027 864 6088
rachel@hoskinghouse.com
www.hoskinghouse.com

Double: $150–$220

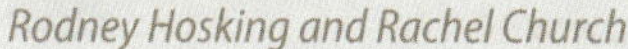

3 Bedrooms: 1K 2Q
Bathrooms: 3 ensuite

Rodney Hosking and Rachel Church

With its period architecture, luxuriously appointed suites, extensive gardens, and warm hospitality, guests of Hosking House will immediately feel the pampering benefits of this unique boutique environment. Located in the CBD of New Plymouth, Hosking House benefits from all this dynamic city has to offer. 'Hosking House – in the heart of New Plymouth.' Hosking House's owners Rodney Hosking and Rachel Church have turned the classic and elegant walls of one Victoria road, into a fabulous place to stay in this vibrant city.

- Bathrooms: large, soaking tubs and walk in showers.
- Full breakfast
- Children welcome
- Weddings and functions
- No smoking on property
- Internet available

Stratford Lodge B&B — Stratford

B&B
0.1 km N of Stratford

3514 State Highway 3, Stratford 600 metres N of PO, Stratford 4394
(06) 765 8324
stallardbb@infogen.net.nz
www.stratfordlodge.co.nz

Double: $98   Single: $65
Children: $12–5 to 15 yrs

4 Bedrooms: 2D 2T 2S
Bathrooms: 4 ensuite, 1 guest share

Billieanne and Corb Stallard

Graceful 'Upstairs Downstairs' comfort. A down to earth gardeners rest Aga-cooked or continental breakfast included. Free self-catering kitchen, tea, coffee, biscuits. Homely or private. Own key. Optional separate lounge. Restaurants, taverns, shops nearby. Rooms are antique, romantic with TV, heaters, electric blankets, serviced daily. Gardens, BBQ, row boat, bush bath, river walks. 15 minutes to Mount Egmont ski fields, tramping. Centrally located easy distance to New Plymouth, museums, famous gardens, tourist attractions. Interests include gemstones, travel, art. Welcome.

- Family Room (4 people) $120
- Accommodation only with use of guest kitchen
- Accommodation only
- Pet-free home
- Children welcome
- Internet available

Whanganui · Bushy Park Homestead

B&B
24 km N of Wanganui

791 Rangitatau East Road, RD8 Kai Iwi
Wanganui, 4578
(06) 342 9879 or (0800) BUSHYP (287.497) – NZ onl
info@bushypark.co.nz
www.bushypark.co.nz

Double: $125–$155   Single: $90–$125
Children: Foldaway beds and cot available

6 Bedrooms: 3Q **1**D **2**T
Bathrooms: 4 guest share

Theo and Viv Perry

- Dinner: Fully licensed and dinner by prior arrangement
- Continental breakfast
- Pet-free home
- Children welcome
- Weddings and functions
- Non-smokers only
- Internet available

Established for over a century, Bushy Park Homestead and Forest has a unique location in an ancient rainforest. Bushy Park is a Category One Historic Places Trust registered building in a forest setting and is a Top 25 Australasian Ecological Restoration Project. A pest-proof fence surrounds the 240 acre sanctuary creating a 'mainland island' which protects endangered birds from all predators. Enjoy the relaxed atmosphere with wonderful self-guided bush walks where the native forest has been preserved. You will see 'Ratanui', regarded as New Zealand's largest northern rata.

Taumarunui · Matawa Country Home

Farmstay
5 km NE of Taumarunui

213 Taringamotu Road, Taumarunui
(07) 896 7722
costleyj@farmside.co.nz
www.bnb.co.nz/taumarunui.html

Double: $100–$120
Single: $70–$80

2 Bedrooms: 1K **1**T
Bathrooms: 1 guest share

Shirley and Allan Jones

- Dinner by arrangement
- Continental breakfast

Our spacious home is situated 5 km from the centre of Taumarunui surrounded by a peaceful one acre garden with a native bush backdrop filled with NZ native birds. The bedrooms open on to a large verandah. Laundry available. A stream runs along one boundary of the 80 acre property suitable for walks and summertime swimming. A golf course is located within two km, along with guided mountain walks, canoeing, hot pools, scenic flights, skiing, trout fishing and white-water rafting are all within an hours drive.

Fernleaf Farmstay/Bed and Breakfast — Owhango, Taumarunui

B&B Farmstay
15 km S of Taumarunui

58 Tunanui Road, RD 1, Owhango 3989
(07) 895 4847 or 0800 FERNLEAF or 027 362 2993
fernleaf.farm@xtra.co.nz
www.fernleaffarmstay.co.nz

Double: $110–$140
Single: $90–$110

4 Bedrooms: 3Q 1T
Bathrooms: 2 ensuite, 1 guest share

Carolyn and Melvin Forlong

Relax in the tranquil Tunanui valley mid way between Wellington and Auckland. Only 500 metres from SH4 – close for convenience – far enough away for peace and quite. Melvin is three rd generation to farm Fernleaf – his Romney flock has been recorded for 80 years. Experience local attractions – a tour of our beautiful farm, fascinating local glow worms, Trout fishing in the Whanganui/Whakapapa rivers, the world famous Tongariro crossing, Forgotten Highway. Magnificent local bush walks. 42 traverse and other cycling pathways.

- Full breakfast
- Children welcome
- No smoking on property
- Internet available
- Beautiful country setting
- Close to Tongariro National Park
- Log fire in winter
- Dinner by arrangement

Mitredale — Ohakune

Homestay Farmstay
6 km SW of Ohakune

208 Smiths Road, RD, Ohakune
(06) 385 8016 or 027 453 1916
mitredale@ihug.co.nz
www.bnb.co.nz/mitredale.html

Double: $130
Single: $70

2 Bedrooms: 1D 2S
Bathrooms: 1 family share, 1 guest share

Audrey and Diane Pritt

We farm sheep, empty dairy cows and run a boarding kennel in a beautiful peaceful valley with magnificent views of Mount Ruapehu. Tongariro National Park for skiing, walking, photography. Excellent 18 hole golf course, great fishing locally. We are members of Ducks Unlimited (a conservation group)and our local wine club. We have three labradors. We offer dinner traditional farmhouse (Diane, a cook book author with new kitchen), or breakfast with excellent home-made jams. Take Raetihi Road, at Hotel/BP Service Station corner. 4 km to Smiths Road. Last house 2 km.

- Comfortable, cosy electric blankets on all beds
- Dinner: $55pp by arrangement
- Continental breakfast
- Pets welcome
- Internet available

Ohakune

Penguins B&B

B&B
27 km NW of Waiouru

56 Goldfinch Street, Ohakune, 4625
(06) 385 9411
douglas.richard@xtra.co.nz
www.penguinsnz.co.nz

Double: $75–$85
Single: $75–$75

eftpos
NEW ZEALAND LIMITED

4 Bedrooms: 3Q **1**D **3**S
Bathrooms: 1 ensuite, 1 guest share

Douglas and Richard

- Full breakfast
- Children welcome
- No smoking on property
- Internet available

We are a relaxed and informal Edwardian Villa Bed and Breakfast situated close to Mount Ruapehu in the township of Ohakune.

Being close to Mount Ruapehu, Tongariro and Whanganui national parks we are considered the place to stay regarding tramping, walking, canoeing and mountain biking activities. let us book your activity for you. shuttle service is from the door.

Tongariro alpine crossing booking service.

Mountain biking booking service.

If you would like dinner
most hosts require 24 hours notice.

Tarata Fishaway Lodge

**Luxury B&B Farmstay • Separate Suite •
Apartment with Kitchen • Cottage with Kitchen
• Luxury River Retreats Farmstay**
26 km SE of Taihape

925 Mokai Road, RD 3, Taihape
(06) 388 0354 or 027 279 7037
fishaway@xtra.co.nz   www.tarata.co.nz

Double: $130–$240   Single: $70–$180
Children: under 5 $20 Children 6 to 12 yrs $45.00
VISA MasterCard

9 Bedrooms: 5KT **4**Q **4**S
Bathrooms: 5 ensuite, 1 private

Stephen and Trudi Mattock

- Ourdoorsmark (Outdoors New Zealand Safety
  Audit Certified)
- 3 Private spa pools
- Bathrooms: honeymoon suite has spa bath and
  spa pool
- Dinner: $47pp by arrangement
- Full breakfast
- Approved pets welcome
- Children welcome
- Internet available

We are very lucky to have a piece of New Zealand's
natural beauty. Tarata is nestled in bush in the
remote Mokai Valley where the picturesque
Rangitikei River meets the rugged Ruahine Ranges.
Wilderness and unique trout fishing are right at
our doorstep. Stephen offers guided fishing and
scenic rafting trips for all ages. Raft through the
gentle crystal clear waters of the magnificent
Rangitikei River, spot the many trout, visit Middle
Earth and a secret waterfall, stunning scenery you
will never forget. Come on a farm tour meeting
our many friendly farm pets including Panda the
llama and Teddy the Alpaca. Stay in our Homestead,
Tree House or River Retreat and relax on the large
decking amidst native birds and trees. Soak in your
own private spa pool with million dollar views of
the Rangitikei River. Peace, privacy and tranquillity
at its best! We will even deliver a candle light dinner
to your door. We think Tarata is truly a magic place
and we would love sharing it with you.

Honeymoon Retreat, Trout Fishing, Scenic Rafting,
Visit LOTR, Bungy, Mini Golf with a difference,
swimming pool, spa pools, bush walks, spotlight
safaris, campouts and farm pets

Mangaweka — Mt Huia Farmstay

Farmstay

9 km E of Mangaweka

906 Ruahine Road, Mangaweka, 4774
(06) 382 5726
info@mthuia.co.nz
www.mthuia.co.nz

Double: $195
Single: $145

VISA MasterCard

2 Bedrooms: 1K 1D
Bathrooms: 2 ensuite

Virginia and Neil Travers

- Bathrooms: self-contained coattge has 2 bathrooms.
- Dinner: Hosted 3 course dinner with complementary drink $50
- Full breakfast
- No smoking on property
- Internet available

Off SH1 via a dramatic bluff road and just two hours from Taupo and exactly half way between Rotorua and Wellington.

A farm tour by 4WD quad bike or vehicle is an option, and often gives guests the opportunity to see the dogs at work on our 800 acre sheep and cattle farm.

The rooms each have their own access and parking. The wide deck or shaded verandah are the perfect spot to relax and enjoy the peace and tranquility of the countryside and garden.

Take time to enjoy your journey
and the company of your hosts.
Sometimes less is more.

Hawkes Bay
Tiniroto
Wairoa
2
5
Bay View
Napier
Taadaler
Hastings
Havelock North
50
2
2
Waipukurau
52
0 Kilometres 40
0 Miles 24

Mahanga Beach, Mahia Peninsula | Reomoana

B&B • Apartment with Kitchen • Bedroom with trundle bed for children
50 km N of Wairoa

629 Mahanga Road, R.D. 8 Mahanga Beach, Mahia, Hawkes Bay 4198
(06) 837 5898
reomoana@gmail.com
www.reomoana.co.nz

Double: $130–$150   Single: $75
Children: $30

VISA MasterCard

5 Bedrooms: 2Q 1T 2S
Bathrooms: 1 ensuite, 1 private

Louise Schick

- Dinner by arrangement $40
- Continental breakfast
- Pets welcome
- Children welcome
- Internet available

'Reomoana' – The voice of the sea. Overlooking the Pacific with breathtaking views this rustic home with handcrafted features combines New Zealand and Hungarian creativity. Situated on a hillside the property is grazed by sheep and cattle, where walks may be enjoyed through QE two convenanted native bush. 5mins. walk to 8Kms. of white sandy beach, a recreational paradise for swimming, surfing and fishing. Attractions: – Morere Hot Springs, Marae visits, Golf-course and fishing charters. 6Kms. to Cafe Mahia and Sunset Point Restaurants. Pet cat 'Tilly'

Please let others know how you enjoyed your B&B experience.
Add a comment to the listing on the internet.
www.bnb.co.nz.

B&B Farmstay • The Lodge (Self-contained)
12 km N of Napier

263 Hill Road, Eskdale, Hawkes Bay, PO Box 136 Bay
View, Hawkes Bay, 4149
(06) 836 6666 or 027 28 15738
thefarmstay@xtra.co.nz
www.thefarmstay.com

Double: $120–$180   Single: $90–$110
The Lodge: Double from $150   Single $110
Extras $30pp

VISA MasterCard

3 Bedrooms: 1K 1KT 2D 2S
Bathrooms: 1 guest share, 1 private

Roslyn and Don Bird

- 2 in The Farmstay, 1+ loft in 'The Lodge'
- Bathrooms: 'The Farmstay' guests (max 4) share
  luxury bathroom and separate toilet
- Breakfast available in The Lodge $15pp
- Dinner: $55pp 3 course with wine
- Full breakfast
- Pets welcome by arrangement
- Children welcome
- Weddings and functions
- Internet available

Enjoy genuine kiwi hospitality at our tranquil
countryside escape overlooking the picturesque
Esk Valley. Our 'farmstay and superior self-contained
'lodge' offers private, sunny, relaxing peaceful
surrounds. spectacular views. Feel the comforts
of home as we tempt you with fine wine, farm
produce, baking, and preserves. Experience our
FARM life, Sam (friendly Hunterway), Allie-cat, feed
sheep, cows, pigs, chickens. Try milking goats, or
bottle-feeding lambs (seasonal).

Its a wine lovers paradise! Don a third generation
Hawke's Bay winemaker – is passionate about the
wine industry and happy to share his knowledge
over dinner or help plan your personalized winery
adventure. Explore the world's art deco capital
Napier 12 minutes drive, and Hawke's Bay's many
regional attractions within 30 minutes. Experience
mountain biking at Eskdale mtb park, fishing the
Esk River, cast for snapper off the beach, bush walks,
visit art studios, wineries, rural cafes, all these within
five minutes or just relax! Unwind on the Deck
to the chorus of native birds in the surrounding
gardens and at day's end spend time romancing
over the wonderful night sky.

Napier — A Room with a View

B&B Homestay
1.5 km N of Post Office

9 Milton Terrace, Napier
(06) 835 7434 or 027 249 2040
roomwithview@xtra.co.nz
www.bnb.co.nz/mcgregor.html

Double: $130–$130
Single: $90–$90

VISA MasterCard

1 Bedroom: 1Q
Bathrooms: 1 private

Robert McGregor

- Surcharge on credit card payments
- Bathrooms: private with bath & shower, directly oppposite bedroom.
- Continental breakfast
- Pet-free home
- Internet available

Since my wife died, I've continued to enjoy companionship, conversation and laughter with guests. Fourth generation property, 140 year old garden, spacious room, sea view. 15 minute walk to restaurants at historic Port Ahuriri or our world famous Art Deco city centre. Private bathroom. Free laundry, transport, internet. Off-street parking. Complimentary refreshments on arrival during check-in period (4.30 6.30pm). Smoke-free inside. I'm interested in travel, gardening, the arts, and especially local history – until retirement I was CEO of the Art Deco Trust.

Napier — Hillcrest

B&B Homestay
1.2 km N of Napier Central

4 George Street, Hospital Hill, Napier
(06) 835 1812
lyons@inhb.co.nz
www.hillcrestnapier.co.nz

Double: $120–$125
Single: $90

VISA MasterCard

2 Bedrooms: 1D **2**S
Bathrooms: 1 guest share

Nancy and Noel Lyons

- Bathrooms: directly opposite bedrooms & separate toilet
- Continental breakfast
- Pet-free home
- Not suitable for children

If you require quiet accommodation just minutes from the city centre, our comfortable home provides peace in restful surroundings. Relax on wide decks overlooking our garden, or enjoy the spectacular sea views. Explore nearby historic places and the botanical gardens. Your own lounge with tea/coffee making; laundry and off-street parking available. We have travelled extensively and welcome the opportunity of meeting visitors. Our interests are travel, music, bowls and embroidery. We will happily meet you at the travel depots. Holiday home at Mahia Beach available.

Snug Harbour

B&B Homestay
5 km S of Napier

147 Harold Holt Avenue, Napier, 4112
(06) 843 2521
donmcld@clear.net.nz
www.snugharbour.co.nz

Double: $110–$140
Single: $90–$90

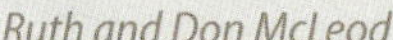

2 Bedrooms: 1Q 1T
Bathrooms: 1 ensuite, 1 family share

Ruth and Don McLeod

Ruth and Don welcome you to their comfortable home with its rural outlook and sunny attractive patio. The garden studio with ensuite and tea making facilities has its own entrance. We are situated on the outskirts of Napier City, the art deco city of the World, and in close proximity to wineries and many other tourist attractions. We both have a background in teaching, with interests in travel, gardening and photography.

- Twin room has super single beds
- Dinner: $40 by arrangement
- Full breakfast
- Pet-free home
- Internet available

Cobden Garden Homestay

Luxury B&B Homestay
1 km N of Napier

1 Cobden Crescent, Bluff Hill, 4110
(06) 834 2090 or 0800 426 233
info@cobden.co.nz
www.cobden.co.nz

Double: $210–$265
Single: $180–$235
Children: negotiable

3 Bedrooms: 1K 2KT
Bathrooms: 3 ensuite

Rayma and Phillip Jenkins

Come enjoy our hospitality and colonial villa high on Bluff Hill. Enjoy spacious bedrooms comfortably furnished with; quality bedding, lounge furniture, TV with DVD player, refreshments, robes, hairdryer. Relax in the garden, on the veranda or in a guest lounge. Check emails on the net book or use the complimentary Wi-Fi. Join us for complimentary tasting of local wine and hors – d'oeuvres each evening. Choose breakfast from a selection of homemade and local foods. Your stay will be memorable. Three unobtrusive cats in residence.

- Full breakfast
- No smoking on property
- Internet available

Napier — Seaview Lodge

B&B Homestay
0.5 km N of Napier Central

5 Seaview Terrace, Napier
(06) 835 0202 or 021 180 2101
cvulodge@xtra.co.nz
www.aseaviewlodge.co.nz

Double: $170–$180
Single: $130–$140

VISA MasterCard

3 Bedrooms: 1K 1KT 1S
Bathrooms: 1 ensuite, 2 private

Catherine and Evert Van Florenstein

- Continental breakfast
- Pet-free home
- Not suitable for children
- No smoking on property
- Internet available

Seaview Lodge is a lovingly renovated, spacious late Victorian home. This inner city, beachside bed and breakfast offers a warm welcome and spectacular views. Enjoy breakfast on the lower verandah while watching the waves break on the shore. In the evening relax in the spacious guest lounge or on the upstairs balcony. Situated across the road from the beach, hot pools and conference complex and a three minute stroll to the city centre. The 2008/2010 edition of the 'Lonely Planet' guide promoted Seaview Lodge as their pick for Napier.

Napier — Art Deco Te Awa

B&B
3 km S of Napier

19 Te Awa Avenue, Napier
(06) 835 1618 or 027 211 0023
kaypat1@xtra.co.nz
www.bnb.co.nz/Art Deco Te Awa.html

Double: $160–$160

3 Bedrooms: 1Q 1D 1T
Bathrooms: 3 ensuite

Kay and Rod Goodspeed

- Continental breakfast
- Pet-free home

Art Deco Te Awa is spacious, executive quality accommodation. Ideal for visiting NZ's Art Deco City. Breakfast includes locally grown fresh fruit, home made muesli and preserves. Quality beds with fine linen. Guest rooms include one spacious double room with ensuite bathroom, one queen with ensuite bathroom and one twin with ensuite bathroom, all with heated towelrail, hairdryer and complimentary toiletries. Five minutes to city centre. Ten minutes to airport. Walking distance to the beach and 18 hole golf course. Easy access to Hawke's Bay's wineries.

Kerry Lodge

B&B Homestay • Cottage with Kitchen
8 km SW of Napier

7 Forward Street, Greenmeadows, Napier
(06) 845 2317
kerrylodge@xtra.co.nz
www.kerrylodge.co.nz

Double: $180–$260   Single: $130–$130
Children: $45

4 Bedrooms: 2K **2**T
Bathrooms: 1 ensuite, 1 guest share, 1 private

Fiona and Brent Rollings

Set in tranquil gardens, we invite guests to share the warmth and comfort of our home. Our large rooms offer heating, refreshment facilities and colour television. A mobility ensuite and wheelchair access is available for guests convenience. We have off street parking and the laundry is available for great use. Your day with us begins with a scrumptious breakfast and a chat to help plan your day's activities. Relax in our sparkling pool or indoor spa. Situated near Church Road and Mission wineries. Our dog Hogan and cat Tabitha wait to welcome you.

- Full breakfast
- Pets welcome
- Children welcome
- No smoking on property
- Internet available

119ongeorges

Napier

B&B Homestay
2Km km S of CBD

119 Georges Drive, Napier, 4110
(06) 843 3609 or 021 718 396
info@119ongeorges.co.nz
www.119ongeorges.co.nz

Double: $150–$150
Single: $130–$130

2 Bedrooms: 1KT **1**Q
Bathrooms: 2 ensuite

Wendy and Peter Murphy

119 on georges is centrally located in peaceful and elegant surroundings to the many attractions in Napier and Hawke's Bay. We offer off-street parking and are close proximity to city centre rich with Art Deco architecture, art galleries, restaurants, cafés and theatres, fabulous shopping, heated pools on Marine Parade, 18 Hole Golf Course, cycle and pathways.

There are tea and coffee making facilities available and a scrumptious breakfast is served in our dining room.

Evening meal available by prior arrangement.

- Full breakfast
- Not suitable for children
- No smoking on property
- Internet available

Napier – Taradale

Omarunui Homestay

B&B Homestay
12 km S of Napier

69 Omarunui Road, Napier, 4183
(06) 844 9396 or 021 071 0159
kate.ladson@slingshot.co.nz
www.omarunuihomestay.co.nz

Double: $140–$160
Single: $120–$140

1 Bedroom:
Bathrooms: 1 ensuite

Kate and Roger Ladson

- Superking
- Full breakfast
- Not suitable for children
- No smoking on property
- Non-smokers only
- Internet available

Welcome to our quiet, relaxing home situated approximately midway between Napier and Hastings. The spacious sunny guest room has private access to the garden and a comfortable sitting area. We are ideally situated for visits to wineries, golf courses and the kilometres of safe cycleways and are close to shops and restaurants in the Napier suburb of Taradale. There is a small, solar heated pool in the garden which you are welcome to use. One unobtrusive cat in residence.

Napier

Chyreen Bed and Breakfast

B&B
0.5 km N of Information Centre

20 Brewster Street, Bluff Hill, Napier, 4110
(06) 835 0727 or 021 215 8762
chyreenbnb@gmail.com
www.napierbnb.com

Double: $120–$135
Single: $90

VISA MasterCard

3 Bedrooms: 1Q 1D 1S
Bathrooms: 1 guest share

Sharon and Michael

- All rooms have a sea view.
- Full continental breakfast included in the room price.
- Continental breakfast
- Not suitable for children
- No smoking on property
- Internet available

Drink in the stunning ocean views from our home on Napier's Bluff Hill with a mere five minute walk to the Art Deco city centre. Appreciate comfort, quiet and privacy in our 1920s character home.

Enjoy a delicious continental breakfast upstairs with views across the bay to Cape Kidnappers. Free Wi-Fi, guest lounge with library, TV, DVD, fridge and tea/coffee-making facilities. Off-street parking.

Sharon and Michael look forward to making your stay memorable.

Grandvue Country Stay

B&B Homestay
14 km SW of Hastings

Grandvue, 2596 State Highway 50, R D 5 Hastings 4175
(06) 879 6141 or 027 668 0252
homestays@xtra.co.nz
www.bnb.co.nz/grandvuehomestay.html

Double: $110–$135   Single: $70
Children: negotiable

VISA MasterCard

2 Bedrooms: 1KT 1Q
Bathrooms: 1 ensuite, 1 family share

Dianne and Keith Taylor

- Dinner: $35 pp
- Full breakfast
- Pet-free home
- Children welcome
- No smoking on property
- Internet available

Retired and moved from our farm but still the same genuine and caring hospitality. Enjoy with us in a relaxed atmosphere in our extensive private garden the wonderful views over vineyards in the Gimlett Gravels and Ngatarawa/Bridge Pa Triangle area, and to Havelock North hills in the distance. Comfortable beds with firm mattresses make for a good nights sleep (electric blankets in winter.) Sit and chat when time allows over a generous breakfast cooked or continental with homemade preserves and goodies – inside or alfresco. Dinner available on request.

Our interests include tramping, bushwalks, gardening, travel and genealogy. Having travelled extensively we do enjoy meeting local and overseas visitors. Let us advise you on all the wonderful things to do and see while in our lovely Hawkes Bay. There are many wineries close by with restaurants, Safari trips to the Gannet Colony, Orchard tours, Trout fishing, six golf courses, Panoramic views from Te Mata Peak, Havelock North with it's boutique shops and cafés and Napier the Art Deco City of the world are just a few. We can arrange tours for you too, and also advise you on your travels through New Zealand. After more than 24 years of hosting we have an ever increasing circle of friends with many returning.

Hastings City | McConchie Homestay

Homestay
1 km N of Hastings Central

115A Frederick Street, Hastings, 4122
(06) 878 4576
barbaramcconchie@gmail.com
www.bnb.co.nz

Double: $110
Single: $70
Children: $30

VISA (MasterCard)

2 Bedrooms: 1Q 2S
Bathrooms: 1 guest share

Barbara and Nina McConchie

- Bedroom with 2 single beds opens out to a deck.
- Dinner: $30 pp by arrangement
- Full breakfast
- Children welcome
- No smoking on property

Enjoy our peaceful garden back section, no traffic noises, yet central to Hastings City. My cat says 'Hi'. Nearby are parks, golf courses, wineries, orchards and the best icecream ever. Short trips take you to spectacular views, Cape Kidnapper's gannet colony, or Napier's art deco, hot pools, or just relaxing and enjoying great hospitality. Directions: from Wellington, arriving Hastings City, turn left into Eastbourne Street, right into Nelson Street, right into Frederick Street, cross Caroline Road. Driveway on right. 115A first house off driveway.

Havelock North, Hastings | Wharehau

B&B Homestay
16 km S of Havelock/Hastings

1604 Middle Road, Havelock North, RD 11, Hastings 4178
(06) 877 4111 or 022 165 7584
ros.phillips@xtra.co.nz
www.wharehau.co.nz

Double: $130   Single: $65
Children: half price

VISA (MasterCard)

4 Bedrooms: 2Q 2T 1S
Bathrooms: 1 family share, 1 guest share

Ros Phillips

- Beach bach $130/150
- Dinner: $30
- Full breakfast
- Pets welcome
- Children welcome
- Internet available

Wharehau is in the beautiful Tuki Tuki valley – a great base for Hawkes Bay experience. Quarter of an hour travel from Hastings or Havelock North in the midst of Wine Country. Close to golf courses, Splash Planet, gannets and art deco. Or enjoy the peace and space on the farm. Weather permitting a farm 4WD tour is available. Walks available locally. Trout fishing (local guide can be hired) in the Tuki Tuki River. Comfortable beach bach at Kairakau Beach is available for rent.

Havelock House

Luxury B&B
3 km S of Havelock North

77 Endsleigh Road (cnr of Endlseigh Drive),
Havelock North, Hawkes Bay
(06) 877 5439 or mobile 021 152 3755
dianaarnold@xtra.co.nz
www.havelockhouse.co.nz

Double: $180–$250   Single: $160–$220
Children: are welcome

3 Bedrooms: 1K 1KT 1Q
Bathrooms: 3 ensuite

Diana and Jeff Arnold

You wont want to leave – charming stylish accommodation nestled in four acres designed for your relaxation and comfort. Enjoy its spacious ensuite rooms, elegant gardens, friendly service from your hosts Diana and Jeff, and amazing breakfasts. Relax in the large guest lounge, use the snooker table, swimming pool and all weather tennis court or sit in the garden and just relax with a glass of local Hawke's Bay wine.

Just four minutes drive from Havelock North with its boutique shopping, galleries, and great cafés.

- Dinner: A variety of restaurants in Havelock North village
- Full breakfast
- Pet-free home
- Children welcome
- Non-smokers only
- Internet available

Bluebell Lodge and Cottages

Boutique Self-contained Cottages
5 km S of Havelock North or Hastings

137 Longlands Road East, R D 2, Hastings 4172
(06) 876 5243 or 027 220 2262
c.lewis@inhb.co.nz
www.bluebell-cottage.co.nz

Double: $140–$280
Children: Extra guests are $30 per person per night

3 Bedrooms: 2K 1KT
Bathrooms: 3 ensuite

Max and Carol Lewis

Max and Carol would love to welcome you to come and stay in one of our spacious and comfortable self-contained cottages in an orchard setting yet close to Havelock North or Hastings. The cottages have comfortable King bed or King and Super King beds (or two singles), ensuites, leather recliner chairs, kitchen, heat pump/air con, SKY TV, DVD player (complimentary DVDs to watch) and verandah to sit out on. The two bedroom cottage also has a dishwasher and washing machine.

- Bathrooms: both cottages have ensuite bathrooms off the bedrooms.
- Breakfast by arrangement
- Children welcome
- No smoking on property
- Internet available

Waipukurau

Woburn Homestead

Luxury B&B

2 km S of Waipukurau

216 Hatuma Road, RD 1, Waipukurau
06.858.9668 or 0274.529.112
heatha@woburnhomestead.co.nz
www.woburnhomestead.co.nz

Double: $250–$300
Single: $0–$150
Children: Not suitable sorry

VISA MasterCard

3 Bedrooms: 3Q
Bathrooms: 3 ensuite

Heatha Edwards and Philip Allerby

- 3 with queen beds and 1 queen has an extra king single in the room
- Dinner: Cheerfully available with a bit of notice!
- Special breakfast
- Not suitable for children
- Weddings and functions
- No smoking on property
- Internet available

Welcome to Woburn Homestead, an exquisite NZ Historic Places Trust built in 1893 with seven bedrooms and six bathrooms. Heatha and Philip adore sharing their home, and there are two tubby Labradors, who relentlessly patrol the grounds for any stray snacks or crumbs! Everything, from the fine quality Italian chandeliers, antique furniture and luxurious Egyptian cotton towels and sheets to the beautifully appointed ensuites, have been carefully chosen to shamelessly pamper you. Our style reflects a high level of service awareness plus attention to detail and presentation. Get away from it all and catch up with your reading, soak up the sun with a glass of wine by the pool or play croquet on the lawn… enjoy a hearty home-cooked meal and warm your toes by one of the gorgeous fireplaces. Retire to your room and indulge yourself with a satin jet massage shower or sink into a deep luxurious soak in the traditional clawfoot bath. You're also invited to browse the library to enjoy a book by the open fire, or join us in the vast country kitchen for some sparkling company or a sound thrashing at cards (but not Bridge, as we're just learning and hopeless!)

Manawatu and Horowhenua
1
3
Feilding
3
Palmerston North
1
57
Waitarere Beach
Levin
Otaki
oro
0 Kilometres 10
0 Miles 6

Feiding

Whakaari Retreat

Luxury B&B Farmstay • Guest House
8 km SW of Feilding

54 Sutherland Road, Palmerston North, 4479
027 481 0822
whakaariretreat@gmail.com
www.whakaariretreat.co.nz

Double: $150
Single: $140
Children: up to 16 years $35

4 Bedrooms: 2Q 1D 2S
Bathrooms: 1 private

Darryl and Maree Pritchard

- Extra adults $50
- Continental provisions supplied
- Pets welcome
- Children welcome
- Non-smokers only
- Internet available

Whakaari Retreat is a purpose built self-contained house accommodating up to eight guests in four bedrooms and is exclusively yours for your stay. There is a spacious bathroom complete with heated floor tiles and heated towel rails. Upstairs is the kitchen with open plan dining and lounge, leading out to the balcony where you can relax and soak up the views. Snuggle up in front of the fire or take a stroll down to the pond – the choice is yours.

Palmerston North

Bradgate

B&B Homestay
3 km NW of Palmerston North Centre

3 Celtic Court, Roslyn, Palmerston North
(06) 355 5956 or 021 024 11864
bradgate@xtra.co.nz
www.bnb.co.nz/bradgate.html

Double: $90
Single: $50

3 Bedrooms: 1Q 1D 1T
Bathrooms: 1 guest share

Frances

- Dinner: $30
- Full breakfast

Welcome to Bradgate, a four bedroomed brick townhouse located in a quiet cul-de-sac. 37 years ago my husband and I came to New Zealand. We owned a restaurant opposite Virginia Lake Wanganui, after retiring we ran a bed and breakfast overlooking the river. Having shifted to Palmerston North it was time to open up our home again. I have a Labrador named Crunchy. I enjoy playing golf, gardening and meeting people. Close to airport, will pick up if required. Non-smoking house, dinner by arrangement.

Country Lane Homestay
Palmerston North

B&B Homestay
13 km E of Palmerston North

52 Orrs Road, RD 1 Aokautere, Palmerston North
(06) 326 8529 or 027 448 5833
countrylane@xtra.co.nz
www.bnb.co.nz/user82.html

Double: $100–$150
Single: $80–$95

3 Bedrooms: 1K 1KT 1Q 1D 1S
Bathrooms: 1 ensuite, 1 family share, 2 private

Fay and Allan Hutchinson

Luxury country living, short distance from Palmerston North, near Manawatu Gorge, below wind farm. 10 km from Pacific College and 2 km from Equestrian Centre. Excellent stop over en route to/from Wellington or East Coast. Our home is newly decorated, with antiques in a country traditional style surrounded by our garden. Sawmill on the property, coloured sheep, horses and calves. Manawatu River borders our property. It is our pleasure to provide home-cooked meals with some local produce. Directions: please phone. A brochure with map is available.

- Dinner: $35–$40
- Full breakfast
- Not suitable for children
- Non-smokers only

Dunes
Waitarere Beach

B&B Homestay
14 km NW of Levin

10 Ngati Huia Place, Waitarere Beach 5510
(06) 368 6246 or 027 819 2750
sand.dunes@xtra.co.nz
waitarere.dunes.googlepages.com

Double: $135
Single: $100

VISA MasterCard

2 Bedrooms: 2Q
Bathrooms: 2 ensuite

Robyn and Grant Powell

Robyn and Grant Powell welcome you to our absolute beachfront retreat. Enjoy beach walks and magnificent views of Kapiti and Mounts Taranaki and Ruapehu. We offer two queen-size bedrooms with own private entrance and deck areas, ensuites, own living areas with TV, tea/coffee making facilities – continental breakfast provided. Situated 14 km north west of Levin, approximately one and a half hours from Wellington and 35 minutes from Palmerston North. Laundry facilities, off-street parking, non-smoking. Dinner by arrangement.

- Dinner: $30
- Continental breakfast
- Pet-free home
- Children welcome
- Non-smokers only
- Internet available

Levin — Fantails Accommodation

B&B • Cottage with Kitchen • Self-contained cottages
1 km E of Levin

40 MacArthur Street, Levin 5510
(06) 368 9011
fantails@xtra.co.nz
www.fantails.co.nz

Double: $145–$165
Single: $130–$150

3 Bedrooms: 1K **2**Q **1**T **2**S
Bathrooms: 2 ensuite, 1 private

Heather Watson

- Self-contained cottages $140–$175
- Dinner by arrangement
- Special breakfast
- Pets welcome
- Children welcome
- Weddings and functions
- Internet available

Heather and Allan welcome you to our special place in Levin – Fantails. We offer B&B, self-catering cottages or our gypsy-style house truck. Maintained to a high standard. Enjoy delicious, home-cooked organic breakfast, homemade butter, cheese and preserves, sourced directly from the garden and farm. Special diets on request. Fantails offers the opportunity to milk our house cow Molly, come face-to-face with thoroughbred horses and Pitt Island sheep. Participate in cheese-making courses and/or sustainable gardening tours. Warm hospitality and humour.

Levin — Ohau Highland Bed & Breakfast

B&B • Separate Suite
7 km S of Levin

138 Muhunoa West Road, Levin, 5570
(06) 368 4729
landpwolfenden@xtra.co.nz
www.ohauhighland.co.nz

Double: $100–$120

1 Bedroom: 1Q
Bathrooms: 1 ensuite

Peter and Lynette Wolfenden

- Continental breakfast
- Not suitable for children
- No smoking on property
- Internet available

Situated in the recently developed lifestyle sub division Western Rise, only seven km South of Levin, 1.4 km off SH1, Ohau Highland Bed and Breakfast is the ideal place for travellers to relax in a quiet, rural environment. Ohau Highland B&B offers a self-contained suite with private access, Sky TV, DVD, wireless internet, continental breakfast and ample off street parking. Enjoy a stroll around our property and meet Basil and Abbi, our friendly Jack Russell terriers, and our delightful, friendly miniature highland cattle.

Wairarapa
Colyton
elding
ewbury
Palmerston North
Oroua Downs
Tokomaru
Foxton
Levin
Otaki
Te Horo
Waikanae
aparaumu
akariki
ui
Upper Hutt
eretaunga
3
2
Eketahuna
Masterton
Carterton
2
Greytown
53
Martinborough
0
Kilometres
20
0
Miles
12

Masterton — Tidsfordriv Rural Retreat

B&B Homestay • Rural Lifestyle farmlet.
10 km SW of Masterton

54 Cootes Road, Matahiwi R.D. 8, Masterton, 5888
(06) 378 9967
ghansen@contact.net.nz
www.bnb.co.nz/tidsfordriv.html

Double: $120   Single: $70
Children: $30 under 13 years

2 Bedrooms: 1Q 2S
Bathrooms: 1 private

Glenys Hansen

- 1 Queen room, 1 twin room
- Wireless Internet – free
- Dinner: $30 by arrangement includes pre-dinner drink
- Full breakfast
- Pet-free home
- Children welcome
- Internet available

A warm welcome awaits you at 'Tidsfordriv' – a 64 acre farmlet – seven kilometres off the main bypass route. Enjoy the comforts of a modern home set in parklike surroundings with large gardens and lakes. Bird watch with ease and enjoy the peaceful serenity of this 'Rural Retreat'. Glenys invites you to join her for dinner and enjoy good conversation about gardening, conservation, travel and local history. Stay more than one night and enjoy visits to Pukaha Mount Bruce Wildlife Centre, Castlepoint and other Wairarapa attractions.

Masterton — Mas des Saules

B&B Homestay Farmstay • Luxury Gypsy River Camping
1 km E of Masterton

35A Pokohiwi Road, Homebush, 5810
(06) 377 2577 or 027 620 8728
mas-des-saules@wise.net.nz
www.mas-des-saules.co.nz

Double: $135   Single: $90
Children: Under 3 – no charge, 3–5 $25, over 5–$40

2 Bedrooms: 2Q
Bathrooms: 1 guest share

Mary and Steve Blakemore

- Dinner: $45 – three courses with wine, shared with the hosts.
- Full breakfast
- Pets welcome
- Children welcome
- Internet available

Hidden down a tranquil country lane, discover our authentic French Provencal farmhouse with its landscaped garden, stream, and courtyard. Swimming and trout fishing in nearby river. Our children have departed, leaving us with two cats, our small dog, and cattle on our small farm. Guest lounge and bathroom with bath and shower. Open fire and central heating. Wi-Fi available. Enjoy farmhouse cooking with fresh vegetables from our large country garden, barbecues and picnic lunches. We are a well-travelled couple who enjoy helping guests discover the unspoilt Wairarapa.

Llandaff

B&B Farmstay
0.5 km NW of Urban Boundary

183 Upper Plain Road Masterton,
(06) 378 6628 or 021 359 562
llandaff@xtra.co.nz
www.llandaff.co.nz

Double: $110–$140
Single: $80–$120
Children: $30

5 Bedrooms: 1K **2**Q **1**D **1**T
Bathrooms: 2 ensuite, 2 guest share

Elizabeth and Robin Dunlop

Elegantly restored, the homestead boasts beautiful native NZ timbers throughout, wood panelled rooms, polished floors, old pull-handle toilets, a 'coffin' bath, open fireplaces and cosy woodburning kitchen stove. Explore the historic buildings including stables, washhouse, produce shed, gardener's shed, pavilion and dove cote. Enjoy tea in the large glass house. See the vintage farm machinery and 1916 Overland car. Relax in the majestic garden beneath 130 year old trees, or wander the farm and see the animals. Bike riding, croquet and petanque are available to guests. Enjoy a cooked breakfast with dinner available on request.

- One bathroom with both shower and bath
- Dinner: $35
- Full breakfast
- Pets welcome
- Children welcome
- Weddings and functions
- Internet available

Oak House

B&B
0.5 km NW of Martinborough

45 Kitchener Street, Martinborough, 5711
(06) 306 9198
chrispolly.oakhouse@xtra.co.nz
burings.co.nz

Double: $120–$140
Single: $60–$70

VISA MasterCard

3 Bedrooms: 2Q **2**S
Bathrooms: 1 ensuite, 1 guest share

Polly and Chris Buring

Our characterful 88 year old Californian bungalow offers gracious accommodation. Our spacious lounge provides a relaxed setting for sampling winemaker Chris's wonderful products. Our guest wing private entrance, bathroom (large bath and shower) and separate toilet. Our Garden Room has ensuite facilities. Bedrooms enjoy afternoon sun and garden views. Breakfast features fresh fruits, croissants, home-preserved local fruits and conserves. Creative cook Polly matches delicious dishes (often local game) with Chris's great wines. Tour our winery with Chris. Meet our friendly cats.

- Dinner by arrangement
- Special breakfast
- Not suitable for children
- No smoking on property

Martinborough — The Martinborough Connection

B&B
1 km S of village square

80 Jellicoe Street, Martinborough, 5711
(06) 306 9708 or 027 438 1581
martinboroughconnection@xtra.co.nz
www.martinboroughconnection.co.nz

Double: $135–$145
Single: $115–$120
Children: $15 additional in room with extra bed

VISA · MasterCard · eftpos NEW ZEALAND LIMITED

4 Bedrooms: 4Q 1S
Bathrooms: 4 ensuite

David and Lorraine Murray

- One room has a sofa bed in addition to queen
- $30 additional adult in room with extra bed
- Full breakfast
- Pet-free home
- Children welcome
- Internet available

Bed and breakfast accommodation situated within the Martinborough wine village. Originally built in 1889 the property has been fully restored retaining its original character. Open your bedroom door to a sunny verandah and garden. Start the day with a scrumptious breakfast, before visiting Martinboroughs wineries, or Cape Palliser with its spectacular coastline, lighthouse,& furseal colony. Relax in the guest lounge with its open fire or outside in the lovely gardens. Wireless internet and Sky TV available We look forward to hosting you.

Martinborough — Martinborough Experience B&B

B&B
1 km SE of Village Square

84 Venice Street, Martinborough, 5711
(06) 306 9912 or 027 446 7378
info@martinboroughexperience.co.nz
martinboroughexperience.co.nz

Double: $140–$160
Single: $110–$130
Children: $15 extra on foldaway bed

eftpos NEW ZEALAND LIMITED

3 Bedrooms: 3K
Bathrooms: 3 ensuite

Bob and Dawn Knight

- $30 extra adult on foldaway bed
- Bathrooms: 1 with double spa bath
- Full breakfast
- Children welcome
- Internet available

Motel style quality Bed and Breakfast situated in a peaceful location, just five minute walk to the Village, restaurants, cafés, arts and crafts. All rooms have ensuite (one with double spa bath), Super King beds (convert to singles if required), fridge, TV, couch, tea and coffee making facilities, with café table and chairs to sit outside in the sun. Scrumptious breakfast served in the privacy of your room.

Foldaway beds, port-a-cot and BBQ are available on request.

Ample off street parking.

Wellington
Kapiti Island
Kapiti Coast
Waikanae
Paraparaumu
Raumati
Manaka
1
2
1
2
Lower Hutt
Eastbourne
Ohariu Valley
Johnsonville
See
Wellington City
next page
Aro Valley
Brooklyn
Vogeltown
Mt Victoria
Hataitai
Mt. Cook
Mornington
Melrose
Karaka Bay
Seatoun
Island Bay
Breaker Bay
Palmer Head
Wellington
International
Airport
0
Kilometres
10
0
Miles
6

Wellington City
Johnsonville
Khandallah
Ngaio
Wadestown
Interisland
Ferry Terminal
Karori
Wellington
Central
Oriental Bay
Roseneath
Aro Valley
Mt Victoria
Mt. Cook
Vogeltown
Island Bay
Wellington
International
Airport
1
2
1

Manaaki Bed & Breakfast

B&B • Separate Suite • Apartment with Kitchen • Kitchenette
1 km E of Otaki

102 Rahui Road, Otaki, 5512
027 478 3220
manaaki.bnb@gmail.com
www.manaakibnb.co.nz

Double: $130–$140
Single: $100–$110
Children: Extra guest $30

1 Bedroom: 1Q 1S
Bathrooms: 1 ensuite

Sharon and Sam

Manaaki is situated opposite the Otaki Racecourse and a short walk from the popular outlet shopping area and cafés. Enjoy a continental breakfast including seasonal fruits, cereals, fresh bread and preserves, tea and coffee available at your leisure. Relax on your private patio or take a walk in Manaaki's country gardens. Private off street parking is provided. There are activities available on the Kapiti coast to accommodate all tastes including, mountain biking, horse racing and several quality golf courses, walking tracks and beautiful beaches.

- Continental provisions supplied
- Children welcome
- No smoking on property

Our B&Bs range from homely to luxurious,
but you can always be sure of superior hospitality.

B&B Seperate Suite Cottage with Kitchen
5 km SW of Waikanae

26 Konini Crescent, Waikanae Beach, Kapiti Coast 5036
(04) 904 6610
konini@paradise.net.nz
www.konini.co.nz

Double: $140–$175   Single: $100–$175
Children: $20 under 13 years. Extra Adult $35

3 Bedrooms: 2Q 2S
Bathrooms: 2 ensuite

Maggie and Bob Smith

- Cottage 2 bedroom Homestead Suite 1 bedroom
- Book online at www.konini.co.nz and save!
- Dinner: cafés/Restaurants within walking
- Breakfast by arrangement
- Pet-free home
- Children welcome
- Internet available

Welcome to KONINI. Imagine a long walk or swim at the endless sandy ocean beach, a game of golf on the adjoining links, or simply sitting on the verandah and enjoying the peace and tranquillity of the large garden. Being only one hours drive from the Interisland ferries it is the perfect stop off point to repack and do laundry. Easy walking to Cafe' and Restaurants. Enquire about Kapiti Island Nature tours. One nights stay may not be enough.

THE HOMESTEAD SUITE: A traditional B&B in its own wing of the main house. The suite comprises Queen bedroom with adjoining private sitting room overlooking the garden and ensuite bathroom. Continental Breakfast is included in tariff. Double $140 Single $100

THE COTTAGE: Self contained and situated in the garden. Tastefully furnished offering a spacious 70 Sq Meters of self-catering accommodation with fully equipped kitchen. Two bedrooms (one Queen and one Twin), lounge with cable TV, Shower room, and laundry facilities. Breakfast by arrangement. Double $175

Directions: Turn off SH1 at traffic lights to the Beach. Four km to automotive garage. Take right fork then next right. 1 km to Konini Cres.

Sea Haven

B&B Homestay
4 km SW of Paraparaumu

325 Rosetta Road, Raumati Beach, Paraparaumu
(04) 902 0047 or 021 0279 8803
jan-laurie@paradise.net.nz
www.bnb.co.nz/SeaHaven1.html

Double: $120
Single: $95

VISA MasterCard

1 Bedroom: 1Q
Bathrooms: 1 private

Jan and Laurie Bason

Welcome to our spacious smoke-free home. Our guest room opens to a small garden, with seating amongst native ferns, shrubs and trees. 250 metres to restaurants, village shops, beach, bowling green and Marine Gardens. Kapiti Miniature Railway is situated at Marine Gardens with various locomotives running on Sunday afternoons weather permitting. Laurie, a railway enthusiast, has a miniature locomotive and collection of railway memorabilia. Paraparaumu Beach Golf Club is within five kms. Kapiti Golf Club is within approximately eight kms.

- Continental breakfast
- Pet-free home
- Not suitable for children
- No smoking on property
- Internet available

Judy & Bob's Place

B&B Homestay
2 km S of Lower Hutt

11 Ngaio Crescent, Woburn, Lower Hutt
(04) 971 1192 or 021 510 682
bob.vine@paradise.net.nz
www.bobvine.gen.nz/blog

Double: $140–$175
Single: $70–$90

VISA MasterCard Diners Club International AMERICAN EXPRESS

2 Bedrooms: 1Q 2S
Bathrooms: 1 private

Judy and Bob Vine

Located in Woburn, a picturesque and quiet central city suburb of Lower Hutt, known for its generous sized houses and beautiful gardens. Within walking distance of the Lower Hutt downtown, 15 minutes drive from central Wellington, its railway station and ferry terminals; airport 25 minutes; three minutes walk to Woburn Rail Station. Private lounge and TV. Love to entertain and share hearty Kiwi style cooking with good New Zealand wine. Laundry facilities. Transfer transport available. Free Wi-Fi.

- Bathrooms: limit: 1 booking a time to obviate bathroom sharing
- Dinner: $40
- Full breakfast
- Pet-free home
- Non-smokers only
- Internet available

Lower Hutt

Rose Cottage

B&B Homestay
0.5 km SE of Lower Hutt

70A Hautana Street, Lower Hutt, Wellington
(04) 566 7755 or 021 481 732
gellen@xtra.co.nz
www.bnb.co.nz/rosecottagelowerhutt.html

Double: $115–$135
Single: $95–$115

2 Bedrooms: 1KT **1Q**
Bathrooms: 1 ensuite, 1 family share

Maureen and Gordon Gellen

- Dinner: $35 by arrangement
- Full breakfast
- Not suitable for children

Relax in the comfort of our cosy home which is just a five minute walk to the Hutt City Centre and 15 minutes to ferries. Originally built in 1910 the house has been fully renovated. Interests, travel, sports and live theatre. As well as TV in guest room there's coffee and tea-making facilities. Breakfast will be served in our dining room at your convenience. Unsuitable for children. We look forward to welcoming you into our smoke-free home which we share with Scuffin our cat.

Harbourview, Lower Hutt

Harbourcity View B&B

B&B Homestay
1.5 km SW of Lower Hutt

14 City View Grove, Harbourview, Lower Hutt 5010
(04) 586 0557 or 027 688 3306
harbourcityview@xnet.co.nz
www.harbourcityviewbnb.com

Double: $140–$170
Single: $90–$130
Children: by arrangement

3 Bedrooms: 1S
Bathrooms: 1 ensuite, 1 guest share

Mary Quayle

- Bathrooms: ensuite has shower over bath
- Guest share has shower
- Dinner: $25p.p. by arrangement
- Full breakfast
- Not suitable for children
- No smoking on property
- Internet available

Welcome to my home in a peaceful setting surrounded by a bush reserve with panoramic views of Wellington harbour and Hutt River. 15mins by train or car to central Wellington to visit Parliament, Botanical Gardens, Cable Car, Te Papa, Zealandia, Ferry. Alternatively hike in the Regional Parks or play golf on nearby courses. At the end of the day relax in the garden with a view to the sea. Enjoy tea/coffee facilities with home baking in the conservatory. Tours arranged, Airport/Ferry transfers. Laundry available, Off street parking.

FernTree Hideaway

B&B • Apartment with Kitchen • Boutique
12 km E of Wellington

7 Huia Road, Days Bay, Eastbourne
(04) 562 7692 or 027 616 9826
relax@ferntreehideaway.co.nz
www.ferntreehideaway.co.nz

Double: $160–$190   Single: $150–$150
Children: $25

VISA MasterCard

1 Bedroom: 1K
Bathrooms: 1 private

Robyn and Roger Cooper

Ride our private cable car through native bush to FernTree Hideaway. Self-contained romantic retreat overlooking Wellington harbour. Enjoy sparkling sea views and bellbird song; breakfast on your garden patio; relax with books, TV, DVDs, CDs. Open plan lounge/dining/kitchenette, luxury bath/shower, free Wi-Fi, phone. 200 metres to beach, cafés, galleries. Days Bay ferry to Central Wellington (20 minutes) berths near Te Papa and The Stadium. Inter-island ferry 20 minutes. 'This place is Dreamland – a Kiwi Shangri-la.' Self-catering optional.

- 1 king bedroom, 2 sofabeds in lounge
- Extra adults $35
- Breakfast by arrangement
- Pet-free home
- Children welcome
- Internet available

Please let your hosts know if you have to cancel.
They will have spent time preparing for you.

Eastbourne

The Walnut Tree

Luxury B&B
2 km S of Eastbourne Village

335 Muritai Road, Eastbourne, Wellington, 5013
(04) 562 8768 or 027 439 3886
jasmin@thewalnuttree.co.nz
www.thewalnuttree.co.nz

Double: $160   Single: $130
Children: $40 – property Not suitable under 8 years of age

3 Bedrooms: 1KT 1Q 1S
Bathrooms: 1 private

Jasmin and Alan Macdonald

- Bathrooms: private semi-ensuite
- Dinner: Anti-pasto platter by prior arrangement. See website for details Full breakfast
- No smoking on property
- Internet available

Enjoy glorious views, birdsong and total privacy from the top storey of our renovated multi-level country character home. We offer delicious food, three charming Bedrooms, a sumptuous upstairs Lounge with widescreen TV, garden balcony and outdoor spa.

Easy stroll to the beach and bush, or cafés and boutiques in Eastbourne village. The Wellington bus stops right at the front gate.

Our two young adult children and two spoilt Siamese cats live with us too. The welcome mat is out, the croissants are hot – we'd love your company!

Johnsonville, Wellington

Cherswud

B&B Homestay
8 km N of Wellington CBD

121 Helston Rd, Johnsonville, Wellington, 6037
(04) 477 6767 or 021 060 7815
stay@cherswud.com
www.cherswud.com

Double: $130
Single: $80

2 Bedrooms: 2Q
Bathrooms: 2 private

David and Marilyn McDonald

- Dinner: 3 courses $40 pp, by prior arrangement. Gluten-free options.
- Full breakfast
- Pet-free home
- Internet available

Welcome to Cherswud, our authentically restored 1919 home located just ten easy minutes from the Interislander ferry. Our accommodation includes two lounges, a conservatory overlooking a lovely sheltered garden, two warm and bright queen rooms, each with its own private bathroom, one of which has a spa bath. On the menu are delicious meals, including home-made bread and gluten-free options. Dinner (pre-arranged) is served with New Zealand wine, although several restaurants are within 12 minutes' walk. Warm, welcoming hospitality. A genuine 'home away from home'.

The Loft in Wellington

B&B • Separate Suite
7 km N of Wellington

6 Delhi Crescent, Khandallah, Wellington
(04) 938 5015 or 021 448 491
info@theloftinwellington.co.nz
www.theloftinwellington.co.nz

Double: $120
Single: $95

1 Bedroom: 1Q
Bathrooms: 1 ensuite

Phillippa and Simon Plimmer

The Loft in Wellington offers comfort and style in a beautifully appointed self-contained studio (no cooking facilities). Enjoy complete privacy with your own entrance. Cable TV, off-street parking and laundry facility available. 10 minutes from downtown Wellington. Close to ferry terminal. 300 metres to local train and bus. 15 minutes train ride direct to Westpac Stadium. 500 metres from Khandallah Village and local restaurants. Studio Not suitable for pets. We have three young children.

- Continental provisions supplied
- Pet-free home
- Not suitable for children
- No smoking on property
- Internet available

Ngaio Homestay

B&B Homestay • Apartment with Kitchen
7 km N of Wellington

56 Fox Street, Ngaio, Wellington 6035
(04) 479 5325
enquiries@ngaiohomestay.co.nz
www.ngaiohomestay.co.nz

Double: $150–$160   **Single: $120–$130**
Children: negotiable

5 Bedrooms: 1Q 1D 2T 3S
Bathrooms: 3 ensuite, 1 private

Jennifer and Christopher Timmings

Welcome to Wonderful Wellington! Come to Ngaio Homestay and enjoy personal hospitality in our unusual open plan character home (built 1960). Our comfortable double ensuite room has double doors opening onto a deck and 'jungle' bush garden. Fridge/tea/coffee facilities provided in room. Or stay in either the Queen or Twin bed apartment (can convert to Superking bed). Self catering and weekly rates offered. Perfect for relocating, sabbatical, work/study or holiday.

Do come and relax here. You will be comfortable and welcome.

- Bathrooms: shower & bath in apartments, shower in ensuite B&B
- Continental breakfast
- Pet-free home
- Children welcome
- Non-smokers only
- Internet available

Wadestown, Wellington

Harbour Lodge Wellington

B&B
2 km N of Wellington

200 Barnard Street, Wadestown, Wellington
(04) 976 5677 or 021 032 6497
lou@harbourlodgewellington.com
www.harbourlodgewellington.com

Double: $180–$250
Children: negotiable

VISA MasterCard AMERICAN EXPRESS

2 Bedrooms: 2K
Bathrooms: 2 ensuite

Lou and Chris Bradshaw

- Continental breakfast
- Children welcome
- Internet available

Let your stresses be gently lulled away in the luxurious comfort of this beautiful lodge. Admire the fabulous views of Wellington Harbour from the large sunny deck. Take a spa. Laze in the comfort of a large guest lounge with stunning harbour views. All this is only a few minutes drive from central Wellington, ferry terminal or Wellington Stadium. Children of all ages welcome, no pets please.

Wadestown, Wellington

Ahu Mairangi

B&B
2 km NW of C.B.D

128 Weld Street, Wadestown, 6012
landline (04)4737157 or freephone 0800 678 031
james.quinn@xtra.co.nz
www.bnb.co.nz/AhuMairangi.html

Double: $160–$180
Single: $110–$120

2 Bedrooms: 1Q **1**D
Bathrooms: 1 ensuite, 1 private

James and Helen

- 1 with ensuite and 1 with own bathroom
- Neg.rates for longer stays
- Dinner by arrangement
- Continental breakfast
- Pet-free home
- Not suitable for children
- Internet available

Located high up on the hills above Wellington City for awesome views and maximum sun. Our recently modernised home has a large guest bedroom with ensuite which has both bath and shower. Also a second smaller double bedroom with adjoining bath room and separate w.c. Both rooms have peaceful bush views so come and enjoy a relaxing stay in our beautiful city. As we adjoin the town belt there are some great walks for the fitter guests. Courtesy transfer from ferry, airport or car hire. Dinner optional extra.

B&B Homestay
5 km SW of Wellington

23 Parkvale Road, Karori 6012, Wellington
(04) 476 6110 or 0274 535 080
ctool@ihug.co.nz
bnb.co.nz

Double: $120–$125
Single: $80–$85
Children: half price (under 12)

2 Bedrooms: 1Q 1T 1S
Bathrooms: 1 guest share

Murray and Elaine Campbell

- Bathrooms: separate toilet, full bathroom/shower next to guest bedrooms
- Dinner: $35 by arrangement
- Continental breakfast
- Pets welcome
- Children welcome
- No smoking on property

Welcome to our home right in the village of Karori, but only ten minutes from the central city.

Dine with us, or eat out at the local taverns, cafés, enjoy our local village shopping centre, library, Post Office and other amenities all within a few minutes walking distance. As we are on the main bus route, guests, can park their car off street and take the bus into the city. We are happy to pick you up from ferry, train, bus or airport terminals and of course make sure you do not miss your onward connection. We are situated close to the Karori Wildlife Sanctuary, Botanic Gardens and Otari-Wilton's Bush, Cable Car, historic Thorndon's boutique shopping centre and restaurants.

'Absolutely Positively Wellington' is a dynamic ever changing compact city making it easy to walk from one place to the next and with simply the most friendly helpful people. Take advantage of Wellington's cultural events: orchestra, ballet, opera, galleries and theatres. Visit our fabulous modern museum Te Papa or take a shuttle ferry across the harbour.

Guests have the sole use of a separate toilet and a full sized bathroom next door to the bedrooms. Relax and make yourself at home – use our laundry, garden, lounge, email/internet facilities.

Aro Valley, Wellington — Millie's Bed & Breakfast

B&B Homestay
2 km SW of Information Centre

33 Holloway Road, Aro Valley, Wellington 6021
(04) 381 2968 or 021 254 7308
miriam.busby@paradise.net.nz
www.milliesbb.co.nz

Double: $130
Single: $90
Children: $40

2 Bedrooms: 1D 1S
Bathrooms: 1 family share

Miriam Busby

- Bathrooms: one bath and shower available for guests to use.
- Dinner: $25 for Colonial cottage cuisine.
- Full breakfast
- Children welcome

Named after Millie, the pet cat, at Millie's you awake to the sound of native birdsong. The house is nestled in a bushy valley near the Karori Sanctuary. Situated on a heritage trail, Millie's is close to a bus-stop, Aro Street cafés, restaurants and shops. 20 minutes walk to city. Free off-street parking available. Complimentary breakfast. One extra divan bed in kitchen. Deck with BBQ. Dinner, scenic drives, walks and therapeutic art sessions are extra services available.

Mt Victoria, Wellington — Austinvilla

B&B • Apartment with Kitchen
0.5 km E of Courtenay Place

11 Austin Street, Mount Victoria, Wellington
(04) 385 8334
info@austinvilla.co.nz
www.austinvilla.co.nz

Double: $195–$245

VISA MasterCard eftpos

2 Bedrooms: 2Q
Bathrooms: 2 ensuite

Zarli and Mark

- Continental breakfast
- Not suitable for children
- No smoking on property
- Internet available

Prime location: Quiet, leafy residential setting in one of Mount Victoria's elegant Victorian villas, yet within minutes walk of restaurants, shops, waterfront precinct and Te Papa. Close to public transport and short drive to airport, ferries, and Westpac Stadium.

2 self-contained apartments with individual entrances each with queen bed, ensuite (bath and shower), kitchen, living/dining area, cable TV, phone and Wi-Fi access. Both offer privacy, sun and city views. One having its own patio/garden. Laundry facilities and off-street parking available.

Panorama

B&B
2 km E of Central city

1 Robieson Lane, Roseneath
(04) 801 8691 or 021 801 869
pegmackay@hotmail.com
www.wellingtonpanorama.co.nz

Double: $140–$170
Single: $100–$120

2 Bedrooms: 2Q
Bathrooms: 1 guest share, 1 private

Peg Mackay

Lie in bed and enjoy the panorama of ships, ferries and tugs and enjoy the sun, peace and privacy of our warm modern home above Oriental Bay. You have your own deck and sitting room with TV and refreshments. Five min walk up to Mount Victoria or 15–20 minute walk down to Oriental Bay, the city, theatres, galleries and Te Papa: the Museum of New Zealand. Taste NZ in the many nearby cafés and restaurants. Ferry/Airport 10 minutes, city five minutes drive. AND you can park right at our door! Wireless Internet available.

- Two queen with harbour views
- Long term rates on application
- Bathrooms: 1 guest bath
- Continental breakfast
- Internet available

Maida Vale B&B

B&B
1 km E of Wellington CBD

6 Maida Vale Road, Roseneath, Wellington
027 332 1570 or (04) 970 5184
bess.sutherland@clear.net.nz
www.maidavalebnb.co.nz

Double: $150–$180
Single: $60
Children: child negotiable

2 Bedrooms: 1K 1S
Bathrooms: 1 ensuite

Bessie Sutherland

Our centrally located home has spectacular views across the harbour to the city centre. The larger room has an ensuite. Both rooms are on the ground floor and have their own entrance (our family lives above). The city centre, restaurants, theatres and museums are a five minute drive away or, alternatively, a 20 minute walk along the waterfront. The airport and ferry terminals are 10–15 minutes away. The family will greet you with a warm welcome as will Zoe, the Jack Russell terrier.

- Main room is spacious with harbour views.
- Weekly rates negotiable
- Continental breakfast
- Children welcome
- No smoking on property
- Internet available

Roseneath, Wellington — Sub Rosa

Luxury B&B • Guest House
1 km N of wellington city central

Thane Rd, Roseneath Wellington, 6011
021–058–0780 or 021–1888–245
redandbluedream@hotmail.com
www.bnb.co.nz/8383.html

Double: $120–$140
Single: $100–$120
Children: 60 extra

VISA · MasterCard · eftpos NEW ZEALAND LIMITED

2 Bedrooms: 1K 1Q
Bathrooms: 1 guest share, 1 private

Robin St Helens

- Bathrooms: 2 rooms available – share bathroom if both rooms booked otherwise private bathroom
- Breakfast by arrangement
- Children welcome
- No smoking on property
- Internet available

Sub Rosa - secret, private, intimate - the perfect description of our Roseneath hideaway. Lie in bed and enjoy panoramic views of the harbour and Wellington's busy maritime traffic from the peace and privacy of your private balcony in our modern home perched high above Oriental Bay. 5 min walk up to Mt Victoria or 15-20 minute walk down to Oriental Bay, the city, theatres, galleries and Te Papa: the Museum of New Zealand.

Enjoy NZ hospitality in the many nearby cafes and restaurants. Ferry/Airport 10 minutes, city 5 minutes drive.

Vogeltown/Newtown, Wellington — Finnimore House

B&B Homestay
3 km S of Wellington CBD

2 Dransfield Street, Vogeltown, Wellington
(04) 389 9894
w.f.ryan@xtra.co.nz
www.finnimorehouse.co.nz

Double: $100–$130
Single: $90–$110
Children: $30

VISA · MasterCard

3 Bedrooms: 3Q 2S
Bathrooms: 1 guest share, 1 private

Willie and Kathleen Ryan

- Twin rate $120–$140. Extra person $30. Seaonal rates vary.
- Full breakfast
- Children welcome
- No smoking on property
- Internet available

Welcome to our historical manor five minutes drive from downtown Wellington. We offer warm Irish hospitality, spacious Victorian rooms with tea/coffee/fridge facilities, full cooked breakfast at your convenience. Willie offers enthusiastic guidance to Wellington's attractions. Our location is close to: airport, ferries, Newtown, restaurants, supermarkets, Basin Reserve, hospital, zoo, Massey University, National School of Dance and Drama. Secure private parking on-site, convenient public transport. Laundry facilities free if staying three nights or more (otherwise a charge applies). Special rates may apply to major events.

Botanica Homestay

Botanica Homestay is a classic villa surrounded by beautiful, mature gardens, located in a quiet cul-de-sac on the Miramar Peninsula in Wellington, where you will sleep on good quality beds in stylishly decorated rooms, or relax on a comfortable couch in the conservatory. You can watch a movie on a flat-screen TV, sit in the gardens and enjoy the flowers and trees or drive the scenic route around the bays and arrive in Wellington City in only 10 to 15 minutes.

In the bed-and-breakfast area of the Botanica Homestay you will have the entire downstairs floor for your private use, catering for up to six guests. This includes a 'main' bedroom with a queen-size bed, a second bedroom with a king-size bed, a conservatory (or sunroom) with views of the front garden, a lounge with Sky TV, a computer, and a top-quality double sofa bed for an additional two people, an outside sitting area, and a modern bathroom for your private use.

You'll also enjoy free wireless Internet and the use of a desktop computer, fridge, microwave, DVD player, SKY and Nespresso machine.

Luxury B&B Homestay

3 km S of Wellington Airport

34 Ashleigh Crescent, Miramar, Wellington, 6022
(04) 976 8058 or +64–27–5400055 or +64–21–809045
contact@botanicaaccommodation.com
www.botanicaaccommodation.com

Double: $150–$170
Children: Under 5 years free, 5–12 years $20

VISA MasterCard

2 Bedrooms: 1K 1Q 1D
Bathrooms: 1 guest share

Jos Maas and Lucien Dol

10%

- All beds (including the double sofabed) are of excellent quality.
- Price is for 1–2 people, extra people $40 per night/ per person. Max. 6 people.
- Bathrooms: modern bathroom with shower, toilet and basin.
- Breakfast by arrangement
- Children welcome
- No smoking on property
- Internet available

Self-contained

6 km S of Wellington City Central

326 The Esplanade & 116 The Esplanade, Island Bay, Wellington
(04) 472 4177 or 027 442 5555
bruce@thelighthouse.net.nz
www.thelighthouse.net.nz

Double: $180–$230

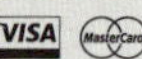

1 Bedroom: 1Q
Bathrooms: 1 private

Bruce Stokell

- Full breakfast provisions
- Not suitable for children
- No smoking on property

Island Bay – 10 minutes city centre, 10 minutes airport, 20 minutes ferry terminal. The Lighthouse is on the south coast and has views of the island, fishing boats in the bay, the beach and rocks, the far coastline, the open sea, the shipping and, on a clear day, the South Island. There are local shops and restaurants. The Lighthouse has a basic kitchen and bathroom on the first floor, the bedroom/sitting room on the middle floor and the lookout on the top. Romantic.

The Keep is a stone tower just two minutes from The Lighthouse. It has a lounge/basic kitchen on one level and a bed with ensuite on the next level. Also a spa bath in the bedroom. It is very cosy and has excellent views of the sea, especially in a storm. Stairs from the bedroom lead to a hatch which opens on to the roof.

South Island

Marlborough
French Pass
Pelorus Sound
Kenepuru Sounds
Queen Charlotte Sound
Mahau Sound
Anakiwa
Picton
6
63
Renwick
Blenheim
1
able Bay
0 Kilometres 20
0 Miles 12

Marlborough
French Pass
Pelorus Sound
Kenepuru Sounds
Queen Charlotte Sound
Mahau Sound
Anakiwa
Picton
able Bay
63
Renwick
Blenheim
6
1
Kilometres
0
20
Miles
0
12

B&B Homestay
1 km E of Picton

20 Lincoln Street, Picton, 7220
0 3 573 8160 or 0 21143 2224
alisonandgeoff@retreat-inn.co.nz
www.retreat-inn.co.nz

Double: $135–$145

2 Bedrooms: 2Q 2S
Bathrooms: 1 ensuite, 1 private

Alison and Geoff

Set in peaceful bush surroundings, Retreat Inn Homestay/B&B offers you comfort, rest, quietness. A choice of guest bedrooms – ground floor queen room (ensuite, bath and shower) with outside access to fern/seating area. Upstairs – queen (or twin) room, adjacent private bathroom. Gluten free breakfast option. Marlborough province is diverse, unforgettable – come stay two or three nights and explore what we have to offer. Flat off-street parking.

- All are firm beds with electric blankets
- Room rate $135–$145
- Continental breakfast
- Not suitable for children
- Internet available

Grandvue

B&B Homestay • Apartment with Kitchen
0.5 km SE of Picton Central

19 Otago Street, Picton 7220
(03) 573 8553 or 0800 49 1080
enquiries@grandvuepicton.co.nz
www.grandvuepicton.co.nz

Double: $135–$145   Single: $75–$110
Children: $45

3 Bedrooms: 2Q 1T 1S
Bathrooms: 1 ensuite, 1 family share

Rosalie and Russell Mathews

On the hills above Picton, Grandvue is a quiet haven in a secluded garden with a grandview. It's a five minute walk to the shopping area, restaurants, the waterfront and bushwalks. Russell, retired, enjoys boating, fishing and gardening. Rosalie an enthusiastic quilter, loves cooking and gardening. Both enjoy meeting people. The accommodation is spacious, warm, quality and self-contained with kitchen and ensuite. Other rooms available in our home. Feast on magnificent views from our conservatory while enjoying a wholesome breakfast. Courtesy transport, parking and laundry facilities.

- Our queen or twin or single is share our facilites but there are no other guests using these facilities.
- Dinner: N/A
- Continental breakfast
- Pet-free home
- Children welcome
- Internet available

Tanglewood

B&B • Separate Suite • Apartment with Kitchen
16 km SW of Picton

1744 Queen Charlotte Drive, The Grove, RD 1, Picton
(03) 574 2080 or 027 481 4388
tanglewood.hearn@xtra.co.nz
www.tanglewood.net.nz

Double: $165–$195   Single: $130–$150

4 Bedrooms: 2KT 1Q 2S
Bathrooms: 4 ensuite

Linda and Stephen Hearn

Modern architectural home nestled amongst the native ferns overlooking Queen Charlotte Sounds. Enjoy our luxury Super King/Twin ensuite rooms with balcony and views; or a self-contained guest wing which includes Queen and two Single beds (with ensuites), lounge, kitchen and sunny balcony/BBQ area. Relax in our jacuzzi surrounded by beautiful native garden and birds or view the glow-worms. Generous breakfast provided before your day's pursuits, swimming, fishing, kayaking, walking the Queen Charlotte Walkway or exploring Marlborough Wineries. Fifth generation Kiwi hospitality at its best.

- Self-contained $195–$300.00
- Dinner: $50
- Full breakfast
- Internet available

Marlborough

Mahau Sound, Pelorus

Ramona

B&B Homestay
33 km SW of Picton

460 Moetapu Bay Road, Mahau Sound,
Marlborough
(03) 574 2215 or 027 247 6668
illes@clear.net.nz
www.bnb.co.nz/ramona.html

Double: $150   Single: $90
Children: We can accomodate 3 children

VISA MasterCard

2 Bedrooms: 1Q **2T 1**S
Bathrooms: 1 private

Phyl and Ken Illes

- Tea &&& coffee available in conservatory
- Bathrooms: hair dryer in bathroom
- Continental breakfast
- Pet-free home
- Children welcome
- No smoking on property
- Internet available

Our waterfront home on the beautiful Mahau Sound has been designed for you to share. Our guest floor has its own conservatory, here you can view the passing water traffic. Awake to the call of bellbirds and tuis, and after breakfast stroll around our large garden, or fossick on the beach. We are 15 mins from the South end of Queen Charlotte walkway. Launch tours of the Kenepuru and outer Pelorus Sound depart from Havelock (30 minutes by road from Ramona). Day trips by road into Pelorus and the wine region of Marlborough are reccomended. Phyl's interests included writing, quilting, gardening and oilpainting.

Queen Charlotte Drive Picton

Waterfront Bed & Breakfast

B&B Homestay
11 km SW of Picton

Queen Charlotte Drive, 2383 Queen Charlotte
Drive, Little Ngakuta Bay, RD 1, Picton Marlborough
(03) 573 8584 or 027 748 4172
waterfront@farmside.co.nz
www.waterfrontbnb.co.nz

Double: $175–$195
Single: $140–$195

2 Bedrooms: 2Q
Bathrooms: 1 ensuite, 1 private

Vicki and David Bendell

- 24 hour notice (to catch the fish)
- Dinner: with notice $60pp BBQ or fish followed by cheese platter
- Full breakfast
- Children welcome
- No smoking on property
- Internet available

Our waterfront accommodation is as close to the water as you can get. Seperate from our cottage are the aptly named and themed Boatshed and Pacific rooms with ensuite, private bathroom and Italian cotton linens. A long jetty outfront is ideal for swimming, fishing or an evening stroll to see the water fluoresce. Please join us for a meal on the deck over-looking the water. Not just another B&B but an accommodation experience with a young ideal NZ family.

French Twist

B&B • Separate Suite

440 Port Underwood Road, RD1 Picton, 7281
(03) 573 8823
jennychater9@gmail.com
www.bnb.co.nz/8417.html

Double: $150
Single: $150

1 Bedroom: 1Q
Bathrooms: 1 ensuite

Jenny Chater

French Twist is separate accommodation from the house. It has it`s own balcony, is private and quiet with sweeping views of Queen Charlotte Sound. The bedroom has a comfortable Queen size bed and Sky TV. The bathroom has a bath and shower. Off this is a den with tea/coffee facilities and a fridge for drinks and snacks. Breakfast to start your day is homemade muesli, fruit and yogurt followed by toast, tea or coffee.

Jenny can give you ideas for your daily pursuits.

- Queen Bed
- Cooked breakfast by request
- Bathrooms: shower over bath
- Dinner: Upon request
- Continental breakfast
- Not suitable for children

Beaver B&B

Blenheim

Homestay • Cottage with Kitchen
1 km SW of Blenheim Central

60 Beaver Road, Blenheim, 7201
(03) 578 8401 or 021 626 151
rdhopkins@xtra.co.nz
marlborough.co.nz/beaver/

Double: $110–$110
Single: $90–$90

VISA MasterCard

1 Bedroom: 1Q
Bathrooms: 1 ensuite

Jen and Russell Hopkins

10%

Our self-contained unit has its own entrance and off-street parking-5 minutes drive from central Blenheim and 10 minutes drive from the wineries and the Aviation Heritage Centre.

The bed is queen-size. The mini-kitchen has a microwave, small sink and fridge containing items for a self-serve continental breakfast to have at your leisure. The bathroom has a large bath and a separate shower and toilet. Two cats live with us.

- Continental provisions supplied
- Not suitable for children
- No smoking on property
- Internet available

Blenheim | Philmar

B&B Homestay
3.5 km S of Post Office

19 Hillside Terrace, Witherlea, Blenheim, 7201
(03) 577 7788
philmar9@xtra.co.nz
www.bnb.co.nz/philmar.html

Double: $100
Single: $80

2 Bedrooms: 1Q 1T
Bathrooms: 1 guest share

Wynnis and Lex Phillips

- Dinner: $20pp by arrangement
- Continental breakfast
- No smoking on property
- Internet available

Welcome to our home 3.5 km from the town centre. Guests can join us in our spacious sunny living areas. We both enjoy all sports on TV and our other interests include wood turning, handcrafts and the Lions organisation. Blenheim has many wineries, parks, craft shops, art galleries and golf courses. Not far from Picton, Nelson and Kaikoura whale watching. We share our home with our pets, Lucy-Lu and Louie. Smoking is not encouraged. Just phone to be picked up at airport, bus or train.

Blenheim | Henry Maxwell's Central Lodge B&B

Luxury B&B
0.0 km NW of central Blenheim

28 Henry Street, Blenheim
(03) 578 8086 or 0800 436 796 or 027 485 5142
graymere@xtra.co.nz
www.henrymaxwells.co.nz

Double: $127–$147
Single: $87

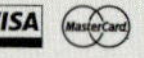

4 Bedrooms: 3Q 1T 1S
Bathrooms: 3 ensuite, 1 private

Diana and Graham Westenra

- 3 large comfortable rooms, one small single,
- Bathrooms: bath in the large bathroom
- Full breakfast
- Pet-free home
- Children welcome
- Internet available

Welcome to Henry Maxwell's Bed and Breakfast and Accommodation. A gracious 90 year old home, Guests have spacious quiet rooms, three with ensuites, one with a private bathroom. Comfortable beds and chairs, TV, tea, coffee, and complimentary port. Breakfast in the unique dining room (maps and charts) is memorable, kitchenette facilities. Guest laundry, wireless, library. Five minutes stroll to town, restaurants, shops, theatre. Off-street parking. Very suitable for extended stays, conference and wedding parties. Discounts. Affordable luxury.

Ashwood Bed & Breakfast

B&B Homestay
4 km SW of Post Office

17 Ashwood Drive, Blenheim, 7201
(03) 579 1700 or 027 313 0125
maureen.reg@xtra.co.nz
www.ashwoodbnb.co.nz

Double: $115–$120
Single: $78–$88

2 Bedrooms: 1Q 2T
Bathrooms: 1 guest share

Maureen and Reg Sagar

Reg and Maureen welcome you to Ashwood Bed and Breakfast in our warm, modern home adjacent to the foothills of the Wither Hills Farm Park. We offer a continental breakfast, or cooked by arrangement, served in our dining room looking out to the beautiful Richmond Ranges. You can be assured of a good nights sleep in comfortable beds in a quiet neighbourhood.

 five Minutes drive from the centre of Blenheim, we are also near the Provincial Museum, the Aviation Centre and many local wineries.

- Dinner: $35pp with 24 hours notice
- Continental breakfast
- Pet-free home
- Not suitable for children
- Internet available

Chardonnay Lodge

B&B · Cottage with Kitchen
6min km N of Blenheim

1048 Rapaura Road, Rapaura, Blenheim
(03) 570 5194
info@chardonnaylodge.co.nz
www.chardonnaylodge.co.nz

Double: $160
Children: $30 (5 years and over)

2 Bedrooms: 2Q 2S
Bathrooms: 2 ensuite

Karen and David Rees

We offer excellent accommodation and facilities, including secluded solar heated swimming pool, private spa, sun lounges, BBQ,a full sized tennis court. Central to superb vineyards and restaurants, with Blenheim just six minutes away we provide high standard self-contained villas set in one acre of beautifully landscaped grounds. You will find everything you and your family need for a comfortable and relaxing stay. We are 2.2 km from the Spring Creek turn off on SH1. Location map, pictures and information on web site.

- Continental provisions supplied
- Children welcome
- Internet available

Blenheim | The Grove

B&B
4 km N of Blenheim

94 Rowley Crescent, Blenheim, 7202
35794923 or 021 134 1510
rossuter@hotmail.com
www.thegroveblenheim.com

Double: $130–$130

1 Bedroom: 1K
Bathrooms: 1 ensuite

Ros Suter and Debs Simpson

- Continental provisions supplied
- No smoking on property
- Internet available

We welcome you to stay in our beautiful home on the edge of Blenheim within a four minute drive of the town centre and its many restaurants, cafés and shops. Set in four acres, the accommodation offers you complete peace and tranquillity. You can amble through the large garden, olive groves and fruit orchard, feed the Kunekune pigs or just relax in your own private courtyard garden.

A continental breakfast is left in your fridge so that you may take it at your leisure either in your room or in the private courtyard.

Blenheim | St Leonards Vineyard Cottages

B&B • Cottage with Kitchen
3 km SW of Blenheim

18 St Leonards Road, RD1 Blenheim, 7271
(03) 577 8328 or 0064 27 686 1636
stay@stleonards.co.nz
www.stleonards.co.nz

Double: $120–$320
Single: $120–$320
Children: No charge under 16 years

VISA MasterCard

6 Bedrooms: 5Q **1**T
Bathrooms: 2 ensuite, 3 family share

Paul and Daphne Radmall

- Bathrooms: one cottage has a bath and shower, others all have showers.
- Dinner: N/A
- Continental provisions supplied
- Pet-free home
- Children welcome
- No smoking on property
- Internet available

We have five individual cottages, each offering a unique experience. There is an outdoor heated swimming pool (for summer use), good quality complimentary bikes for touring the wineries and free use of the laundry. We also have wireless internet broadband.

All cottages have flat screen TV, Freeview, DVD, radio, BBQ, hairdryer, iron and board. We keep a few sheep, Fallow deer and free range hens who will provide you with fresh eggs for breakfast. St Leonards is a haven set within the grape vines.

Nelson,
Golden Bay

Pakawau
Collingwood
Parapara
Tukurua
Pohara
Takaka
60
Abel Tasman
National Park
Marahau
Split Apple Rock
Kaiteriteri
Riwaka
Motueka
Motueka Valley
Ruby Bay
Mapua
Upper
Moutere
6
Nelson
Richmond
Kilometres
0
20
Miles
0
12
6
63
Murchison
65
Nelson
Lakes
St Arnaud

Nelson

Harbour View Homestay B&B

B&B Homestay
2 km SW of Central Nelson

11 Fifeshire Crescent, Nelson
(03) 548 8567 or 027 247 4445
harbourview-homestay@xtra.co.nz
www.bnb.co.nz/harbourbb.html

Double: $150–$170
Single: $135–$150

VISA MasterCard

3 Bedrooms: 2Q 2S
Bathrooms: 2 ensuite, 1 private

Judy Black and David Beets

- Enquire about available discounts
- Continental breakfast

Our home is above the harbour entrance. Huge windows capture spectacular views of beautiful Tasman Bay, Haulashore Island, Tahunanui Beach, across the sea to Abel Tasman National Park and mountains. Observe from the bedrooms, dining room and outside deck, ships and pleasure craft cruising by as they enter and leave the harbour. If you can tear yourself away from our magnificent view, within walking distance along the waterfront there are excellent cafés or enjoy fish and chips on the beach. We welcome you for a memorable stay.

Marybank, Atawhai, Nelson

Mike's B&B

B&B Homestay
6 km NE of Nelson CBD

4 Seaton Street, NELSON, 7010
(03) 545 1671
mikecooper@actrix.co.nz
www.bnb.co.nz/hosts/kent

Double: $95–$100
Single: $95–$95

VISA MasterCard

2 Bedrooms: 2Q
Bathrooms: 2 ensuite

Mike Cooper and Lennane Cooper-Kent

- Two double queen size beds
- Bathrooms: showers in ensuite bathroom
- Dinner: $45 pp with prior notice
- Full breakfast
- No smoking on property
- Internet available

5 minutes NE of Nelson City our home is in a quiet neighbourhood with extensive views over Tasman Bay to the mountains beyond. Our guests' accommodation is almost self-contained and includes ensuite bedrooms, a kitchenette with a fridge/freezer, microwave and complimentary tea and coffee making facilities, a small lounge with TV and part of our collection of books. Laundry facilities, internet access and off street parking are available. Our interests include travel, education, volunteer work abroad and our young friendly kerry-blue terrier.

Peppertree B&B

B&B • Separate Suite
0.75 km SW of Nelson Central

31 Seymour Avenue, Nelson 7010,
(03) 546 9881 or (03) 021 074 6540
c.sygrove@clear.net.nz
www.bnb.co.nz/peppertreebb.html

Double: $135
Single: $135
Children: $25

VISA MasterCard

1 Bedroom: 1Q 1D 1S
Bathrooms: 1 ensuite

Richard Savill and Carolyn Sygrove

Enjoy space and privacy in our heritage villa, only 10 minutes riverside walk from Nelson's city centre. The master bedroom has an ensuite bathroom and walk-in wardrobe. Your private adjoining rooms include a large lounge with double innersprung sofabed, single bed, Sky TV, fridge, microwave, kettle etc. Also sunroom with cane setting and private entrance. Central heating and airconditioning for all year round comfort. Wireless internet and off-street parking available. Children are welcome. We have one daughter aged 17 and a friendly Cavoodle called Mia.

- Extra adult $35
- Dinner: $40–$50 by arrangement
- Continental breakfast
- Children welcome
- No smoking on property
- Internet available

Te Maunga Historic House

B&B Homestay • Apartment with Kitchen
1 km E of Nelson Cathedral

15 Dorothy Annie Way @ 82 Cleveland Trc.,
Nelson City
(03) 548 8605 or 021 201 2461
temaungahouse@xtra.co.nz
www.nelsoncityaccommodation.co.nz

Double: $120–$135   **Single:** $80–$95
Children: negotiable

VISA MasterCard

3 Bedrooms: 2D 1T 1S
Bathrooms: 1 guest share, 2 private

Anne Kolless

Anne welcomes you to her family's 1930's registered Heritage House. Only five mins to downtown this stunning unique Arts and Crafts style, native woods example is mostly original with modern facilities. Te Maunga sits on a knoll, in rambling gardens, giving commanding views over Nelson, sea and valleys. Your special continental style breakfast includes local produce, home-made breads, and preserves. Relax and enjoy your aperitif, while taking in the amazing views. Self-catered unit next door! NZQA Food Safety Cert. Free Wireless Broadband link.

- Self-catered $145
- Bathrooms: showers & tub-shower
- Continental breakfast
- Pet-free home
- Children welcome
- No smoking on property
- Internet available

Experience the peace and charm of the past in our fully restored circa 1880s B&B, one of Nelson's original family homes. Situated beside the beautiful Maitai River, Sussex House has retained all the original character and romantic ambiance of the era. It is only minutes' walk from central Nelson's award-winning restaurants and cafés, the Queens Gardens, Suter Art Gallery and Botanical Hill (The Centre of NZ) and many fine river and bushwalks. The five sunny bedrooms all have TVs and are spacious and charmingly furnished. All rooms have access to the verandahs and complimentary tea and coffee facilities are provided. Breakfast includes a variety of fresh and preserved fruits, hot croissants and pastries, home-made yoghurts, cheeses and a large variety of cereals, rolls, breads and crumpets. Other facilities include: wheelchair suite; free email/internet station; fax; courtesy phone; laundry facilities; separate lounge for guest entertaining; complimentary port; tea and coffee facilities; very sociable cat (Riley). We have lived overseas and have travelled extensively. We speak French fluently.

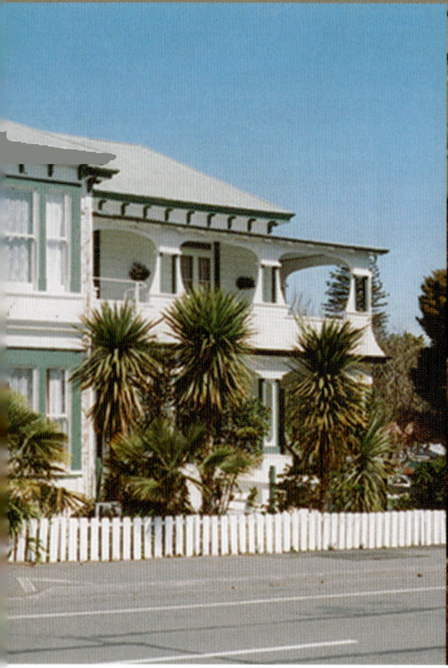

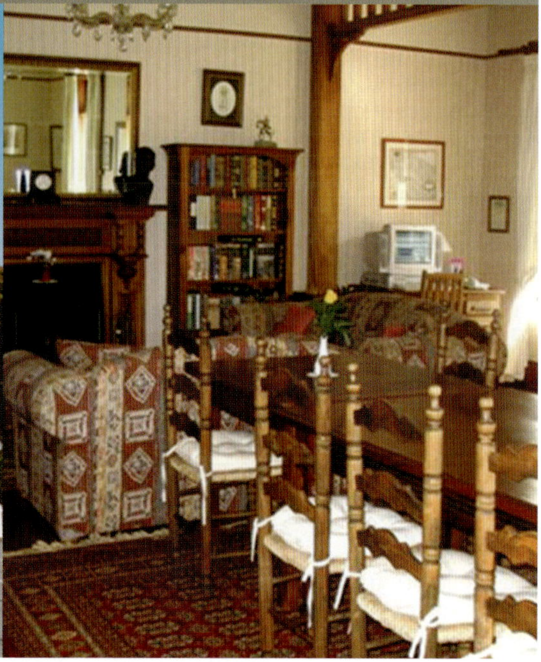

B&B

1 km E of Nelson Central

238 Bridge Street, Nelson
(03) 548 9972 or 0800 868 687
reservations@sussex.co.nz
www.sussex.co.nz

Double: $150–$180
Single: $110–$150
Children: $20

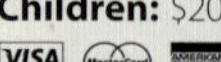
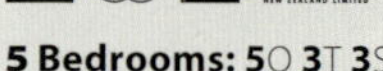

5 Bedrooms: 5Q 3T 3S
Bathrooms: 4 ensuite, 1 private

Victoria and David Los

- Continental Buffet Breakfast
- Continental breakfast
- Children welcome

Baywick Inn

Luxury B&B • Cottage with Kitchen
0.5 km E of Nelson City Centre

51 Domett St, Nelson, 7010
(03) 545 6514 or 027 454 5823
baywicks@iconz.co.nz
www.baywicks.com

Double: $165–$250   **Single: $130–$200**
Children: over 12
Total capacity 8 guests

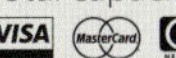 

5 Bedrooms: 5Q 1T
Bathrooms: 4 ensuite, 1 private

Janet Southwick & Tim Bayley    

- Sleeps 3 in B&B and 1 or 2 in Cottage
- Free Wi-Fi
- Dinner platters available $50 to $60
- Full breakfast
- Not suitable for children
- No smoking on property
- Internet available

– Fabulous gourmet breakfast
– Genuine Kiwi/Canadian hospitality
– Three enchanting bedrooms
– Executive one or two bedroom cottage
– Free Wi-Fi
– Off street parking
– Walking distance to restaurants and shops
– Walk to Centre of New Zealand
– All for an affordable price.

Welcome to the Baywick Inn, a heritage luxury bed and breakfast located in a quiet garden setting along the Maitai River, just a five minute walk to the central city to some of Nelson's best restaurants and cafés as well as many artists studios, shops and other Nelson attractions and just a short walk across the river to the Centre of NZ.

Janet Southwick and Tim Bayley spent almost a year restoring this 1885 Victorian villa into three luxurious B&B rooms and in 2010 built a 'Victorian' designed Cottage, using many of the original Inn's features. It is located in the Brookside garden, just steps away from the main house. Here we have two very special, luxurious queen guest rooms, the Courtyard Suite and Brookview.

Nelson — Cambria House

Luxury B&B
0.5 km N of Nelson City Centre

7 Cambria St, Nelson, 7010
(03) 548 4681 or 21548468
cambria@cambria.co.nz
www.cambria.co.nz

Double: $295–$355
Single: $255–$310
Children: $60 p.n. extra for rollaway in Lodge Suite

6 Bedrooms: 4K 2KT 2Q
Bathrooms: 6 ensuite

Karel and David Wallace

- Full breakfast
- Pet-free home
- Children welcome
- No smoking on property
- Internet available

Inner city location in a quiet, leafy street, just five minutes walk to cafés, restaurants and shopping. Cambria House has modern facilities (free wireless) with gracious ambience and Victorian charm. It is the classic small accommodation alternative, combining style, luxury and service. The guest living room opens onto a sunny deck and secluded gardens. Breakfast is a gourmet delight with extensive use made of Nelson's fresh produce. Hosts, Karel and David are very knowledgable locals. Your comfort, happiness and privacy are important to us.

Nelson — Warwick House – Boutique Hotel

B&B • Boutique Hotel
0.5 km SE of Nelson City

64 Brougham St, Nelson, 7010
(03) 548 3164 or 21688243
info@warwickhouse.co.nz
www.warwickhouse.co.nz

Double: $149–$295
Single: $129–$255
Children: over 10 years only. Victorian suite is best

6 Bedrooms: 2K 2KT 2Q
Bathrooms: 6 ensuite

Nick and Jenny Ferrier

- Dinner: 5–10 mins walk to central Nelson restaurants.
- Full breakfast
- Weddings and functions
- Internet available

Warwick House is a spectacular 1854 early Victorian mansion. It offers unique boutique accommodation only 5–10 mins. walk from beautiful Nelson city. The verandah and Bayview Suite have views over Nelson city to the sea. The Victorian and the Daisy Jenner are available as self catering with optional breakfast in the Grand Ballroom.

Enjoy the gardens, Walk Vicki the lovely black Labrador Secure off street parking and free Wi-Fi Broadband Experienced hosts who can help you will all your activity planning in the area.

Antiquarian Guest House

B&B
1 km SE of Richmond

12A Surrey Road, Richmond, Nelson
(03) 544 0253 or (03) 544 0723
souchebys@clear.net.nz
souchebys@clear.net.nz

Double: $110–$145
Single: $95
Children: $15

3 Bedrooms: 1K 1Q 1T
Bathrooms: 1 ensuite, 1 private

Robert and Joanne Souch

Bob and Joanne Souch welcome you to their peaceful home only two minutes from Richmond (15 minutes drive south of Nelson) – excellent base for exploring National Parks, beaches, arts/crafts, ski fields etc. Relax in the garden, beside the swimming pool or in our large TV/guest lounge. Tea/coffee facilities, home-baking and memorable breakfasts. Our family pet is Gemma (friendly border collie). As local antique shop owners we know the area well.

- Full breakfast
- Pets welcome
- Children welcome
- No smoking on property

Clayridge House and Cottages

B&B Farmstay • Cottage with Kitchen
3 km NW of Mapua

77 Pine Hill Road, Ruby Bay, Nelson, 7173
35402548 or 027 447 2099
info@clayridge.co.nz
www.clayridge.co.nz

Double: $220–$280
Single: $170–$190

5 Bedrooms: 2K 3KT
Bathrooms: 1 ensuite, 2 guest share

Marion and Peter Copp

Situated on a ridge at Ruby Bay, in the centre of the beautiful Nelson region, lies Clayridge House and Cottages. With panoramic views of Tasman Bay, mount Arthur and the nearby mountain ranges. You can choose either bed and Breakfast in our luxurious Mount Arthur Suite, in the homestead, or one of our two spacious comfortable two bedroom self-contained cottages, you can self-cater or have a delicious continental breakfast tray delivered to your cottage (extra charge). The tariff for the Mount Arthur suite in the Homestead, includes a cooked or continental breakfast.

- Bathrooms: our two cottages have one bathroom and two bedrooms
- The Mount Arthur suite has a king/twin bed
- Full breakfast
- Children welcome
- Internet available

Ruby Bay, Nelson — The Foxes

Luxury B&B • Private Suites
1 km N of Mapua

304 Pomona Road, Upper Moutere, Near Mapua,
Nelson, 7173
(03) 540 3472
enquire@thefoxes.co.nz
www.thefoxes.co.nz

Double: $350
Single: $350

VISA MasterCard

2 Bedrooms: 2KT
Bathrooms: 2 ensuite

Margaret and Derek Fox

- 2 Luxury Suites
- Total Capacity for 4 guests
- Full breakfast
- Internet available

Relax, unwind and enjoy the inside and outside living spaces and the panoramic views at this luxury rural retreat in Ruby Bay.

The property offers two luxuriously appointed, spacious suites, each with their own entrance, private balcony and ensuite bathroom. There is a private guest lounge which opens onto a wide balcony offering spectacular views over the Tasman Bay. The Foxes Luxury Boutique B&B is also the ideal base from which to explore and enjoy the many activities Nelson and Abel Tasman region.

Motueka — Motueka Homestay

B&B Homestay • Apartment with Kitchen
1.4 km E of Motueka

186 Thorp Street, Motueka
(03) 528 9385
info@Motueka-Homestay.co.nz
www.motueka-homestay.co.nz

Double: $130–$150   Single: $75–$90
Children: $20

VISA MasterCard

4 Bedrooms: 3Q **1**D **2**S
Bathrooms: 2 ensuite

Rebecca and Ian Williams

- 2 Bedroom Apartment with Kitchen, Sleeps 4 or 5
- Apartment with Kitchen – from $200
- Dinner by arrangement
- Full breakfast
- Children welcome
- Internet available

We are 1.4 km to Motueka shopping centre and 1.2 km to 18 hole golf course. A spacious two bedroom self-contained apartement + two bedrooms both with own ensuite. The guest lounge has tea and coffee making facilities and fridge. Motueka is the stop-over place for visitors to explore Abel Tasman and Kahurangi National Parks. Golden Bay and Kaiteriteri golden sands beach is 10 km away. We have a Jack Russell dog. Visa and Mastercard accepted.

Doone Cottage Country Homestay

Motueka Valley, Motueka

B&B Homestay
26 km S of Motueka

2281 Motueka Valley Highway, Rural District No 1,
Motueka 7196
(03) 526 8740
doone-cottage@xtra.co.nz
www.doonecottage.co.nz

Double: $140–$195
Single: $110–$160

VISA MasterCard

3 Bedrooms: 2KT **1**Q
Bathrooms: 3 ensuite

Glen Davenport

10%

Charming 130yr old cottage welcoming guests for over 30 years. Secluded natives/flower gardens in mountain setting overlooking Motueka River Valley. Five Trout rivers – Guiding available. In-house Guestrooms plus Private Garden Chalet. Enjoy countrystyle B and B, homemade breads, preserves, free range eggs etc. Sheep, chickens, ducks, donkeys. Short distance Abel Tasman, Kahaurangi, Nelson Lakes National Parks, Or just relax and soak up the country atmosphere of yesteryear in this special place. Nelson 45 mins. Motueka 20 mins. Picton 2½ hours Westcoast three hours.

- Dinner by arrangement/ nearest restaurants 5–20 minutes away.
- Full breakfast
- Not suitable for children

Tasman 360

Motueka Valley, Abel Tasman

B&B
6 km SW of Motueka

90, Mytton Heights, Motueka, 7196
(03) 528 9995 or + 44 1637 860 898
gandrbodsworth@btinternet.com
www.tasman360.co.nz

Double: $160–$180
Single: $120–$135

1 Bedroom: 1Q
Bathrooms: 1 ensuite

Garry and Rebecca Bodsworth

With amongst the most amazing views in New Zealand, Tasman 360 is a family run bed and breakfast in the stunning Nelson Tasman region.

Panoramic sea views with breathtaking vistas of mountains, river valleys, orchards, vineyards and Islands.

In an elevated position, nestled in three acres of lush garden with native song birds. A perfect place to relax and unwind after a hectic day and plan tomorrow's adventures.

- Full breakfast
- Pet-free home
- Children welcome
- No smoking on property
- Internet available

Motukea | Vistara Bed & Breakfast

B&B Farmstay
20 km SW of Motueka

2035 Motueka Valley Highway, R.D.1
Motueka, 7196
(03) 526 8288 or 021 079 7919
stay@vistara.co.nz
www.vistara.co.nz

Double: $105   Single: $80
Children: $20 per night

3 Bedrooms: 2Q 2T
Bathrooms: 2 guest share

Bruce and Guruvati Dyer

- 2 Queensize beds and 2 twin bed
- Dinner: $20 dinner per person
- Full breakfast provisions
- Pets welcome
- Children welcome
- No smoking on property
- Internet available

We welcome you to Vistara a relaxed peaceful haven situated on our seven acre property adjacent to the Motueka River.

Vistara is ideal for families with great river swimming, native birds and bush, a beautiful garden, mountain scenery and Jess our Jack Russell dog. We also have milking goats and their three kids, sheep and chickens. Attractions include great river swimming, native birds and bush, a beautiful garden and mountain scenery.

Bedrooms feature polished floors and charming décor.

Kaiteriteri | Bellbird Lodge

Luxury B&B
16 km N of Motueka

Bellbird Lodge, Sandy Bay Road, Kaiteriteri, RD2, Motueka, 7197
(03) 527 8555
stay@bellbirdlodge.co.nz
www.bellbirdlodge.co.nz

Double: $270–$350
Single: $220–$275

2 Bedrooms: 2KT
Bathrooms: 2 ensuite

Anthea and Brian Harvey

- Two Super-King/Twin
- Full breakfast
- Pet-free home
- Not suitable for children
- Internet available

Welcome to Bellbird Lodge, where warm friendly hospitality, superb food and fine accommodation await you. Nestled on the hillside in a tranquil setting with panoramic sea views, Bellbird Lodge is close to Kaiteriteri Beach with its stunning golden sands, the gateway to the Abel Tasman National Park. Both the guest rooms are on the ground floor and have free Wi-Fi, TV/DVD, tea/coffee making facilities, fridge, own entrances, sea or bush views and outdoor terraces.

We look forward to welcoming you soon.

Split Apple Rock Homestay
Split Apple Rock, Abel Tasman

B&B Homestay
17 km NW of Motueka

116 Tokongawa Drive, Split Apple Rock, RD 2,
Motueka 7197
Landline (03) 527 8182 or Mobile 021 137 9145
splitapplerock@gmail.com
www.splitapplerock.com

Double: $165–$180   Single: $135–$165
Children: Price by arrangement/under 14 yrs

2 Bedrooms: 1Q 1T
Bathrooms: 2 ensuite

Thelma and Rodger Boys

Enjoy 180 degree panoramic sea views of Tasman Bay and Abel Tasman National Park. Our Eco-log home rooms have private entrances and decking. Situated within walking distance of golden sand beaches, five minutes drive to Marahau and the start of Abel Tasman National Park where walking, kayaking, boating, swimming and more are available. Two cats in residence. Directions: on the Marahau/Kaiteriteri Road take the Tokongawa Drive turn-off, 1.2 km up Tokongawa Drive the 'Split Apple Rock Homestay' sign is on your right.

- Twin has 2 single beds. Cot available.
- Dinner: $40 pp by arrangement
- Full breakfast
- Children welcome
- No smoking on property
- Internet available

The Devonshires
Tata Beach, Takaka

B&B Homestay
15 km NE of Takaka

32 Tata Heights Drive, Tata Beach, RD 1, Takaka,
Golden Bay
(03) 525 7987
jthomas@bnb.co.nz
www.bnb.co.nz/thedevonshires.html

Double: $100   Single: $70
Children: Not suitable

1 Bedroom: 1Q
Bathrooms: 1 ensuite

Brian and Susan Devonshire

The Devonshires live at Tata Beach and invite you to enjoy their comfortable home and stroll to the nearby beautiful golden beach. A tranquil base for exploring the truly scenic Golden Bay, the Abel Tasman Walkway, Kahurangi National Park, Farewell Spit, amazing coastal scenery, fishing the rivers or visiting interesting craftspeople. Brian, an educator, wine and American Football buff is a keen fisherman. Susan enjoys crafts, painting, gardening and practising her culinary skills. Charlie Brown and Hermione are the resident cats. Longer visits welcomed.

- Dinner: $25–$30 by arrangement
- Full breakfast

Takaka — Garden Retreat Bed and Breakfast

B&B

8 km N of Takaka

598 Stae Highway 60 Takaka/Collingwood
Highway, Takaka, 7182
(03) 525 6121 or 027 272 4200
relax@gardenretreat.co.nz
www.gardenretreat.co.nz

Double: $140–$165   Single: $90–$110
Children: 5 years and over only. Tarrif by arrangement

3 Bedrooms: 2Q 1T
Bathrooms: 1 ensuite, 1 guest share

Diane and Alan McIntosh

10%

- Bathrooms: the guest share can be reserved as a private bathroom for an extra small charge.
- Continental breakfast
- Children welcome
- Non-smokers only

Only eight kms from Takaka and surrounded by lush sub-tropical gardens and orchards, this is your perfect place to relax and unwind.

Enjoy wandering around the gardens or farm and orchards …you may even find a juicy peach, nectarine or citrus to snack on, or have a quiet chat with the friendly sheep.

Garden Retreat has three large upstairs bedrooms with lovely garden views. The Queen and Twin which share a bathroom may also reserve this bathroom for private use for extra charge.

Parapara — Hakea Hill House

B&B

20 km NW of Takaka

PO Box 35, Collingwood, 7054
(03) 524 8487
vic.eastman@clear.net.nz
www.virtualbay.co.nz/lizaeastman

Double: $150
Single: $100
Children: $50 each

3 Bedrooms: 2Q 6S
Bathrooms: 2 guest share

Vic and Liza Eastman

- Three bedrooms, two have large balconies
- Bathrooms: both have bathtub and shower
- Dinner: Family dinner by arrangement
- Full breakfast
- Children welcome
- Internet available

Hakea Hill House at Parapara, Golden Bay, is our modern and spacious two-story home. Two guest rooms have large balconies; the third for children has bunk beds and a cot. American and New Zealand electric outlets are installed. Television and tea or coffee are available in the main guest rooms. Telephone and broadband are by arrangement. Vic is a physician, now retired, with a particular interest in astronomy and all forms of engineering and electronic design. Liza is an accomplished fabric artist, quilter and tutor. A tour of her studio and personal tutorials are available by arrangement. To check out her work visit.

Twin Waters Lodge

Luxury • Lodge
9 km N of Collingwood

PO Box 33, Collingwood
(03) 524 8014
twin.waters@xtra.co.nz
www.twinwaters.co.nz

Double: $200–$250
Single: $175–$200

4 Bedrooms: 1KT 3Q
Bathrooms: 4 ensuite

Trish and Mike Boland

Nestled harmoniously beside a tidal estuary and just fifty metres from a sandy beach, Twin Waters features curved timber ceilings, panoramic windows and multilevel decks. The elegant interior has ample space for guests to enjoy its charm and tranquility. Waking to tuis singing, breakfasting in the sun, sipping wine on the decks overlooking the estuary, or savouring a delicious dinner, there's sure to be a special moment to remember. Trish and Mike and their feline companions look forward to welcoming you at Twin Waters.

- Dinner by arrangement
- Full breakfast
- Not suitable for children
- Internet available

Nelson Lakes Homestay

Homestay
85 km S of Nelson

RD 2, State Highway 63, Nelson 7072
(03) 521 1191
Home@Tasman.net
www.nelsonlakesaccommodation.co.nz

Double: $145
Single: $110

2 Bedrooms: 2KT 1Q
Bathrooms: 2 ensuite

Gay and Merv Patch

Nestled on the sunny slopes of the St Arnaud Mountain Range, 4 kms east of St Arnaud. Our spacious modern home is designed for the comfort and convenience of our guests. Spacious ensuite rooms, with doors opening on to our native garden, large comfortable lounge and terrace to relax on at the end of the day and admire the magnificent mountain views.

Nelson Lakes National Park, is a beautiful region of picturesque lakes, forests mountains and rivers.

- Full breakfast
- Pet-free home
- Not suitable for children

West Coast

67

Carters Beach
Cape Foulwind
Westport
6
Charleston
69
Punakaiki
Barrytown
7
Greymouth
Hokitika
Ruatapu
Kilometres
0
60
Miles
0
36
6
Franz Josef
Fox Glacier
Castle Hill Village
Lake Coleridge
Darfield
Mt Hutt
Methven
Staveley
Rakaia
Mount Cook
Ashburton
6
Lake Tekapo
Kimbell
Ealing
Burkes Pass
Fairlie
Geraldine

Steeples Cottage, Studio & B&B

Cape Foulwind, Westport

B&B Homestay • Separate Suite • Apartment with Kitchen • Cottage with Kitchen • Self-contained Cottage
11 km S of Westport

48 Lighthouse Road, Cape Foulwind, Westport
(03) 789 7876 or 0800 670 708
thesteeples@xtra.co.nz
www.steeplescottage.co.nz

Double: $100–$130   Single: $90–$100
Children: $25 persons over 4

4 Bedrooms: 4Q 1S
Bathrooms: 2 ensuite, 1 private

Pauline and Bruce Cargill

Peaceful rural accommodation, lovely gardens, magnificent sea views, rugged coastline, beautiful beaches, tranquil sunsets. swimming, surfing, fishing, kayaking mountain biking. Walk the popular seal colony walkway, Great dining The Bay House Restaurant or friendly Star Tavern. Local attractions 18 golf course, Coaltown Museum, jet boating, horse riding, underworld and white water rafting, caving, bush walks, unlimoy trips, all year swimming centre, full gymnasium and Punakaiki National Park. We have a Jack Russell and cat. Laundry and off-street parking. Whitebait meals by arrangment, free wireless internet available. Sky TV.

- Bathrooms: 1 cottage ensuite, studio ensuite, 1 private or guest share
- Dinner: Whitebait meal by arrangement
- Continental provisions supplied
- Children welcome
- Internet available

Bellaville

Carters Beach, Westport

B&B • Separate Suite
3 km S of Westport

No 10 State Highway 67 A, Carters Beach, Po Box 157, Westport
0800 789 845 or (03) 789 8457
bellaville@xtra.co.nz
www.bnb.co.nz/bellaville.html

Double: $120
Single: $100
Children: $15

1 Bedroom: 1Q 1S
Bathrooms: 1 ensuite, 1 private

Marlene and Ross Burrow

Hear the sound of waves pounding our safe swimming beach. Ouiet sunny extra large, studio room, private entrance, parking at door. No steps, no traffic noise. Private ensuite, large bathroom, bath, shower separate toilet. Ideal family unit. Electric blankets, TV, fridge, tea and coffee and home-baking. Laundry available. Close to all activities, coastal walks, seal colony. 3mins walk to licensed café/bar, golf course, playground. Have travelled extensively overseas and in NZ. Don't rush, stay a day or two, you will be glad you did. Wi-Fi Available.

- Extra large room with rollaway available
- $25 Adult
- Bathrooms: bath With separate shower
- Full breakfast
- Pet-free home
- Children welcome
- Internet available

Carters Beach, Westport

Carters Beach B&B

B&B
4 km S of westport

Main Road Carters Beach, On State Highway 67A, Westport
(03) 789 8056 or 0800 783 566 or 027 589 8056
cartersbeachaccom@xtra.co.nz
www.bnb.co.nz/cartersbeachbb.html

Double: $100–$130
Single: $70–$90

3 Bedrooms: 2Q 1T
Bathrooms: 1 ensuite, 1 private

Sue and John Bennett

- Very spacious
- Continental breakfast
- Pet-free home
- Children welcome
- Internet available

Carters Beach – a lovely relaxed atmosphere, Situated only 4 km south of Westport. Three minute walk to our beach, with fully licenced resturant/ café and bar. Golf links, world famous seal colony and Bay House Cafe within a few minutes drive. Our rooms are very spacious with TV and tea/coffee making facilities. Own private entrance-ways with sun decks. Laundry facilities available by arrangement. Ideal accommodation for couples travelling togeather. We look forward to meeting and sharing our local knowledge with you. Cheers, Sue and John Bennett.

Barrytown, Punakaiki

Kallyhouse

B&B Homestay • Apartment with Kitchen
20 km N of Greymouth

13 Cargill Road, Barrytown, Runanga, RD 1, 7873, Westland
(03) 731 1006
kallyhouse@xtra.co.nz
www.kallyhouse.co.nz

Double: $125–$160   **Single: $100**
Children: yes

VISA MasterCard

4 Bedrooms: 3Q 1T
Bathrooms: 1 ensuite, 1 guest share

Kathleen and Alister Schroeder

- Wireless internet available
- Continental breakfast
- Pet-free home
- Children welcome
- No smoking on property
- Internet available

We have a new spacious home on a quiet rear section, a garden setting, native bush backdrop and sea views. We offer a self-contained flat downstairs, with queen room and twin beds in spacious living area. Kitchen, bathroom, washing machine, parking and separate entrance. Also two queen rooms upstairs. Breakfast with host. Punakaiki Pancake Rocks and adventure activities in Paparoa National Park, 10-minutes north. Greymouth 20 minutes south. Turn at Allnations Hotel, past three houses on left, up lane, house on left. Licensed Restaurant handy.

Ardwyn House

Homestay
0.5 km N of Greymouth Central

48 Chapel Street, Greymouth
(03) 768 6107
ardwynhouse@hotmail.com
www.bnb.co.nz/ardwynhouse.html

Double: $90–$100
Single: $60–$65
Children: half price

VISA MasterCard

3 Bedrooms: 2Q 3S
Bathrooms: 1 guest share

Mary Owen

Ardwyn House is three minutes walk from the town centre in a quiet garden setting offering sea, river and town views. The house was built in the 1920s and is a fine example of an imposing residence with fine woodwork and leadlight windows, whilst being a comfortable and friendly home. Greymouth's ideally situated for travellers touring the West Coast being central with good choice of restaurants. We offer a courtesy car service to and from local travel centres and also provide off-street parking.

- Full breakfast
- Children welcome

Maryglen Homestay

B&B Homestay • Bed and Breakfast
3.5 km S of Greymouth

20 Weenink Road, Karoro, Greymouth
(03) 768 0706
maryglen@bandb.co.nz
www.bandb.co.nz

Double: $125–$150   Single: $95–$125
Children: negotiable

VISA MasterCard

3 Bedrooms: 2KT 1Q 1S
Bathrooms: 3 ensuite

Allison and Glen Palmer

Large Native ferns and bush surround our hillside home overlooking the sea. Our guests comment – amazing location. The sound of the surf will lull you to sleep. Off the main road, quiet location, two rooms have deck entrances. Amazing sunsets, Complimentary transport available from bus/train. Let us share our wonderful coast with you as we help you plan your days-scenic tours, bush walks, Misty, our cat will welcome you. Trans-scenic train (a must), Shantytown, Punakaiki Pancake Rocks. Your home away from home.

- 1 family room – sleeps 3–4. plus 2 super king/twin rroms
- Full dinner (pre-notice)
- Bathrooms: all private
- Dinner: Snack $20-full $45
- Special breakfast
- Children welcome
- Internet available

Greymouth | Oak Lodge

B&B • Cottage with Kitchen

3 km NE of Greymouth

286 State Highway 6, Coal Creek, Greymouth, 7803
(o3) 768 6832 or 0800 625 563
relax@oaklodge.co.nz
www.oaklodge.co.nz/westland-rates.htm

Double: $150–$250   Single: $150–$200
Children: 12 years and over are welcome. Tariff as adult

6 Bedrooms: 3KT **2**Q **1**T
Bathrooms: 5 ensuite, 1 private

Shirley and Alastair Inman

- 5 Bed and Breakfast bedrooms in Lodge & 1 bedroom in self-contained cottage.
- Breakfast available for cottage at an extra charge
- Full breakfast
- Pet-free home
- Not suitable for children
- Internet available

Full of character and charm, Oak Lodge is a quality B&B just three minutes north of Greymouth with a rural outlook. There are five large comfortable bedrooms waiting for you, all on the second floor, four have ensuites and one a private bathroom. Each room has its own TV, chairs and bath robes. There is also a guest lounge with tea and coffee making facilities, TV, microwave and leather lounge.

Oak Lodge has been designed with your relaxation in mind. Soak in the hot tub, relax in the sauna, play a game of tennis or Billiards. Feed the Sheep or relax in the garden.

A continental and full breakfast is served each morning, choose from the breakfast menu, perhaps just a fresh muffin or pastry with a cuppa or a coffee. The choice is yours.

Friendly, relaxing atmosphere. Alastair and Shirley have been sheep and cattle farmers in the past and extend a warm welcome to you.

Also available is Oak Tree Cottage a one bedroom, self catering cottage, superking bed, full kitchen, washing machine and deck area, sleeps 2.

Children 12 yrs and over are welcome, tariff same as adult.

Amberlea B&B — Hokitika Central

B&B
1 km E of Post Office

146 Gibson Quay, Hokitika, 7810
(03) 755 7346 or 027 697 1130
rpsmsymons@hotmail.com
www.bnb.co.nz/AmberleaBB.html

Double: $120–$150
Single: $100–$120
Children: welcome. Under 5 years $10. Under 12 years $30

4 Bedrooms: 3Q **1**T
Bathrooms: 2 ensuite, 1 guest share

Sharyn and Butch Symons

Sharyn and Butch along with their cats invite you to their quiet friendly home situated beside the Hokitika River. Relax in the lovely gardens or watch the sunsets over the Tasman Sea and the Southern Alps. We are a five minute walk from the town centre and all of its tourist attractions, resturants and beach. Visit the Hokitika Gorge. Visit our great greenstone, paua, gold and ruby rock shops or relax at the beach or lakes enjoying the clean air.

- All upstairs. Queen beds in ensuite rooms
- Bathrooms: all bathrooms have showers
- Full breakfast
- Pets welcome
- Children welcome
- Internet available

Berwick's Hill — Ruatapu

B&B Homestay
12 km S of Hokitika

Ruatapu, 106 Ruatapu-Ross Road, State Highway 6, RD 3, Hokitika 7883
(03) 755 7876
berwicks@xtra.co.nz
www.berwicks.co.nz

Double: $100–$130
Single: $60–$80

VISA MasterCard

2 Bedrooms: 2KT **1**Q
Bathrooms: 1 ensuite, 1 private

Eileen and Roger Berwick

Welcome to Berwick's Hill. We offer you a friendly and relaxed stay in our comfortable home. Magnificent views of the Tasman Sea and the Southern Alps are seen from the main living areas. Experience the sunsets and sunrises. We are close to Lake Mahinapua, bush walks, Mananui Bush and Beach walk, golf course. On our lifestyle farm we have sheep, Belted Galloway cattle and a farm dog also hens. We and our cat look forward to meeting you.

- Heater in bedrooms
- Bathrooms: 1 bath in ensuite
- Dinner: $40 by arrangement
- Full breakfast

Franz Josef — Ribbonwood Retreat

Luxury B&B • Cottage with Kitchen
5 km N of Franz Josef

26 Greens Road, Franz Josef Glacier
(03) 752 0072
ribbon.wood@xtra.co.nz
www.ribbonwood.net.nz

Double: $240–$320
Children: under 6 stay for free

VISA MasterCard

3 Bedrooms: 1K 3Q 1S
Bathrooms: 2 ensuite, 1 private

Julie Wolbers and Jonathan Crofton

- Bathrooms: luxurious tiled bathrooms, private bathroom next to room.
- Dinner: A variety of restaurants in Franz Josef village
- Full breakfast
- Pet-free home
- Children welcome
- Internet available

Welcome to our part of paradise. Ribbonwood has stunning mountain, glacier and forest views from our modern home and cottage.

Hosts Julie is an international school teacher and Jonathan a wildlife ranger.

Ribbonwood is five minutes drive from busy Franz Josef village. We offer comfortable new beds, high pressure showers, home-cooked breakfast, free Wi-Fi and a wealth of knowledge of local attractions and activities. At Ribbonwood we pride ourselves on our friendly personalised advice.

Fox Glacier — Fox Glacier Mountainview B&B

B&B Homestay • Cottage
3 km SW of Fox Glacier

10 Williams Drive, Fox Glacier, West Coast, South Island.
64+3+751 0770
info@foxglaciermountainview.co.nz
www.foxglaciermountainview.co.nz

Double: $185–$325   **Single:** $165
Children: welcome. Portacot available

VISA MasterCard eftpos

3 Bedrooms: 3K
Bathrooms: 3 ensuite

Karen Simpson (K2)

- SuperKing or SuperKing twins
- Wi-Fi available. TV in all rooms.
- Full breakfast
- Children welcome
- Internet available

Welcome to my peaceful hideaway set on eight acres of pure nature at its best. This modern country home has it all. With wide-open landscape, breathtaking views of Mount Cook and Mount Tasman, and surrounded by bush-clad hills with magnificent reflections on my own special pond.

I have a cosy self-contained cottage (for two) with ensuite. Inside my home, are ensuited super king/twin bedrooms.

Three bedrooms have private access. There are two bedrooms, with an adjoining bathroom between, ideal for a family of four.

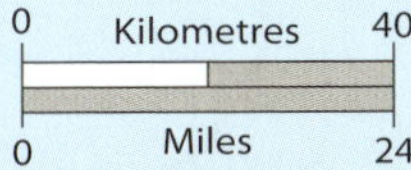
Canterbury
Reefton
Kaikoura
Hanmer Springs
7
1
Inchbonnie
Hawarden
73
Okuku
Oxford
Rangiora
Ohoka
Kaiapoi
Christchurch,
see next page
Mt Hutt
72
Westhaven
Okains Bay
Methven
Banks
Peninsula
Rakaia
Akaroa
Ashburton
Akaroa
Harbour
1
0
Kilometres
40
0
Miles
24

Christchurch
City
1
Christchurch
International
Airport
1
Burnside
Bryndwr
Avonhead
Merivale
Ilam
Riccarton
Christchurch
Central
1
Cashmere
Murray Aynsley
Sumner
75
Lyttelton
Lincoln
Lyttelton
Harbour
Tai Tapu
0
Kilometres
5
0
Miles
3

Bay-View HomeStay

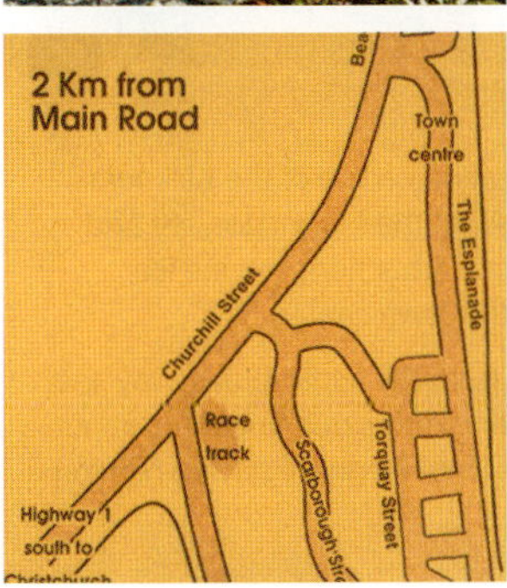

Homestay
130 km SW of Blenheim

296 Scarborough Street, Kaikoura
(03) 319 5480
bayviewhomestay@xtra.co.nz
www.bayviewhomestay.wordpress.com

Double: $125–$130
Single: $75
Children: under 14 $30

3 Bedrooms: 1Q 1T 1S
Bathrooms: 1 ensuite, 2 private

Grandma Margaret Woodill

- Free Wireless Internet
- Full breakfast
- Pets welcome
- Children welcome
- Internet available

Margaret Woodill is the classic Kiwi grandmother who has lived in her Kaikoura peninsula home with its sweeping views of sea and mountains since 1934.

She and her late husband, Bob began taking in passing travellers over 25 years ago, just before the whales and dolphins turned the township into a tourist destination. When her four children left home, opening a bed and breakfast seemed a good use for spare rooms and has become a joy!

In her one-acre garden she grows tomatoes to go with her home-laid eggs and the breakfast bacon. She bakes her own bread, makes muesli, preserves and jam and this traditional kiwi breakfast is available as early as required for whale/dolphin watching guests. Enjoy breakfast whilst taking in the magnificent mountain view.

This family home near the Lookout on Scarborough Street is in a quiet spot only five minutes from the Kaikoura township, off the main highway south. The house rests on an acre of colourful garden and has plenty of off-street parking. A guest lounge, sunny deck and several outdoor seating areas are available for guest use.

Margaret will happily meet the bus or train.

Kaikoura Peninsula — Austin Heights Scenic Bed & Breakfast

Luxury B&B • Separate Suite
2 km NE of Kaikoura township

19 Austin Street, Kaikoura, 7300
(03) 319 5836 or 0800 080 324 Reservations only
austinheights@xtra.co.nz
www.austinheights.co.nz

Double: $150–$265   Single: $150–$265
Children: Not suitable

4 Bedrooms: 2K 2Q 1D
Bathrooms: 3 ensuite, 1 private

Lynley and John McGinn

- Dinner: Not available. Great restaurants & Cafes.
- Full breakfast
- Pet-free home
- Not suitable for children
- No smoking on property
- Internet available

Austin Heights is situated on a prime location on top of the Kaikoura Peninsula with a stunning Panoramic view of the Mountains, sea and coastline. Central to all of Kaikoura's unique attractions marine life activities. Only a five minute drive from the town center.

Our guests enjoy all the home comforts from their spacious, sunny and clean ensuite units which have large sliding doors opening directly out onto a long balcony. Private entrance to units. Plenty of private parking space. Laundry facilities available.

Kaikoura — Bendamere House Bed & Breakfast

Luxury B&B
0.2 km SE of .2

37 Adelphi Terrace, Kaikoura
(03) 319 5830 or 0800 107 770
bendamerehouse@xtra.co.nz
www.bendamere.co.nz

Double: $180–$220
Single: $160–$200

5 Bedrooms: 5K 2T 3S
Bathrooms: 5 ensuite

Kerry and Julie Howden

- All ensuite rooms
- Extra Adult-$40
- Special breakfast
- Not suitable for children
- Internet available

Kerry and Julie welcome you to Kaikoura's Bendamere House B&B which offers you five quality ensuite rooms all with private balconies where you can enjoy the breathtaking ocean and mountain views. Relax in our expansive lawns and rose gardens or take a short stroll into the Kaikoura township. All rooms have sleepyhead beds, silent fridges, heat pumps, tea/plunger coffee/bathrobes and more. Free wireless Internet and coin operated laundry facilities as well as secure offstreet parking.

The Point Bed & Breakfast

B&B Homestay
4 km NE of Kaikoura town centre

85 Fyffe Quay, Kaikoura, 7300
(03) 319 5422 or 027 740 2836
pointsmith@xtra.co.nz
www.pointbnb.co.nz

Double: $130–$155
Single: $110–$125

VISA MasterCard

2 Bedrooms: 2Q
Bathrooms: 2 ensuite

Peter and Gwenda Smith

Your hosts Peter and Gwenda welcome you to The Point, Kaikoura. Built in the late 1800's Enjoy the quiet and unique waterfront location of our 125 year old home, situated on a 90 acre Drysdale Sheep farm. We have working dogs, one pet dog and a cat. While enjoying your breakfast – enjoy breathtaking views of the sea and the Kaikoura Seaward Mountain range. Facilities include wireless internet, gardens and veranda seats, guest lounge and off street parking. Ideally situated for Peninsula and Seal colony walks. Our daily Sheep Shearing Show provides a typical Kiwi Attraction for guests making this a popular stay.

- Queen bed with electric blanket.
- Continental breakfast
- Not suitable for children
- Internet available

Fyffe Country Lodge   **Kaikoura**

B&B
6 km S of Kaikoura

State Highway 1, Kaikoura
(03) 319 6869
fyffe@xtra.co.nz
fyffecountrylodge.com

Double: $270–$675
Single: $160–$250

VISA MasterCard   eftpos

6 Bedrooms: 6K
Bathrooms: 7 ensuite

Chris Rye

Fyffe Country Lodge is a small luxury lodge with an award winning restaurant close to whalewatching in Kaikoura. The lodge is beautifully created of rammed earth with Canadian cedar shakes on the roof, its rustic charm gives the property a timeless atmosphere. At Fyffe you can expect to find the finest of linens, individually decor'd rooms/suites, a superb menu sporting fresh local delicacies. Excellent service and gracious hosts. Fyffe has a class all of its own. Not suitable for young Children or Pets.

- 4 Superior rooms
- 2 Suites
- Suites from $495
- Dinner: $75 pp
- Full breakfast
- Not suitable for children
- Weddings and functions
- No smoking on property
- Internet available

...oura

Inn the Bay B&B

B&B

188 km N of Christchurch

196 Esplanade, Kaikoura, 7300
(03) 319 7553 or 027 358 5193
innthebay@gmail.com
www.innthebay.co.nz

Double: $120–$150
Single: $150
Children: $30 per child if extra bedding required

VISA · MasterCard

2 Bedrooms: 2Q **1**S
Bathrooms: 2 ensuite

Luke Poharama and Kylie Smith

- Dinner: May be available upon request
- Continental breakfast
- Pets welcome
- Children welcome
- No smoking on property
- Internet available

Waterfront accommodation, central to shops, restaurants, activities and main attractions. Stunning mountain and ocean views from main balcony. Two spacious lower level bedrooms with ensuites. Shared guest lounge with TV and DVD player, self service tea/coffee and breakfast station. Continental breakfast and wireless internet included in tariff. Private backyard with BBQ facilities and free off street parking.

Kaikoura

Ruth's

B&B

3 km E of Kaikoura

281 Scarborough Street, Kaikoura, 7300
(03) 319 7070 or 027 230 3602
ruthlintott@xtra.co.nz
www.bnb.co.nz/8455.html

Double: $90–$120
Single: $90–$100

1 Bedroom: 1Q
Bathrooms: 1 private

Brian and Ruth Giles

- Continental provisions supplied
- Not suitable for children
- No smoking on property
- Internet available
- 32 inch flat screen TV
- Tea and coffee making facility
- Refrigerator, microwave and toaster

We are a recently retired couple who love gardening, fishing, hunting and overseas travel. We share our home with a small 15 month old cavalier king charles / low-chen cross dog who is very lovable and smart. Our property is surrounded by many NZ native trees, which provide a haven for many birds including the Bell-bird. This is a very quiet and relaxing part of Kaikoura. There are many beautiful walk tracks within walking distance of our home that provide amazing panoramic sea and mountain views.

Hairdryer and washing machine is available if required.

The Dutch Station

B&B • Apartment with Kitchen • Countrystay: B&B-room and self-contained apartment
3 km NE of Hawarden

135 Bentleys Road, R D 1, 7385
(03) 314 2200 or 021 261 3461
info@thedutchstation.co.nz
www.thedutchstation.co.nz

Double: $125–$190   Single: $85–$85
Children: $25; please contact us first; cot available

4 Bedrooms: 1K **1**Q **2**S
Bathrooms: 1 ensuite, 1 private

Rein Bakker/Gertruud Steltenpool

The Dutch Station is located in a rural peaceful environment in North Canterbury on 17 ha with great views on the Alps. European style accommodation, friendly hosts and own Dutch golf course. Fishing, walks, lakes, Maori rock art, Kaikoura (whales), Hanmer Springs, Christchurch all within approximately1 hour. Self-contained unit: two bedrooms, bathroom, fully equipped kitchen, living, satellite TV. B&B-room (ensuite): coffee/tea facilities, satelite TV, extra bed.

- Dinner by arrangement
- Full breakfast
- Pets welcome
- Children welcome
- Weddings and functions
- No smoking on property

Petes Farm Stay B&B and Cottage

B&B Farmstay • Cottage with Kitchen
5 km SW of Rangiora

45 Mairaki Road, Rangiora R.D.1, 7471
(03) 313 5180 or 027–221–8989
petesfarm@xtra.co.nz
petesfarm.co.nz

Double: $160–$180   Single: $100–$120
Children: half price

VISA MasterCard

6 Bedrooms: 1K **1**KT **2**Q **1**D **4**S
Bathrooms: 1 ensuite, 1 family share, 2 private

Gaye and Peter Hurst

Welcome to Pete's Farm B&B.

We are situated 25 minutes from Christchurch Airport and City. Also just seconds off Inland Scenic Route 72.

See a sheep shearing and dog demo.

Relax in our new home and experience first hand the quietness and great views we get from every room in the house.

- Included in price is sheep shearing demo and farm tour
- Dinner: $40 per person.
- Continental breakfast
- Children welcome
- Internet available

Oxford — Hielan House Countrystay B&B

B&B Homestay Farmstay • Countrystay
54 km SW of Christchurch

74 Bush Road, Oxford, North Canterbury
(03) 312 4382 or 0274 359 435
hielanhouse@ihug.co.nz
www.hielanhouse.co.nz

Double: $165–$185   Single: $130–$145
Children: price on application

VISA MasterCard

2 Bedrooms: 1KT 1Q 1T 1S
Bathrooms: 1 ensuite, 1 private

Shirley and John Farrell

- 1 King/Twin Room, 1 Queen with King Single in private lounge.
- Dinner available by arrangement
- Full breakfast
- Pets welcome
- Children welcome
- Internet available

Quality upstairs guest rooms with relaxing areas, ensuites, separate entrance. TV/DVD, tea/coffee facilities, fridges, hairdryers, bathrobes, slippers. Complimentary laundry, internet, sauna, spa, outdoor swimming pool, golf clubs to use. Bicycles. Safe parking. Enjoy John's breakfasts, dinners with home-grown meaTVegetables. Relax, unwind on six acres in peaceful, rural Oxford or stay longer and make us your base for day trips to Arthurs Pass, Hamner, Akaroa. Situated three mins from Inland Scenic Route 72, via Bay/Bush Roads. We enjoy meeting people and look forward to spoiling you.

Kaiapoi — Morichele

B&B
15 km N of Christchurch

25 Hilton Street, Kaiapoi
(03) 327 5247
morichele@kinect.co.nz
www.bnb.co.nz/morichele.html

Double: $130
Single: $100
Children: negotiable

2 Bedrooms: 1D 1T
Bathrooms: 1 private

Helen and Richard Moore

- Comfortable
- Dinner by arrangement
- Full breakfast

Helen and Richard+ Sooky the cat provide comfortable accommodation in a beautiful garden setting, close to rivers, beaches, golf course and walks. With off-street parking, own entrance, sitting/dining area with fridge, tea and coffee making facilities, TV and video. Cafes and restaurants within walking distance alternatively, if you prefer, you are welcome to bring back takeaways or barbeque in the garden. Ski fields, Hanmer Springs themal reserve, Akaroa (home of the Hector's Dolphin) and Kaikoura (whale watching) are less than two hours away.

Olive House Bed & Breakfast

B&B

10 km N of Christchurch CBD

5 Sharnbrook Lane, Regents Park, Redwood,
Christchurch, 8051
(03) 352–5168 or 0274 555 548
burtt@clear.net.nz
www.bnb.co.nz/5609.html

Double: $170–$200   Single: $130–$150
Children: Under 5 free, older $25 per night

3 Bedrooms: 2Q **1**S
Bathrooms: 2 guest share

John and Ping Burtt

Olive House is situated 10 minutes from Christchurch International airport and located close to the junction of the North/South/West bypass. Our Mediterranean styled home offers peace and comfort that all travelers demand. Our tree lined lane and manicured property offer you a stay to remember. We share our house with TauTau, a little white Maltese terrier, and we take a great deal of pride in our service.

We are close to shops, restaurants, and the bus stop for the city service is 1 minutes walk away. We have a nature walk starting at the end of our lane.

- Bathrooms: 2 x Queen bedrooms share ensuite bathroom including spa.
- Dinner: By Negotiation
- Full breakfast
- Children welcome
- No smoking on property
- Internet available

Blossom Tree Homestay

B&B Homestay

8 km NW of City Centre

29 O'Connor Place, Burnside, Christchurch 8053
(03) 358 2635 or 027 458 2044
blossomtree@xtra.co.nz
www.bnb.co.nz/blossomtree.html

Double: $120–$130
Single: $80–$90
Children: $20

3 Bedrooms: 1Q **1**D **2**S
Bathrooms: 1 guest share, 2 private

Lorna Watson

Located five minutes from Christchurch Airport, free transfer to and from airport, car hire depots very close, 15 minutes from City Centre. Good bus services closeby. Russley Golf Course and a variety of excellent restaurants and cafés nearby. Modern and sunny home, along with it's owners, Lorna and Lyndsay and lovely cat Gabby, welcomes bed and breakfast guests. Enjoy lovely surroundings and a generous continental breakfast. Off-street parking and laundry facilities available. Wi-fi available. We look forward to welcoming you.

- Continental breakfast
- Children welcome
- No smoking on property

Canterbury

B&B Homestay
7.5 km NW of Christchurch

7 Westmont Street, Ilam, Christchurch 8041
(03) 358 2762
tony.fogarty@xtra.co.nz
www.bnb.co.nz/annetonyfogartyhomestay.html

Double: $100
Single: $60

VISA   MasterCard

2 Bedrooms: 4S
Bathrooms: 1 family share, 1 guest share

Anne and Tony Fogarty

- Dinner by arrangement
- Continental breakfast

Our home is in the beautiful suburb of Ilam, only minutes from Canterbury University and Canterbury/College of Education. Close to Christchurch Airport (five km) and the railway station (5:4 km). A bus stop is 50 metres from our home.(Route three from the Airport past our area, the University, Hospital, through the city to Sumner Beach.) Excellent local and South Island knowledge Dinner by arrangement ($30:00 per person.). Laundry available. Complimentary tea and coffee. Stay with us and get value for money.

Luxury B&B
5 km E of Christchurch Airport

46 Searells Road, Christchurch, 8052
(03) 355 3239 or 027 418 8961
enquiries@heatherston.co.nz
www.heatherston.co.nz

Double: $130–$150
Single: $100–$120

3 Bedrooms: 2KT 1Q 1S
Bathrooms: 3 ensuite

Jan and Murray Binnie

- Breakfast by arrangement
- Not suitable for children
- No smoking on property
- Internet available

Comfortable, convenient and quiet. A superbly situated, purpose-built, modern house with every convenience, only ten minutes from the Airport, and ten minutes from Central Christchurch. Heatherston has a sunny guests' kitchenette/lounge, bedrooms with comfortable beds, refreshment facilities, and television. Ensuites have heated towel rails, hairdryers and toiletries. Heatherston is close to shops and restaurants, and is conveniently located for sight-seeing in the city, or travelling to wineries, walking tracks, golf courses, and skifields. Heatherston is the perfect tranquil retreat!

Thistle Guest House — Riccarton, Christchurch

B&B • Guest House
6 km SW of City Centre

21 Main South Road, Church Corner, Upper Riccarton, Christchurch, 8042
(03) 348 1499 or 0800 93 21 21
stay@thistleguesthouse.co.nz
www.thistleguesthouse.co.nz

Double: $96–$106
Single: $63–$88

VISA MasterCard eftpos

10 Bedrooms: 1K 4Q 3T 4S
Bathrooms: 1 ensuite, 3 guest share

John and Alison Goodfellow

A small friendly guest house offering quality homestyle accommodation. 10 private bedrooms with fridge, tea/coffee facilities and wireless internet access for laptops. Fully equipped guest kitchen, lounge, off-street parking and attractive garden. Laundry facilities and guest telephone also available. Handy to Canterbury University and College of Education and two minutes walk to shops, restaurants and supermarket. On good bus route to city (15 mins) and 10 minutes drive from airport. Courtesy pick-up by arrangement. Weekly rates and tariffs excluding breakfast also available.

- Room only options also available
- Continental breakfast
- Children welcome
- Internet available

Condell Gardens B&B — Bryndwr, Christchurch

B&B
5 km NW of Christchurch City centre

95 Condell Avenue, Christchurch, 8053
(03) 352 8127 or 0800 216 943
condellgardens@xtra.co.nz
www.condellgardens.co.nz

Double: $125–$150
Single: $100–$125
Children: By arrangement

VISA MasterCard

1 Bedroom: 1Q
Bathrooms: 1 ensuite

Barbara and Murray Matthews

We look forward to welcoming you with everything you need for a relaxing visit. Private, peaceful garden setting, a few minutes drive from airport. Spacious, comfortably furnished, air-conditioned guestroom to relax in, with independent entrance and garden views. Own garden doorway. Lounge furniture, tea/coffee facilities, fridge, TV in room. Free wireless broadband. Phone/fax, computer, bicycles, barbeque, laundry facilities available. Generous continental breakfast. Meals, cooked breakfast and special requests by arrangement. Secure off-street parking. On bus route and near cycleway to city centre.

- Dinner by arrangement
- Continental breakfast
- Non-smokers only
- Internet available

Merivale, Christchurch — Leinster B&B

B&B Homestay
2 km N of Christchurch

34B Leinster Road, Merivale, Christchurch
(03) 355 6176 or 027 433 0771
brian.kay@xtra.co.nz
www.leinsterbnb.co.nz

Double: $150–$180
Single: $150–$180
Children: negotiable

VISA MasterCard

2 Bedrooms: 1Q 1D 1S
Bathrooms: 1 ensuite, 1 private

Kay and Brian Smith

- Full breakfast
- Children welcome
- Internet available

At Leinster Bed and Breakfast we pride ourselves on creating a relaxed friendly atmosphere in our modern sunny home. Only five minutes to Art Gallery, Museum, Botanical Gardens, Cathedral Square, Casino, Town Hall etc. 10 minutes from the airport. For evening dining convenience there are excellent restaurants just a leisurely stroll away at Merivale Village. Laundry, Wi-Fi, off-street parking makes us your home away from home. Very quiet bedrooms have TV, electric blankets, heaters, tea/coffee. Well behaved puss and pooch in residence.

Merivale — Rehua Mews Bed And Breakfast

B&B

Flat 1/18 Berry Street, Merivale, Christchurch, 8140
(03) 355 3379 or 021 230 1627
dlawlor@xtra.co.nz
http://rehuamews.co.nz/contact.htm

Double: $145–$190
Single: $95–$135

VISA MasterCard

2 Bedrooms: 1KT 1D
Bathrooms: 1 ensuite, 1 family share

David Lawlor

- Bathrooms: one room has an ensuite the other room has shared facilities.
- Dinner: By Arangement $20 (per two course meal per person)
- Continental breakfast
- Pet-free home
- Not suitable for children
- Internet available

Tucked away in Merivale, Rehua Mews Bed And Breakfast, Just ten minutes to the Central city, Hagley Park and Shopping precincts. Rehua Mews is a place to unwind in a Native Courtyard garden and a relaxing BBQ area.The rooms one Dbl /Twin Ensuite, 1 Dbl share facilities,open onto a sundrenched deck. I will provide you with a delicious continental breakfast (Optional dinner by arrangement only). I look forward to welcoming you to Rehua Mews and the vibrant garden city.

Eliza's Manor Boutique Hotel — Christchurch City

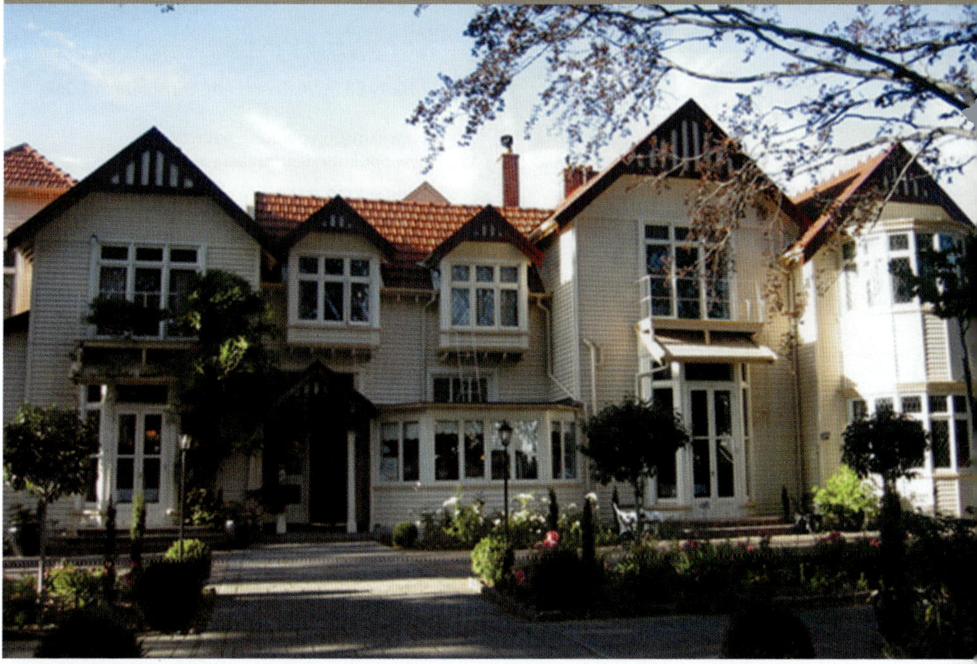

Luxury B&B
1.3 km N of Information Centre

82 Bealey Avenue, City Central, 8013
(03) 366 8584 or 0800 366 859
info@elizas.co.nz
www.elizas.co.nz

Double: $235–$345
Single: $215–$325

VISA MasterCard eftpos

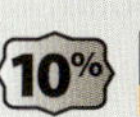

8 Bedrooms: 4K **4**Q **1**S
Bathrooms: 8 ensuite

Ann Zwimpfer & Harold Williams 10% Qualmark ★★★★ plus guest & hosted

- All with ensuites – Heritage and Classic Rooms
- Bathrooms: large tiled walk in showers in all rooms, baths also in Heritage rooms
- Full breakfast
- Pet-free home
- Not suitable for children
- Weddings and functions
- No smoking on property
- Internet available

Eliza's Manor Boutique Hotel offers quality Bed and Breakfast accommodation. A Victorian mansion dating back to the 1860s, Eliza's was restored in 2011 and fully meets the requirements of the latest Building, Structural and Fire Codes. Each of the eight bedrooms has modern ensuite conveniences. A sumptuous breakfast is served as part of the room rate, including fruits, cereals, yoghurts and breads plus a choice of individually cooked breakfast. Enjoy personal service as you unwind at a 'home away from home', where service and attention to detail are a priority. Free wireless internet access and off-street parking are available. Situated on Bealey Avenue on the northern boundary of the Christchurch CBD, 15 minutes by taxi from the airport and railway station and a 15 minute walk to the city centre, arts activities and botanical gardens.

Cashmere, Christchurch — Onuku Bed and Breakfast

B&B
8 km S of Christchurch

27 Harry Ell Drive, Cashmere, Christchurch, 8022

bob.wilkinson@paradise.net.nz
www.onukubedandbreakfast.co.nz

Double: $120–$180
Single: $100
Children: welcome

VISA MasterCard

3 Bedrooms: 2Q 1T
Bathrooms: 2 ensuite, 1 private

Jenny and Bob Wilkinson

- Discount for weekly rates
- Dinner supplied on request
- Full breakfast
- Pets welcome
- Children welcome
- Weddings and functions
- No smoking on property
- Internet available

This special home commands a magnificent site of the north facing Cashmere Hills, which overlooks the city to the mountains and sea.

Jenny is a top bridge player who is happy to arrange a game. Bob is a tour guide by profession, and is also happy to help plan a trip. He is also a golfer who can arrange a match for those enthusiasts.

Reggie, the resident labrador, is a very keen walker who is delighted when guests take him walking the hills.

Murray Aynsley, Christchurch — Pool House

B&B • Separate Suite
4 km SE of City Centre Information

57 Aynsley Terrace, Murray Aynsley, Christchurch, 8022
(03) 337 0380 or 021 131 6441
poolhouse@slingshot.co.nz
www.bnb.co.nz/PoolHouse.html

Double: $155
Single: $110
Children: By arrangement

1 Bedroom: 1KT
Bathrooms: 1 ensuite

Jill and Richard Entwistle

- 1 king/twin bedroom + sofabed in lounge area
- Continental breakfast
- Children welcome
- Non-smokers only

Pool House offers quiet and comfortable, private self-contained accommodation with separate living and sleeping areas, bathroom ensuite. Generous self-serve continental breakfast provided. TV/DVD. Wireless internet. Outdoor pool. Fridge, microwave, kettle and toaster, together with cutlery and crockery for take-away food or for simple self-catering. Tea and real coffee are always available. Hansen Park and the Heathcote River offer gentle riverside walks and children's playground.

Abbott House Sumner Bed & Breakfast

B&B • Self-contained B&B

13 km E of Christchurch Cathedral Square

104 Nayland Street, Sumner, Christchurch, 8081
0800 020 654 or 021 654 344 from overseas
info@abbotthouse.co.nz
www.abbotthouse.co.nz

Double: $120–$140
Single: $100–$120
Children: $10 per extra child/night (Max $50pw)

VISA MasterCard

3 Bedrooms: 3KT
Bathrooms: 1 ensuite, 1 private

Janet and Chris Abbott

Your hosts, Chris and Janet Abbott welcome you to our historic 1870s villa in Christchurch's unique seaside village. Our home is one block from the beach, and an easy ten-minute walk along the beach to Sumner's many cafés, restaurants, boutique shops and cinema. Both suite and studio have king-sized beds, own kitchen areas, TV, DVD and internet access. Off-street parking. Laundry facilities (suite only). Home-baked bread. Wonderful base for many walks, swimming, surfing, mountain biking and road biking.

- Dinner: Several nearby restaurants
- Breakfast provisions first night
- Pets welcome
- Children welcome
- No smoking on property
- Internet available

Dunns Inn Bed and Breakfast

B&B

230 Dunns Crossing Road, Rolleston/
Christchurch, 7614
(03) 347 3477 or 021 123 0217
robyn@dunnsinn.co.nz
www.dunnsinn.co.nz

Double: $110–$130
Single: $100–$120

VISA MasterCard Diners Club

3 Bedrooms: 1KT **2Q**
Bathrooms: 2 ensuite, 1 private

Graham and Robyn Veale

Dunns Inn the Bed and Breakfast accommodation business on the southern edge of Rolleston town. Just the place for a quiet, comfortable night. In a home designed for B&B, including all of the most modern and well placed features imaginable. Two Queen rooms with ensuites, Flatscreen TV, security box. One twin room with access to own private bath and shower. Robyn and husband Graham are new to the Bed and Breakfast Industry from the Host Perspective but we are looking forward to the challenges of running our Bed and Breakfast, we have one child and a very friendly Black lab living at home.

- Continental breakfast
- Children welcome
- Weddings and functions
- No smoking on property
- Internet available

Diamond Harbour

Diamond Harbour Lodge

Luxury B&B
35 km SE of Christchurch

51 Koromiko Cres, Diamond Harbour, R D 1,
Lyttelton, Banks Peninsula, 8971
(03) 329 4005 or 021 103 7080
robyn@diamondharbourlodge.co.nz
www.diamondharbourlodge.co.nz

Double: $160–$200
Single: $150–$180

VISA MasterCard

2 Bedrooms: 2Q
Bathrooms: 2 ensuite

Robyn and Pete Hedges

- Cooked breakfast extra.
- Dinner available by arrangement – 24 hours notice preferred.
- Continental provisions supplied
- Children welcome
- No smoking on property
- Internet available

Nestled into the cliff with 180 degree views of beautiful Lyttelton Harbour, this is the perfect place to relax and unwind. Just 35 minutes drive from Christchurch and eight minute ferry ride to Lyttelton makes a lovely base for exploring Banks Peninsula. All rooms, including the guests lounge, have their own balcony, are double glazed and warm and sunny. Microwave, fridge, sink, and tea and coffee making facilities. Enjoy Linden Leaves toiletries, under floor heating in ensuites and towelling bath robes. Robyn and Pete live on the ground floor with a lively Jack Russell called 'Bertie'

The difference between a B&B and a hotel
is that you don't hug the hotel staff when you leave.

B&B Farmstay

18 km N of Akaroa

1048 Okains Bay Road, Okains Bay, Banks Peninsula
(03) 304 8621
kawatea@xtra.co.nz
www.kawateafarmstay.co.nz

Double: $140–$165
Single: $90–$165
Children: by arrangement

VISA MasterCard

3 Bedrooms: 3Q 2S
Bathrooms: 1 ensuite, 1 guest share, 1 private

Judy and Kerry Thacker

- 1 Queen/Single with Ensuite, 1 Queen/Single, 1 Queen
- Bathrooms: bath, Shower, Separate Toilet
- Dinner: $40
- Full breakfast
- Children welcome
- No smoking on property
- Internet available

Escape to the beauty and tranquility of the country. Enjoy a unique holiday experience in a gracious historic homestead set in beautiful mature gardens, and surrounded by land, farmed by our family for five generations. Kawatea is an elegant, carefully renovated home, built in 1900 from native timber's the house features stained glass windows, handcrafted furniture and much olde world charm. Explore our 1500acre sheep and beef farm and feed the pet sheep. Observe birdlife on the estuary or walk along the scenic coastline to secluded swimming beaches and a seal colony. Learn about Maori culture and the life of early settlers at the acclaimed Okains Bay Museum. Visit Akaroa with its French influence, cafés and galleries. Golf, Kayak or cruise the Akaroa harbour to view Hector Dolphins. Join us in the evening for creative country fare from our garden whilst sharing experiences with fellow travellers. We have been providing farmstays since 1988, and offer thoughtful personal attention and friendly hospitality in a relaxed atmosphere. Directions: Take Highway 75 from Christchurch through Duvauchelle. Turn left at signpost marked Okains Bay. Drive to the top of the Bay – we are 6 km downhill on the right.

French Farm, Akaroa Harbour

Bantry Lodge

B&B • Cottage with Kitchen
70 km SE of Christchurch

French Farm, RD 2, Akaroa
(03) 304 5161 or 027 313 2406
barker.d@xtra.co.nz
www.bantrylodge.co.nz

Double: $140–$160
Single: $90–$100

VISA MasterCard Diners Club

4 Bedrooms: 2Q 1D 1T
Bathrooms: 1 guest share, 2 private

Dolina Barker

- Dinner by arrangement, $50
- Full breakfast
- Pets welcome
- Children welcome
- No smoking on property
- Internet available

This historic home has views across Akaroa Harbour 50 metres away. Groundfloor queen room has french doors to verandah and sea views, private bath. Upstairs queen room with balcony overlooks harbour, private bath. Coffee, tea facilities provided with home-baking. The comfortable sitting room is for relaxing or joining me for a drink. Full breakfast is served in the elegant dining room. Tranquillity and space. A self-contained cottage sleeps four. Linen, breakfast ingredients supplied. One shy cat.

Please let others know how you enjoyed your B&B experience.
Add a comment to the listing on the internet.
www.bnb.co.nz.

Mulberry House

Akaroa

**B&B • Cottage with Kitchen • Our Summerhouse
is available with breakfast or without breakfast**
80 km SE of Christchurch

9 William Street, Akaroa 7520
(03) 304 7778 or 021 610456
anneandjacknz@yahoo.com
www.mulberryhouse.co.nz

Double: $155–$195   Single: $130–$150
Children: Enquire

7 Bedrooms: 3K **2**Q **2**T
Bathrooms: 2 ensuite, 2 private

Anne Craig and Jack Clark

- 3 bedrooms in B&B, 1 in Summerhouse and 3 in Mulberry Cottage
- Vouchers available to give for Christmas, wedding or birthday gift.
- Special breakfast
- No smoking on property
- Internet available
- Featured on Sydney's Channel Seven 'Ernie Dingo's Getaway' as 'the place to stay 'in Akaroa

Experience the very best in homestyle accommodation and delight in the setting of Mulberry House. All rooms are beautifully decorated and feature quality beds and fine linen. There is a choice of double rooms, with or without ensuite, and a twin room which will delight children. The romantic poolside summerhouse has its own kitchen, ensuite and garden to provide total privacy if desired. We also have a beautifully furnished, self-contained cottage with full kitchen. Breakfasts are a specialty and feature a choice of American, European, English, and New Zealand styles.

Champagne breakfasts and other meals by arrangement. Meals can be served outside in the summer months overlooking the pool. Your hosts: Well travelled and semi retired Anne Craig and Jack Clark offer unparalleled hospitality. Fussy about food, both Anne and Jack love to cook: Anne preserves and bakes, and Jack adds his American expertise to breakfasts of pancakes, waffles, omelettes, fresh fruits, and delicious coffee from the espresso machine.

Akaroa

Akaroa Country House

B&B
3 km N of Akaroa

19 Bells Road, Takamatua, Akaroa
(03) 304 7499
takamatua@xtra.co.nz
www.akaroacountryhouse.co.nz

Double: $170–$212
Single: $150

VISA MasterCard

5 Bedrooms: 1KT **3**Q **1**T
Bathrooms: 3 ensuite, 2 private

David and Sue Thurston

- Continental breakfast
- Children welcome
- Internet available

A peaceful rural retreat set amongst bush, birds and creeks. Enjoy the private swimming pool, croquet or petantque. All rooms are private and ensuite, the provencal style The Gardener`s Retreat set in the bush beside the creek with an outside bath. The Gatehouse Cottage is fully self-contained and has a full kitchen, washing machine, two bedrooms, two bathrooms with details on akaroacountryhouse.co.nz. David a cabinetmaker built the house which has many examples of his work including two sleigh beds in the guest rooms. He is happy to welcome visitors to his workshop.

Springston

B&B on Rattletrack

B&B Homestay
5 km SW of Lincoln

353 Rattletrack Road, RD 4, Christchurch, 7674
(03) 329 5817
john-robyn@hotmail.com
www.rattletrack.net

Double: $100–$80
Single: $80–$65

4 Bedrooms: 2Q **2**T
Bathrooms: 1 guest share

John and Robyn Laugesen

- Dinner: $30 for dinner including glass of wine. $10 lunches
- Continental breakfast
- Pets welcome
- Children welcome
- Weddings and functions
- Internet available

John and Robyn look forward to hosting you at our B and B/Homestay. We are located 25 km South of Central Christchurch on lifestyle block in three acres of established garden. Being avid travellers we enjoy meeting people and happy to help with travel plans. We have three dogs who are good with people and other dogs. We have free wireless, computer, sky, kitchen, laundry, table tennis and bicycles available. Close to ski fields, golf courses, restuarants, wineries, and shopping.

Glenview Farmstay

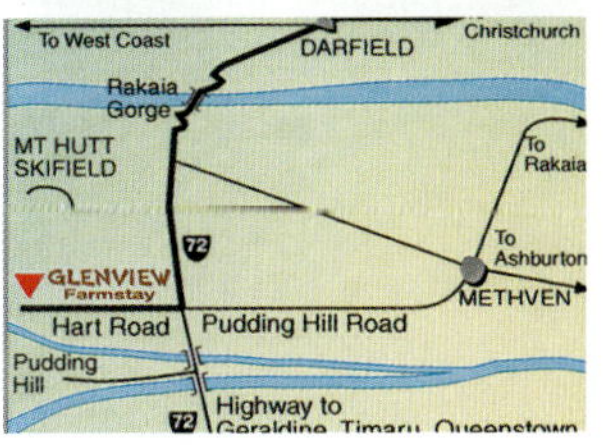

B&B Farmstay · Cottage
11 km SW of Methven

142 Hart Road, Methven, 7782
(03) 302 8620
helenmikejohnstone@yahoo.com
www.bnb.co.nz/glenviewfarmstay.html

Double: $130
Single: $80
Children: $25

5 Bedrooms: 2Q **2**D **1**T **2**S
Bathrooms: 1 ensuite, 1 guest share

Helen and Mike Johnstone

- Bathrooms: ensuite in unit
- Dinner: $35 Gluten Free available
- Full breakfast
- Children welcome
- Internet available

Glenview Farmstay is situated at the base of Mount Hutt Ski Field, with the house designed to look at the mountains and down the Canterbury Plains to the Port Hills. We farm cattle and sheep on our 1200 acre farm. We have several working farm dogs, a pet dog and a very friendly cat. There is a peaceful unit in the garden which is suitable for a couple or a family. It has two bedrooms, one with one queen bed and the other with one double and one single bed, ensuite, TV, tea and coffee facilities and wonderful views. The rooms in the house have separate access, good heating and are non-smoking. Dinner by arrangement with gluten free options available. Free farm tours on request. Methven is only 10 minutes away and we are very close to good fishing, golf, ballooning, horse trekking, para jumping, bush walks and jet boating. Free transfers to local walkways. One hour from Christchurch and we are on the way to Queenstown along Highway 72.

Methven, Mount Hutt

Green Gables Deer Farm

B&B Farmstay

4 km NW of Methven – Mount Hutt Village

185 Waimarama Road, Methven-Mt Hutt Village
(03) 302 8308
greengables@xtra.co.nz
www.nzfarmstay.com

Double: $140–$180
Single: $110–$140
Children: Child $55

VISA MasterCard

3 Bedrooms: 2K 2T
Bathrooms: 2 ensuite, 1 private

Irene and Mike Harris

- Super King Beds
- Dinner: $55pp by arrangement
- Special breakfast
- Children welcome

Set in tranquil surroundings at the foot of Mt. Hutt, Green Gables Deer Farm is withing easy reach of Christchurch (1hr), Kaikoura for Whale Watching and Dolphins (three hours), Mt. Cook (3.5 hours) and Queenstown (approx 5.5 hours).

Our stylish rooms have all the comforts you will require with your own private entrance opening out onto the garden with a backdrop of graceful deer wandering in the paddocks and the ever changing colours of the mountain views. There is plenty of room to stroll, maybe feed the pet deer and meet our friendly dogs or just relax and unwind.

Start your evening meal with a complimentary pre-dinner drink and enjoy the fresh local produce used in our home-cooked meals and desserts.

Activities: – Try out the many summer and winter activities close by – Golf courses at Methven and Terrace Downs (club and cart hire available), Fishing, Hot Air ballooning, Jet Boating, Skiing, 4WD Scenic Tours (available by arrangement), Horse Trekking, Scenic Flights, Ecotours and Alpine Rhododrendon Walks to name but a few. There are even trips to 'Eldoras' the Lord of the Rings film site at Mt. Sunday

Location: – Situated on S/H77 4 kms N/W Methven. From Inland Scenic-Route 72 turn into S/H77 travel 5 kms Green Gables Deer Farm is on the right.

St Ita's Guesthouse

B&B • Guest House
50 km S of Christchurch

11 Rakaia-Barrhill-Methven Road, Rakaia Township,
Mid Canterbury
(03) 302 7546 or 027 488 8673
stitas@xtra.co.nz
www.stitas.co.nz

Double: $140   **Single: $90**
Children: $40

VISA MasterCard

4 Bedrooms: 2Q 1D 4S
Bathrooms: 3 ensuite, 1 private

Miriam and Ken Cutforth

Relax in our elegant and comfortable historic former convent, 600 metres from SH1 in small town New Zealand. Excellent base for exploring Ashburton District. Excellent first and last stop from Christchurch International Airport. Three bedrooms have ensuites and garden views. The fourth the Chapel has a private bathroom. Walking distance to local shops, great cafés, crafts and River Terrace Walkway. Close to golf and salmon fishing, 30 minutes to skiing, jet boating. Wireless available. Dinner by arrangement. Full breakfasts. Share the open fire with our moggie. Friendly oudoor living Black Labrador dog.

- Large, warm rooms with garden views
- Bathrooms: 3 ensuites, 1 private with bath
- Full breakfast
- Pets welcome
- Children welcome
- Internet available

Our B&Bs range from homely to luxurious,
but you can always be sure of superior hospitality.

B&B Homestay

1 km N of Ashburton Info Centre

93 Pages Road, Allenton, Ashburton
(03) 308 6577
jkmcintyre@xtra.co.nz
www.carradalemanor.co.nz

Double: $150
Single: $100
Children: under 12 half price

VISA MasterCard

3 Bedrooms: 2KT **1**Q
Bathrooms: 1 ensuite, 1 private

Karen and Jim McIntyre

- Free Wi-Fi
- Full breakfast
- Internet available

We are one hour from Christchurch International Airport. Our sunny spacious home, which is just off State Highway 1 in Ashburton, is situated in a beautiful, large and sheltered garden by a stream, where you can enjoy peace and tranquility.

After offering hospitality for 16 years on Carradale Farm, we have now retired from Carradale Farm in the country to Carradale Manor in the town where we will continue to operate with those same high standards.

We offer either a fully cooked breakfast, or continental breakfast, served with delicious home made jams and preserves. For your convenience tea/coffee making facilities, and electric blankets are for use in all rooms. Internet access available.

As we have both travelled extensively in New Zealand, Australia, United Kingdom, Europe, North America, Zimbabwe, South Africa, Vietnam and Singapore, we would like to offer hospitality to fellow travellers. Our hobbies include meeting people, travel, reading, photography, gardening, sewing, cake decorating, rugby, cricket, Jim belongs to the Masonic Lodge and Karen is involved in Community Affairs including Probus.

For young children we have a cot and highchair available. Carradale Manor, 'Where people come as strangers and leave as friends'.

South Canterbury
& North Otago
e Bay
Ealing
ley
80
8
Kimbell
Geraldine
Fairlie
79
1
8
Lake Pukaki
Temuka
Twizel
Timaru
8
Lindis Pass
82
1
85
Oamaru
Waianakarua
0   Kilometres   30
0   Miles   18

Geraldine — Rivendell

Apartment with Kitchen • Studio Unit With Fully Fitted Kitchen Shower Room
3 km N of Geraldine

74 Woodbury Road, RD 21, Geraldine
(03) 693 8559 or 021 264 1520
rivendellnz@xtra.co.nz
www.rivendellnz.co.nz

Double: $110

1 Bedroom: 1Q
Bathrooms: 1 ensuite

Erica (Ricky) and Andrew Tedham

- Sofa bed in studio unit
- Self-contained studio unit with kitchen $110
- Accommodation only
- Pets welcome
- Not suitable for children
- Internet available

Set in over three acres, Rivendell is a traditional New Zealand villa and has beautiful secluded gardens. The Mallard Duck unit provides all modern facilities including heat pump. The delightful village of Geraldine with its numerous cafés, restaurants, shops and cinema is only five minutes drive. We offer you a truly warm welcome together with our friendly dogs and animals.

Geraldine — The Downs B&B

Luxury B&B
1.5 km SW of town centre

5 Ribbonwood Road, The Downs, RD 21, Geraldine
(03) 693 7388 or 021 675 249
info@thedowns.co.nz
www.thedowns.co.nz

Double: $200–$220
Single: $150–$150

VISA MasterCard Diners Club International American Express

4 Bedrooms: 3Q 1T
Bathrooms: 3 ensuite, 1 private

Alycen and Myron Cournane

- Rooms have ensuites, TV, armchairs & quality furnishings.
- Bathrooms have heaters, hairdryers & quality toiletries.
- Full breakfast
- Children welcome
- Internet available

Alycen, Myron and Max (the cat) opened this new business early in 2005. The house dates from the 70s but since then has undergone some major alterations. The upper level is now totally for guest use. There are three high quality ensuite guest rooms (one with extra bedroom if required). Free guest laundry. Guestlounge/breakfast room with open bar, tea, coffee etc. Step from the lounge onto the balcony and down to the large lawn and gardens. Enjoy the peace and quiet!

Jones Homestay

Timaru Central

B&B Homestay
1 km NW of timaru

16 Selwyn Street, Timaru
(03) 688 1400
nevisjones@xtra.co.nz
www.bnb.co.nz/jonestimaru.html

Double: $130
Single: $80
Children: half price

VISA MasterCard

3 Bedrooms: 2D 1T
Bathrooms: 2 ensuite, 1 guest share

Margaret and Nevis Jones

Welcome to our spacious character brick home built in the 1920s and situated in a beautiful garden with a grass tennis court. A secluded property with off-street parking and views of the surrounding sea and mountains. Centrally situated, only five minutes from the beach and town with an excellent choice of cafés and restaurants. On arrival tea is served on our sunny verandah. Hosts have lived and worked extensively overseas, namely South Africa, UK and the Middle East, and enjoy music, theatre, tennis and golf.

- Full breakfast
- Pet-free home
- Children welcome

Pleasant View Bed and Breakfast Timaru

Timaru

Luxury B&B Homestay

2 Moore St, Timaru, 7910
(03) 686 6651 or 0021 150 3045
pleasantview@xtra.co.nz
www.pleasantview.co.nz

Double: $125–$140
Single: $95–$110

VISA MasterCard

2 Bedrooms: 1KT 1Q
Bathrooms: 2 ensuite

Rosemary and Ian Rhodes

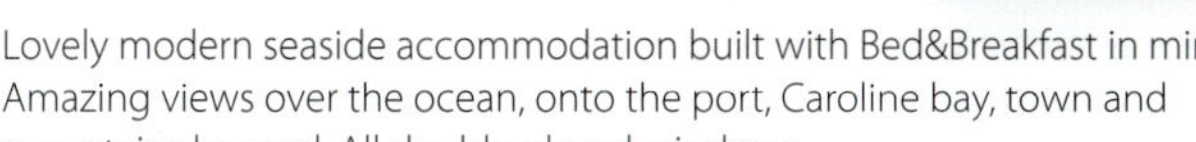

Lovely modern seaside accommodation built with Bed&Breakfast in mind. Amazing views over the ocean, onto the port, Caroline bay, town and mountains beyond. All double glazed windows.

Large visitors comfortable, warm living area also with great views, kitchenette, sky TV, DVD,and free wireless internet.

- 2 bedrooms with attached ensuites
- Extra adult $30
- Full breakfast
- Children welcome
- No smoking on property
- Internet available

Timaru

Centre Hill Cottage

Luxury Farmstay • Self-contained
25 km SW of Timaru

59 Howell Road, Totara Valley, Pleasant Point, Timaru, 7982
(03) 614 7385 or 0274 201120
centre.hill@clear.net.nz
www.centrehillcottage.com
Children: $30 each, children using basinet free

VISA MasterCard

2 Bedrooms: 1Q **2**S
Bathrooms: 1 private

Ian Blakemore

- BBQ available by host at suitable times of season
- Bathrooms: spa bath
- Special breakfast
- Children welcome
- No smoking on property
- Internet available

The cottage offers a cosy charm for those wanting a transforming experience. With stunning views, the cottage nestles amongst mature trees on a Certified Organic farm and features a large living area with a spacious deck, a fully equipped kitchen, a bathroom with underfloor heating and a raised spa bath. Experience the fun of the outdoor bath while stargazing, or open the complimentary bottle of wine and indulge yourself in this magical setting. Centre Hill Cottage is the perfect place to unwind, relax, recharge your batteries and just be in the now. Grass tennis court & swimming pool in season.

Timaru

Solace Country House Bed and Breakfast

B&B Homestay • disabled/access friendly
15 km SW of Timaru

650 Rolling Ridges Road, R.D. 5, Timaru., 7975
(03) 686 1332 or 021 026 16 246 mobile
stay@solacecountryhouse.co.nz
solacecountryhouse.co.nz

Double: $140   Single: $100–$120
Children: Not suitable – enquire for over 12's

VISA MasterCard

2 Bedrooms: 2KT
Bathrooms: 2 ensuite

elaine schlunegger

- Dinner: available on request
- Full breakfast
- Pet-free home
- Not suitable for children
- Weddings and functions
- No smoking on property
- Internet available

Solace Country House, nestled in the rolling hills of South Canterbury, offers tranquillity, very comfortable ensuite rooms (one wheelchair friendly) and nutritious varied breakfasts with local produce. All modern conveniences. Discuss travel and excursion plans over a welcome drink with your host Elaine, who has travelled extensively overseas. Challenging area for walking and cycling. Solace House is ideally suited for small conferences, boutique weddings, retreat/special interest group gatherings. Resources, catering and celebrant can be arranged. Welcome, welcome, welcome.

Rivendell Lodge

Kimbell, Fairlie

B&B Homestay • Countrystay
8 km SW of Fairlie

15 Stanton Road, Kimbell, 7987
(03) 685 8833 or 027 4819 189
joan@rivendell-lodge.co.nz
www.rivendell-lodge.co.nz

Double: $130–$160
Single: $85–$100
Children: negotiable

VISA MasterCard

4 Bedrooms: 3Q 1D 2S
Bathrooms: 2 ensuite, 2 private

10%

Joan Gill

Quality country comfort and hospitality offered in a peaceful historic village on the Christchurch-Queenstown route. Joan is a well-travelled writer, passionate about mountains, literature and local history. I enjoy cooking and gardening and delight in sharing home grown produce. Take time out for fishing, skiing, walking, golf or water sports. Relax in the garden, complete with stream, or come with us to some of our favourite places. Complimentary refreshments on arrival. Laundry facilities available.

- 1 queen, 2 queen + single, 1 double
- Bathrooms: separate spa bath available
- Dinner: $50 per person
- Full breakfast
- Pet-free home
- Children welcome

Tasman Downs Station

Lake Pukaki

Farmstay
27 km SW of Lake Tekapo

Tasman Downs Station, Lake Tekapo 7945
(03) 680 6841
samjane@xtra.co.nz
www.bnb.co.nz

Double: $140–$150
Single: $90–$100

2 Bedrooms: 1Q 1T
Bathrooms: 1 guest share, 1 private

Linda Hayman

We welcome you to a place of unsurpassed beauty located on the shores of Lake Pukaki, with magnificent views of the lake, Mount Cook and Southern Alps. Our local stone home blends in with the natural peaceful surroundings.

This high country station has been in our family since 1914 and runs mainly Angus cattle. Linda and son Ian enjoy sharing their knowledge of farming with guests. An opportunity to experience farm life with friendly hosts. Or visit many nearby attractions. Dinner by arrangement.

- Dinner: $50 pp by arrangement
- Full breakfast

Twizel – Mount Cook

Pinegrove

B&B • Cottage with Kitchen • 2 Cottages with kitchens
1 km N of Twizel

29 North West Arch, Twizel 7944, P.O. Box 88 Twizel
(03) 435 0430 or 021 464 726
aljohpinegrove@hotmail.com
pinegrovetwizel.wordpress.com

Double: $140–$160   Single: $100
Children: $10–$20

2 Bedrooms: 2Q **1**D **2**S
Bathrooms: 2 private

Al and Joh Ingram

- 2 bedrooms in each cottage
- Bathrooms: walk in showers
- Special breakfast
- Children welcome
- Internet available

Rest a while in the beautiful Mackenzie District with its mountains and lakes. We are only 45 mins from Mount Cook and two mins drive to near by restaurants. We welcome you to our sunny cottages situated in an extensive garden with fishpond and tranquil areas to sit in. The cottages are fitted with modern conveniences with your comfort in mind. You can indulge in home baked goodies from the breakfast hamper. We look forward to meeting you and welcoming you to our haven.

Lindis Pass

Dunstan Downs

Farmstay
17 km SW of Omarama

Dunstan Downs, Omarama, 9448
03/4389862
tim.innes@farmside.co.nz
www.dunstandowns.co.nz

Double: $0–$260
Single: $0–$130
Children: half price under 12

2 Bedrooms: 1Q **1**S
Bathrooms: 1 ensuite, 1 family share

Tim and Geva Innes

- Dinner: tarrif includes dinner bed@breakfast
- Full breakfast provisions
- Pets welcome
- Children welcome
- Internet available

Dunstan Downs is a merino sheep station in the heart of the South Island high country. Our home is full of country warmth, you are welcome to join us for dinner (wine served) or bed and breakfast. The surrounding mountains and valleys are an adventure playground, tramping, mountain biking, fishing, farming activities or lazing around soaking up the peace and tranquillity.

No pets inside.

Glen Dendron Farmstay, Garden & Private Golf Course   **Waianakarua, Oamaru**

B&B Farmstay
27 km S of Oamaru

284 Breakneck Road, Waianakarua, R D 90, Oamaru 9495
(03) 439 5288 or 021 615 227
stay@glendendronfarmstay.co.nz
www.glendendronfarmstay.co.nz

Double: $135–$170   **Single:** $110–$135
Children: $50

VISA   MasterCard

4 Bedrooms: 2KT 2Q
Bathrooms: 2 ensuite, 1 guest share

Anne and John Mackay

- Ensuite rooms include TV and tea making facilities
- Bathrooms: spa bath
- Dinner: $40 with wine
- Full breakfast
- Pet-free home
- Children welcome
- Internet available

Our Award Winning Homestay offers tranquility and beauty when you stay in our stylish modern home, spectacularly sited on a hilltop overlooking the picturesque Waianakarua River and surrounded by five acres of landscaped garden. After breakfast, feed the sheep and alpacas. Then take a stroll through the forest, native bush complete with waterfalls and birds or beside the river. Play a round on our private golf course. Later, watch the seals and penguins on a beach nearby. Then, complete a perfect day with our three course dinner with NZ wine before retiring in peace and comfort.

After a lifetime spent in farming and forestry we relish the opportunity to share our home and semi-retired lifestyle with guests. Our adult family lives overseas so we travel frequently and have a great interest in other countries and cultures. We are very keen gardeners, read widely and enjoy antiques. Anne is a floral designer and John a tree connoisseur.

An overnight stay is not enough to do justice to this lovely area – with so much to see, why not stay awhile! The area's many attractions include Oamaru's historic architecture. Garden, heritage and fossil trails.

Oamaru — Ranui Retreat Bed and Breakfast/Homestay

B&B Homestay
8 km S of Oamaru

27 Woolshed Road, Totara, Oamaru, 8D RD
(03) 439 5241
enquiries@ranui-retreat.co.nz
www.ranui-retreat.co.nz

Double: $140–$160
Single: $100
Children: negotiable
VISA MasterCard

2 Bedrooms: 2Q
Bathrooms: 1 ensuite, 1 private

Sheryl Laraman and Family

- Dinner: 35 pp
- Full breakfast
- Pets welcome
- Children welcome
- No smoking on property
- Internet available

Welcome to Ranui Retreat. We are close to historic Oamaru and the main highway to Dunedin. Views of Otago rural landscape stretching to the Kakanui Mountains enhance the rural sense of this five acre property of mature oak, elm and ash trees. There is birdsong aplenty. Character rooms include rich, handmade quilts which add to the relaxed ambience. Join the family for the evening or you may like to retire to other spaces with music and a good book from our library selection.

Oamaru — Forrest Hill B&B

Luxury B&B • Cottage with Kitchen • Two types of accommodation
20 km S of Oamaru

22 Reid Road, 9 O R D, Oamaru, 9495
(03) 439 5233 or 027 539 5233
blanch@netspeed.net.nz
foresthillbb.co.nz

Double: $120–$170
Single: $120–$170

6 Bedrooms: 1K 3Q 2T
Bathrooms: 1 ensuite, 1 family share, 1 guest share

Lesley Blanchard

- Dinner: $30 per person
- Full breakfast
- Pets welcome
- Children welcome
- No smoking on property
- Internet available

Lesley and Brian offer a beautiful location and spacious accommodation for the traveller looking for a peaceful and private place to stay. Their brand new home has three guest bedrooms – one with luxurious ensuite and in a completely private wing – and the cottage on the property, which sits in the forest – also has three bedrooms. Both properties are located on 30 acres of working farmland (sheep and cattle).

The Bed and Breakfast looks out over farmland and forest, the Waianakarua River to the North and out to the Pacific Ocean.

Anne Mieke Guest House — **Oamaru**

Guest House
90 km S of Timaru

47 Tees Street, Oamaru, 9400
(03) 434 8051 (also fax number)
anne.mieke@xtra.co.nz
www.theoamarubnb.com

Double: $90–$130   Single: $60
Children: Under 2 years – free, 2 to 14 years $15, over
14 to 18 $20.00

5 Bedrooms: 3Q 7S
Bathrooms: 2 ensuite, 1 guest share

Des and Sally Cochrane

Fabulous views of the harbour and ocean beyond. Comfortable and clean and very good value. Quiet area of town but close to Historic Precinct, Visitor centre, Blue Penguin colony, shops and restaurants. We welcome inspection. We look forward to giving our guests a happy and comfortable stay.

- Dinner: 2 to 14 years – $15 per night over 14
- Continental breakfast
- Pet-free home
- Children welcome
- No smoking on property
- Internet available

Happy Valley B&B — **Oamaru**

B&B
16 km S of Oamaru

24 Happy Valley Road, Maheno 7.O.R.D,
Oamaru, 9495
(03) 439 5217
info@happyvalleybnb.co.nz
www.happyvalleybnb.co.nz

Double: $159–$159
Single: $139–$139

2 Bedrooms: 2Q
Bathrooms: 2 ensuite

Ann and Lindsay Currie

We welcome you to stay and relax in our new modern self-contained B&B units, quality furnishings, dining table, tea/coffee facilities, fridge, flat-screen TV, warm and comfortable. Quiet farmlet. Complimentary home baking on arrival. Delicious meals served in your unit, breakfast at your leisure. Freerange eggs, home grown produce. Great place to break your journey, relax and unwind. Peaceful location, spacious grounds. 240m off S.H.1., 15 mins south of Oamaru. Discover North Otago, penguins, beaches, award winning dining, historic buildings, Moeraki. Non smoking.

- Dinner by arrangement with fresh vegetables from our garden
- Continental breakfast
- Pet-free home
- Not suitable for children
- No smoking on property

Oamaru

Federation House B&B Inn

B&B Homestay • Inn
0.5 km S of 0.5

60 Tyne Street, Oamaru, 9400
(03) 434 9537
info@federationhouse.co.nz
www.federationhouse.co.nz

Double: $100–$150
Single: $50–$100

VISA MasterCard

4 Bedrooms: 3KT **1**T
Bathrooms: 3 ensuite, 1 guest share, 1 private

Rodger McCaw

- Dinner by arrangement
- Full breakfast
- Pet-free home
- Children welcome
- Weddings and functions
- Internet available

A Welcome Inn – Sound night's sleep assured. An urban haven for discerning guests. This magnificent heritage house has panoramic views of the harbour, ocean and town; close to penguin colonies and restaurants. Refurbished to provide modern facilities, ensuing privacy with ensuite bathrooms and quality King/Twin beds. Tariff varies for guests breakfast requirements with choice of full cooked, continental, or lodging only.

Relax and enjoy Shiner's Saloon. Wireless internet available.

Please let your hosts know if you have to cancel.
They will have spent time preparing for you.

Otago &
North Catlins
Haast
6
Twizel
Kim
P
Omarama
Lindis Pass
Kurow
Wanaka
6
Glenorchy
Danseys Pass
Arrowtown
Cromwell
85
Queenstown
W
6
Garston
1
Wendonside
Otago
Peninsula
sden
Mosgiel
Balfour
Dunedin
8
Waikaka
Gore
Winton
Mataura
Balclutha
Kilometres
0
40
Wyndham
Miles
0
24
cargill
The Catlins
Mokotua
Owaka

Makarora · Makarora Homestead

B&B · Cottage with Kitchen
65 km N of Wanaka

53 Rata Road, Makarora, 9346
(03) 443 1532
info@makarora.com
www.makarora.com
Double: $130–$145
Single: $100–$120

VISA MasterCard

8 Bedrooms: 7Q 1D 7T
Bathrooms: 3 ensuite, 3 guest share

Kenna Fraser and Rick McLachlan

- 3 detached B&B rooms, 5 bedrooms in Homestead
- Dinner: Restaurant is within walking distance (500 m)
- Continental provisions supplied
- Pets welcome
- Children welcome

Makarora Homestead offers a secluded retreat in the midst of the Southern Alps and is perfect for travellers looking for the peace and tranquility of the mountains. We offer a self-contained studio with kitchenette, ensuite and private balcony OR two detached bedrooms each with ensuite, tea/coffee making facilities and shared sundeck. Nestled at the edge of the native forest with panoramic views of the mountains and surrounding wapiti deer farm. Hand feed our tame deer Nigel and various friendly sheep.

Lake Hawea · Bellbird Cottage

Cottage with Kitchen
12 km N of Wanaka

121–125 Noema Terrace, Lake Hawea, 9192
03–443 7056 or 03–443 8678
marge@xtra.co.nz
www.bellbirdcottage.co.nz

Double: $125–$125
Children: extra $10

VISA MasterCard

1 Bedroom: 1Q 1S
Bathrooms: 1 ensuite

Marjorie Sheila and Brian

- Bathrooms: shower and a separate toilet
- Dinner by arrangement
- Continental breakfast
- Pet-free home
- Children welcome
- No smoking on property
- Internet available

Our modern self-contained cottage is situated in beautiful Lake Hawea Village, surrounded by magnificent scenery. The cottage is just 12 kms from Wanaka. It is private and secure, warm and cosy. We are located 30 minutes from major ski fields – Treble Cone and Cardrona. Mount Cook is less than two hours away. The cottage has a fully equipped kitchen, laundry and free wireless internet. Easy to find Noema Terrace leads of themain road Capell Avenue and we are 121–125.

Berryfarm Homestay

B&B Homestay · Separate Suite · Guest lounge
1 km S of Wanaka

83 Orchard Road, Wanaka, Central Otago
(03) 443 4248 or CP 021 494 149
bobannette@menlove.net
www.berryfarmhomestay.co.nz

Double: $150–$180
Single: $150

VISA MasterCard eftpos

3 Bedrooms: 1KT 1D 1T
Bathrooms: 2 ensuite, 1 private

10%

Annette and Bob Menlove

The Berry Farm Homestay extends a warm welcome for visitors who want to stay in beautiful Wanaka, come and enjoy this private residence in a rural setting, and enjoy all that Central Otago has to offer. We are very close to good restaurants, a golf course, ski fields and excellent lake and river fishing.

- Bathrooms: spa and Bath
- Full breakfast
- Children welcome
- No smoking on property
- Internet available

Lake Wanaka Homestay

B&B Homestay · Homestay Bed Breakfast
0.4 km SW of Centre Wanaka

85 Warren Street, Wanaka, Wanaka 9305
(03) 443 7995 or 800443799
wanakahomestay@xtra.co.nz
www.lakewanakahomestay.co.nz

Double: $140–$150   Single: $100–$110
Children: Not suitable for small children

VISA MasterCard

2 Bedrooms: 2D
Bathrooms: 1 guest share, 1 private

Gailie and Peter Cooke

Relax Soak up Breathtaking views Lake and Mountains from our home. Enjoy the very best of Southern Hospility with Peter, Gailie and Kim our Labrador, Just five Minuites easy Walk to Lake. Restuarants,& Shops, Two warm comfortable Doube Bedrooms. Heaters, Electric blankets, Full Cooked Breakfast. Tea, Coffee, Homebaking anytime, No extra, Free Wi-Fi, Off street Parking, Best value homestay, Centre Wanaka, Guests coments,' Absolutely Delightful, so welcoming.what a view,'Valery and David Yorath Suffuck. ' Fabulous Hospitality Delicious Breakfast ' Peter and Diane Hodchan. Wellington.

- Bathrooms: we offer Private our Guests Share, Great shower,
- Dinner: Just 5 minutes walk to Great selection of Resturants
- Full breakfast
- Not suitable for children
- No smoking on property
- Internet available

Wanaka — Beacon Point

B&B • Apartment with Kitchen
3 km N of Wanaka Shops

302 Beacon Point Road, PO Box 6, Lake Wanaka 9343
(03) 443 1253 or 0274 354 847
dan.di@lakewanaka.co.nz
www.beaconpoint.co.nz

Double: $140
Single: $100
Children: $40

2 Bedrooms: 1Q **1**T
Rolla beds: 1
Bathrooms: 1 ensuite

Diana and Dan Pinckney

- Continental breakfast
- Pet-free home
- Children welcome
- No smoking on property

Beacon Point B&B has an acre of lawn and garden for your enjoyment. Leads to a walking track to the village around the edge of the lake. Private spacious studio with ensuite, queen and single beds (two rooms), kitchen, TV, Wi-Fi, sundeck and BBQ. Studio equipped with every need for perfect stay. We enjoy planning your days with you. Our intrests include farming, forestry, fly fishing, real estate, boating, gardening and grandchildren. Turn right at lake – Lakeside Road – then to Beacon Point Road 302.

Albert Town, Wanaka — Riversong

B&B Homestay
6 km NE of Wanaka

5 Wicklow Terrace, Albert Town, Wanaka
(03) 443 8567 or 021 113 6397
info@riversongwanaka.co.nz
www.riversongwanaka.co.nz

Double: $160–$180
Single: $120
Children: $25

VISA MasterCard

3 Bedrooms: 1KT **1**Q **1**S
Bathrooms: 1 ensuite, 1 private

Ann and Ian Horrax

- 1 King/Twin
- Full breakfast
- Children welcome
- Internet available

Riversong is five minutes from Wanaka Township, at Albert Town, on the banks of the majestic Clutha River. At our secluded haven all rooms have river and mountain views, with immediate access to the river. Ann's background is healthcare and Ian's law. We invite you to share the comforts and privacy of our home and garden and Ian's knowledge of the region's fishing and guidance service. We aim to provide a memorable and comfortable stay. We have one outside lab dog. Wireless/broadband available.

The Cedars B&B

B&B
2.4 km E of Wanaka

7 Riverbank Road, RD 2, Wanaka, 9382
Landline (03) 443 1544 or Mobile 021 1208 960
thecedarswanaka@xtra.co.nz
www.thecedars.co.nz

Double: $175–$195
Single: $130–$165
Children: welcome; highchair and portacot available

VISA MasterCard

2 Bedrooms: 2Q 1S
Bathrooms: 1 ensuite, 1 private

Mary and Graham Dowdall

Cead Mile Failte – One hundred thousand welcomes. A warm Irish/Kiwi welcome awaits you at The Cedars, by Mary, Graham, Rough Collie Nessa and cat Cara. Our stone home on 11 acres is close to all Wanaka's attractions and restaurants, has panoramic mountain views, expansive gardens, paddocks with alpacas and sheep, guest lounge with large open fire. We enjoy travelling, dining, music, literature and sports. Full breakfast is served with fresh and home-made produce. We offer evening meals or BBQ by prior arrangement.

- Dinner: three course dinner/BBQ by arrangement with 24 hours notice
- Full breakfast
- Children welcome
- Internet available

Criffel Peak View

B&B • Apartment with Kitchen
0.5 km N of Wanaka

98 Hedditch Street, Wanaka
(03) 443 5511
stay@criffelpeakview.co.nz
www.criffelpeakview.co.nz

Double: $150–$165
Single: $130

VISA MasterCard

3 Bedrooms: 1K 2KT 2Q
Bathrooms: 2 ensuite, 2 private

Caroline Holland

A cosy modern cottage situated in a quiet cul-de-sac, just a short walk from the lake and town. Great mountain views, large sunny deck, friendly young hosts and a crazy cat called Splodge.

Our three guest rooms look out towards the Criffel Range and are equipped with ensuite bathrooms and super king or queen sized beds. The guest lounge has Wireless Internet access, guest computer, tea/coffee making and variety of reading material.

Our apartment is perfect for larger groups and families.

- Bathrooms: all 3 rooms in the B&b have their own bathrooms (2 ensuite, 1 private). The 2 bedroom apartment has one bathroom and 2 toilets
- Full breakfast
- Children welcome
- Internet available

Wanaka — Kanuka Lodge

B&B

12 km E of Wanaka

110 Shortcut Road, SH 8A, Luggate, RD2 Wanaka
(03) 443 7448
hallday@es.co.nz
www.bnb.co.nz/KanukaLodge.html

Double: $0–$125
Single: $100–$100
Children: $25

3 Bedrooms: 1Q 1D 1S
Bathrooms: 1 guest share

Heather and Graeme Halliday

- Full breakfast
- Pets welcome
- Children welcome

Our home is near the Clutha river, 10 minutes drive from Wanaka. It features NZ art and books. We welcome you with a glass of fine NZ wine. At breakfast you must try the Central Otago apricots and Heather's wildflower honey. You can admire the alpine landscape with geologist, photographer and fisherman Graeme, and plan your exploration of Wanaka. We have friendly cats and horses. Heather, originally from Bath in England, gives rides in her vintage buggies and grows the exotic spice saffron.

Wanaka — Websters on Wanaka Lodge and Apartments

Luxury B&B • Guest House • Apartment with Kitchen • Lodge

137 Anderson Rd, Wanaka, 9305
(03) 443 1961 or 027 228 4640
stay@webstersonwanaka.co.nz
www.webstersonwanaka.co.nz

Double: $150–$350
Children: child friendly

8 Bedrooms: 2KT 6Q
Bathrooms: 4 ensuite, 1 private

Liz and Neil Webster

- Self catering apartments available
- Dinner can be provided in lodge by prior arrangment
- Full breakfast
- Children welcome
- No smoking on property
- Internet available

Websters on Wanaka Lodge and Apartments is a boutique luxury accommodation Lodge with self-contained apartments, close to Lake Wanaka township and positioned for maximum sun and excellent alpine views. Our apartments have one, two or three bedroom options. Every aspect is designed around quality comfort and convenience. What makes us special is the warm welcome, the fabulous setting and great guest spaces. You can relax with very special accomodation. Your hosts, Liz, Neil and Megan really understand what it takes to make your stay quite special.

Avalanche B&B Wanaka

B&B • Apartment with Kitchen
2 km SW of Wanaka

74 Bill's Way, Wanaka, 9305
(03) 443 6665 or 027 633 2364
stay@wanakabedandbreakfast.com
www.wanakabedandbreakfast.com

Double: $170–$180   Single: $165–$170
Children: $30 per child. Infants under 3 free of charge

4 Bedrooms: 2Q 1D 1T 1S
Bathrooms: 1 ensuite

Trish and Davy Pattison

Avalanche Bed and Breakfast has spectacular views over farmland to the mountains and Avalanche Glacier. We are 2.5 km from the centre of town and 10 minutes walk to the lake and two quality restaurants. Our spacious self-contained studio with ensuite has a well equipped kitchenette. Delicious home made continental breakfast supplies and baking are provided each day. We offer warm hospitality in our comfortable home, set in a lovely, peaceful garden. We have a small dog, Poppy and an adventurous cat, Tiggy.

- $30 each extra adult.
- Continental provisions supplied
- Children welcome
- No smoking on property
- Internet available

The Hayloft Wanaka

Luxury • Apartment with Kitchen
4 km SE of Wanaka

272 Ballantyne Rd, Wanaka, 9382
(03) 443 8183 or 021 0279 0039
stay@thehayloft.co.nz
www.thehayloft.co.nz

Double: $195–$225   Children: Suitable for infants/toddlers using a portacot supplied

1 Bedroom: 1Q
Bathrooms: 1 private

Julie Jones and John Wellington

Relax in our self-contained strawbale loft apartment set on 16 acres of rolling farmland, enjoying fantastic views of the Southern Alps and just 4 km from Lake Wanaka. The Hayloft has been designed with natural materials and recycled timbers, oozing charm and character. Breakfast provisions are local and organic or free range whenever possible. John is a tour guide and avid walker and will happily share his local knowledge. We have young daughter and two cats.

- Large room with balcony and walk in wardrobe, separate lounge
- See our website for multi day specials
- Breakfast by arrangement
- Children welcome
- No smoking on property
- Internet available

Wanaka

Riverview Terrace

Luxury B&B
3 km NE of Post Office

31 Matheson Crescent, Wanaka, 9305
(03) 443 7377 or 021 156 4639
stay@riverviewterrace.co.nz
www.riverviewterrace.co.nz

Double: $250–$320
Single: $200–$220
Children: by exclusive prior arrangement only

3 Bedrooms: 2K 1KT
Bathrooms: 3 ensuite

Pam and Peter Higgins

- Dinner: by exclusive prior arrangement only
- Full breakfast
- Pet-free home
- Weddings and functions
- No smoking on property
- Internet available

Riverview Terrace is luxury Qualmark five star with unobstructed mountain and river views. Three spacious rooms, private patios, guest lounge, wireless internet, eight seat massaging spa under the stars. Complimentary mountain bikes, close to numerous walking and biking tracks.

Enjoy gourmet cooked breakfasts at a time to suit guests, home baked afternoon tea and coffee freely available, evening appetizers with local Wanaka wines. Laundry and disabled facilities.

All our B&Bs are non-smoking.

Stuart's Homestay **Cromwell**

B&B Homestay
1 km S of live in Cromwell

5 Mansor Court, Cromwell
(03) 445 3636
ian.elaine@xtra.co.nz
www.stuartshomestaybandb.co.nz

Double: $110–$130
Single: $70–$80
Children: by arrangement

3 Bedrooms: 2Q 2S
Bathrooms: 1 ensuite, 1 guest share

Elaine and Ian Stuart

Welcome to our home which is situated within walking distance to most of Cromwell's amenities. We are semi-retired Southland farmers who have been hosting for over 15 years. Cromwell is a quiet and relaxed town with historic gold diggings, vineyards, orchards, trout fishing, boating, walks, close to ski fields. 45 minutes to Wanaka or Queenstown. Share dinner with us or just bed and breakfast. Tea and coffee, home-made cookies available. We enjoy sharing our home and garden with visitors and a friendly stay is assured.

- Dinner: $25 to $35 by arrangement
- Full breakfast
- Pet-free home
- Children welcome
- Internet available

Lake Dunstan Lodge **Cromwell**

Homestay
5 km N of Cromwell

Northburn, RD 3, Cromwell
(03) 445 1107 or 027 431 1415
william.t@xtra.co.nz
www.lakedunstanlodge.co.nz

Double: $120–$140
Single: $90
Children: negotiable

3 Bedrooms: 2Q 3S
Bathrooms: 2 ensuite, 1 guest share

Judy and Bill Thornbury

Friendly hospitality awaits you at our home privately situated beside Lake Dunstan. We are ex-Southland farmers. Our interests include Lions, fishing, boating, gardening and crafts. Bedrooms have attached balconies, fridge, tea and coffee facilities. Guests share our living areas, spa pool and laundry. Local attractions: orchards, vineyards, gold diggings, fishing, boating, walks, four ski fields nearby. Enjoy dinner with us or just relax in the peaceful surroundings. No smoking indoors please. Directions: 5 km north of Cromwell Bridge on SH8.

- Dinner: $30–40 B.A. or by arrangement
- Full breakfast
- Children welcome

Cromwell — Villa Rosa

B&B

2 km E of Info centre

14 Donegal Street, Cromwell, Central Otago
(03) 445 1096 or 027 343 4379
Winsome.blair@gmail.com
Www.villarosa.co.nz

Double: $65–$130   Single: $65–$130
Children: Portacot, Highchair and some toys.
Babysitting. Price by neg

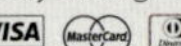   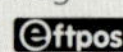

3 Bedrooms: 1Q 1D 1T
Bathrooms: 1 ensuite, 1 guest share

Winsome Blair

- Dinner: Victoria Arms Hotel has a dining room overlooking Lake Dunstan
- Full breakfast
- Pets welcome
- Children welcome
- No smoking on property
- Internet available

Set in a secluded garden, our accommodations include one large queen room with ensuite, a with separate dressing room (suitable for a portacot, if required) and private entrance. The double room and twin room share the guest bathroom, which is spacious and has a separate shower and clawfoot bathtub.

Winsome is also a traveller and apprecitates this opportunity to share her 'corner of the world' with you. Stella the dog will give you a welcoming bark on your arrival, and sleeps inside at night.

Arrowtown — Willowby Downs

B&B Homestay Farmstay
4 km SW of Arrowtown

792 Malaghans Road, R D 1, Queenstown
(03) 442 1714 or 027 222 0964
willowbydowns@xtra.co.nz
www.willowbydowns.co.nz

Double: $150
Single: $100
Children: neg

3 Bedrooms: 2Q 1T 2S
Bathrooms: 2 ensuite, 1 guest share

Pam and David Mcnay

- Double room has 1 Queen 1 single
- Full breakfast
- Pets welcome
- Children welcome

With Pam and David you are assured of a warm and friendly welcome, ex hoteliers they are passionate and practiced in the art of southern hospitality. With tea and coffee on your arrival you can relax in this warm and sunny home environment. 'Willowby Downs' has lovely well appointed guest rooms, electric blankets, TV, laundry options available with guests welcome to the internet, fax and Telephone facilities. Pam and David are able to arrange any extra tour or special events you may require.

Bernsleigh

Arrowtown

Luxury B&B Homestay
0.5 km S of Central Arrowtown

21 Bracken Street, Arrowtown, 9302
(03) 442 1550 or 021 969610 0219 69611
lindapeek@xtra.co.nz
www.bnb.co.nz/BernsleighBB.html

Double: $175–$200
Single: $140
Children: Price negotiable

3 Bedrooms: 2Q 1T 2S
Bathrooms: 1 ensuite, 1 guest share

David and Linda Peek

Welcome to our modern comfortable home situated in a peaceful location overlooking a world-class golf course and panoramic mountain and rural scenes. Private entry leads to your tastefully furnished rooms. Enjoy the sunny sheltered courtyard or cosy indoor atmosphere. Private lounge available. Facilities include: wireless internet, email, fax, laundry along with assistance in further activity planning. A short walk to a range of cafés and restaurants. Golf courses, ski fields, walking tracks nearby. Come and enjoy the warm hospitality of David and Linda.

- Wireless Internet; Laundry available
- Continental breakfast
- Internet available

The difference between a B&B and a hotel
is that you don't hug the hotel staff when you leave.

Queenstown — Willowbrook B&B and Cottages

B&B • Apartment with Kitchen • Cottage with Kitchen

4 km SW of Arrowtown

Malaghans Road, RD 1, Queenstown
(03) 442 1773 or (027) 451 6739
info@willowbrook.net.nz
www.willowbrook.net.nz

Double: $165–$185
Single: $135–$145

7 Bedrooms: 2K 2Q 3T
Bathrooms: 5 ensuite, 1 private

Trish and Tony White

- Rooms: 3 in B&B, 2 in Cottage, 2 in Barn
- Cottage $325 (4 persons)
- Continental breakfast
- Children welcome
- Internet available

Willowbrook offers both Bed & Breakfast and Self-Contained accommodation in an idyllic rural setting below Coronet Peak just 15 minutes from Queenstown. Millbrook Resort and historic Arrowtown are minutes away and we are within easy reach of five skifields and four very picturesque golf courses. A large mature garden contains a tennis court (we have rackets available), a luxurious spa pool and some very friendly sheep.

The MAIN HOUSE (Bed & Breakfast) has 3 centrally-heated double rooms with ensuite/private bathroom and a large guest lounge with an open fire, complimentary tea/coffee and computer, and a built-in fridge for guests to use.

The BARN (Self-Contained) has a super king bed, ensuite bathroom, lounge area, kitchenette and deck with barbeque. The adjoining ANNEX is available for extra members of the same party. Guests are welcome to use the laundry facilities in the Main House.

The COTTAGE (Self-Contained) is a delightful 2 bedroom cottage with full kitchen and laundry facilities, ensuite bathrooms, separate lounge and dining areas, underfloor heating throughout and spacious sundecks with barbeque.

All have Sky TV and free wireless internet. You can expect a warm welcome from Trish & Tony, along with friendly advice and exceptional hospitality.

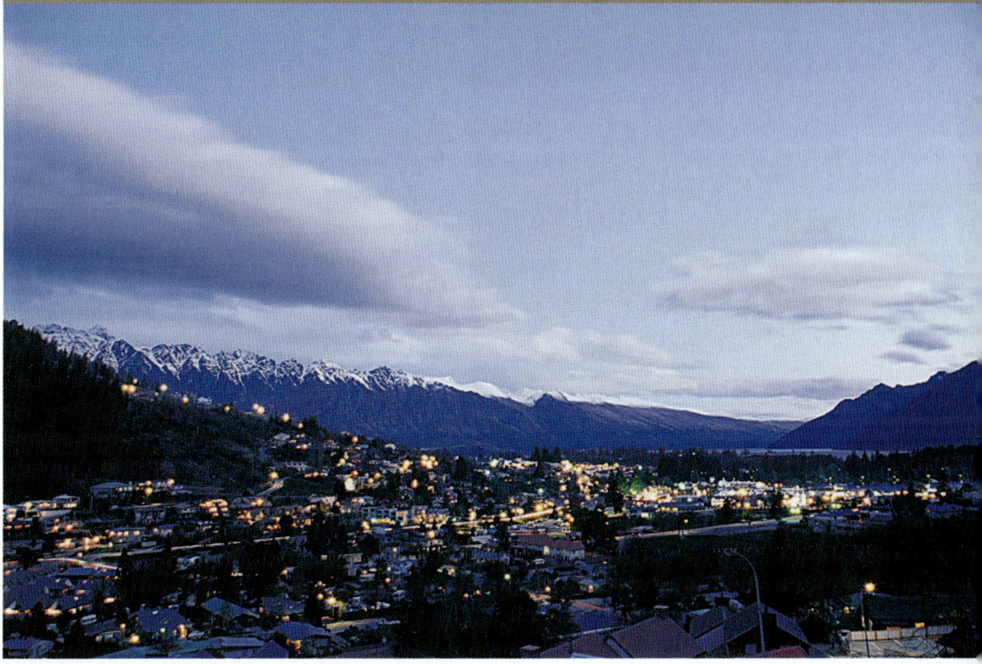

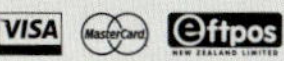

Luxury B&B Hotel • Guest House • Apartment with Kitchen • Private B&B – Hotel
0.8 km NW of Central Queenstown

30 Huff Street, Queenstown 9300
(03) 442 6766 or 0800 89 6766
stay@coronetview.com
www.coronetview.com

Double: $150–$270   Single: $135–$250
Extra in same room: children: $30, adults $40

10 Bedrooms: 6K **3**KT **1**Q
Bathrooms: 10 ensuite

Neil, Karen and Sarah Dempsey

- All with ensuites
- Apartments from $150–$780
- Continental breakfast
- Children welcome
- Weddings and functions
- Internet available

Centrally located just 10–15 minutes walk from town, Coronet View enjoys superb views of Coronet Peak, The Remarkables and Lake Wakatipu. Beautifully appointed rooms offer every comfort in either hosted accommodation or private apartments. Coronet View offers luxurious guest rooms either B&B or fully self-contained private apartments. Guest common areas occasionally shared with gorgeous persian cats include elevated and spacious dining and living areas, outdoor decks, a sunny conservatory, outdoor barbeque, pool and jacuzzi area and wireless internet access. Bed and Breakfast – A home away from home with true kiwi hospitality. Most rooms feature super king beds with lovely quilts, sheepskin electric blankets, tiled ensuites etc. Your hosts are knowledgeable local people who can recommend and book your activities at no extra cost. Apartments on site Queenstown. 1–6 bedroomed ensuited apartments. Most configurations feature ensuites, super king beds, generous living areas, fully equipped kitchens and laundries.

Queenstown

Campbells on Earnslaw

B&B

1.2 km N of Queenstown

9 Earnslaw Terrace, Queenstown
(03) 442 7783
stay@campbellsonearnslaw.co.nz
www.campbellsonearnslaw.co.nz

Double: $175

VISA MasterCard

2 Bedrooms: 1Q 2S
Bathrooms: 1 private

Aderianne and Bevan Campbell

- Extra person $50
- Continental breakfast
- Children welcome
- No smoking on property

We look forward to welcoming you to our home, which has 180 degree spectacular panoramic views of lake, mountains and golf course. Guests own private living room with balcony, TV, fridge, toast, tea and coffee making facilities. Ideal for two couples or family, only one party at a time. Experienced hosts we can advise and arrange your sightseeing and activities. From Frankton Road turn up Suburb Street, right into Panorama Terrace, right into Earnslaw Terrace. We are only a 10 minute stroll into town centre.

If you need any information ask your hosts
they are your own personal travel agent and guide.

B&B Homestay • Apartment with Kitchen
3 km NE of Queenstown Centre

16 Panners Way, Queenstown, 9300
(03) 442 4811 or 027 339 6483
info@larchhill.com
www.larchhill.com

Double: $160–$220
Single: $140–$180
Apartment (sleeps 4) $250–$330

4 Bedrooms: 2K **1**Q **1**T
Bathrooms: 2 ensuite, 2 private

Lesley and Chris Marlow

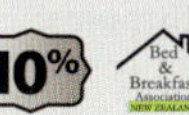

- King; queen; twin; self-contained apartment
- All rooms have ensuite or private bathroom
- Special breakfast
- Children welcome
- Internet available (free WiFi)

Lesley and Chris offer you a warm welcome to Larch Hill in beautiful Queenstown, purpose built on an elevated site overlooking Lake Wakatipu. As featured in 'National Geographic Traveler' and Cathay Pacific's 'Discovery' magazines, all rooms in our comfortable and relaxing homestay have spectacular lake views, with tea/coffee making facilities. Enjoy our warm, restful home with its panoramic views and sunny courtyard surrounded by cottage gardens. We are just a three minute drive from the centre of Queenstown and within walking distance of the lake. Public transport passes our street regularly.

Breakfasts are generous and include homemade bread, freshly baked croissants and pastries, fresh fruit salad, yoghurt, and freshly ground, percolated coffee. Our self-contained apartment is ideal for families or small groups. We can provide pre-arranged complimentary pickups from Queenstown airport. Feel free to use our local knowledge to help plan your itinerary. We are booking agents for Queenstown and Milford tours and activities. We have no pets and are non-smokers, but guests are welcome to smoke outdoors.

From Frankton drive 2.5 kms on State Highway 6A (Frankton Road) towards Queenstown. Turn right into Goldfield Heights at Sherwood Manor. Second left is Panners Way. No. 16 is at the end of the accessway, half-way down Panners Way on the left.

Queenstown · 'Kemnay'

B&B
1.40 km SE of Queenstown

57 Panorama Tce, Queenstown
(03) 442 6270 or 027 243 3181
hfronald@xtra.co.nz
www.bnb.co.nz/'Kemnay'.html

Double: $140–$150
Single: $100
Children: By arrangement

2 Bedrooms: 1Q 1T
Bathrooms: 1 private

Heather and Fraser Ronald

- Bathrooms: bath and shower
- Full breakfast
- Pet-free home
- Children welcome
- Internet available

Heather and Fraser warmly welcome you to their Queenstown Home. Wonderful views of lake and mountains, also overlooks golf course. Queen bed, plus twin, private bathroom. Small comfortable seating area with tea and coffee making facilities. One party at a time. Off street parking. 1.4 km from town centre.

Directions: Approaching Queenstown along Frankton Road, turn right into Hensman Road, then first turn left inot Panorama Tce.

Queenstown · Bearsden Bed and Breakfast

Luxury B&B
8 km SW of Arrowtown

333 Lower Shotover Road, Speargrass Flat, Queenstown, 9371
(03) 442 6656 or 021 222 1325
bookings@bearsden.co.nz
www.bearsden.co.nz

Double: $220–$330   Single: $180–$250
Children: Not suitable under 15 years

VISA MasterCard

2 Bedrooms: 1Q
Bathrooms: 2 ensuite

Margie SlatterySmith and Ned Smith

- Full breakfast
- Pets welcome
- Not suitable for children
- No smoking on property
- Internet available

This luxury B and B is located in a rural setting, yet is only five minutes drive from Queenstown airport and five minutes drive from historic Arrowtown. A choice of two bedrooms with ensuites, views to Coronet Peak, private guest lounge, FREE Wi Fi, outdoor spa, free mountain bikes, hot breakfast choices, freshly made juices, espresso coffee, off street parking, great hosts and friendly Black Lab. Smoke free inside and out.

Evergreen Lodge   Queenstown B&B

Luxury B&B Hotel • Separate Suite • Guest House

28 Evergreen Place, Queenstown, 9400
(03) 442 6636
admin@evergreenlodge.co.nz
www.evergreenlodge.co.nz

Double: $395–$795
Single: $198–$398

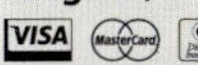  

4 Bedrooms: 4KT **1Q 1D**
Bathrooms: 4 ensuite

Lace and Cyndi

Evergreen Lodge is an award winning property, renowned for its outstanding service and hospitality. A Qualmark 5 Star Guest and Hosted property offering understated luxury and quality. The Evergreen Lodge delivers a unique accommodation experience, combining comfort and warmth with the elegance and sophistication that you should always expect from a private boutique hotel. Situated on the edge of Lake Wakatipu, the Evergreen Lodge boasts stunning views throughout. Its peaceful, natural surroundings convey remoteness and yet it is only minutes from the heart of Queenstown.

- Dinner available on request at extra cost
- Full breakfast
- Pet-free home
- Children welcome
- Weddings and functions
- No smoking on property
- Internet available

Chalet Queenstown

B&B • Guest House

1 Dublin Street, Queenstown, 9300
(03) 442 7117 or 0800 222 457
stay@chaletqueenstown.co.nz
www.chaletqueenstown.co.nz

Double: $195–$245
Single: $175–$220
Children: are welcome, all our king beds can be made into a twin

7 Bedrooms: 7KT
Bathrooms: 7 ensuite

Alex McMillan

Located within a five minute walk to Central Queenstown. This refurbished Swiss style Chalet offers Hosted bed & breakfast accommodation with a warm and stylish atmosphere for your pleasure. Each of our 7 rooms offers a choice of king beds, ensuites, TV, Free Wireless internet, Robes, Docking stations, Fridges, tea/coffee facilities, guest lounge and breakfast served in our dining room . Discover all Queenstown has to offer, with its array of restaurants, shops and adrenalin activities all set dramatic alpine backdrop.

- Dinner: Located within a 5 minute walk to over 50 restaurants
- Full breakfast
- Children welcome
- No smoking on property
- Internet available

Garston

Menlove Homestay

B&B Homestay • Separate Suite
50 km S of Queenstown

17 Blackmore Road, PO Box 39, Garston 9750
(03) 248 8516
mattmenlove@slingshot.co.nz
www.bnb.co.nz/menlove.html

Double: $100
Single: $50

1 Bedroom: 1D 1S
Bathrooms: 1 ensuite

Bev and Matt Menlove

- Dinner: $25 by arrangement
- Continental breakfast

We are organic gardeners and our other interests include lawn bowls, sailing, gliding and alternative energy. Garston is New Zealand's most inland village with the Mataura River (famous for its fly fishing) flowing through the valley, surrounded by the Hector Range and the Eyre Mountains. A fishing guide is available with advance notice. For day trips, Garston is central to Queenstown, Te Anau, Milford Sound or Invercargill. We look forward to meeting you.

Dunedin

Harbourside B&B

B&B Homestay
7 km NE of Dunedin

6 Kiwi Street, St Leonards, Dunedin
(03) 471 0690
harboursidebb@xtra.co.nz
www.bnb.co.nz/harboursidebb.html

Double: $110–$130
Single: $90–$130
Children: $30 sharing with parents

3 Bedrooms: 1KT 2Q 3S
Bathrooms: 1 ensuite, 1 guest share

Shirley and Don Parsons

- Dinner: $30
- Full breakfast
- Pet-free home
- Children welcome
- No smoking on property

We are situated in a quiet suburb overlooking Otago Harbour and surrounding hills. Within easy reach of all local attractions. Lovely garden or harbour views from all rooms. Children very welcome. Directions: drive into city on one-way system watch for Highway 88 sign follow Anzac Avenue onto Ravensbourne Road. Continue approx 5 km to St Leonards turn left at Playcentre opposite Boatshed into Pukeko Street then left into Kaka Road, straight ahead to Kiwi Street turn left into Number 6.

Highbrae Guesthouse

B&B • Guest House • wireless internet availability
1 km SW of Dunedin

376 High Street, Dunedin, 9016
(03) 479 2070 or 027 4328 470
enquiries@highbrae.co.nz
www.highbrae.co.nz

Double: $110–$140   Single: $80–$110
Children: $25 if sharing room with parents

4 Bedrooms: 1K 2Q 1T 1S
Bathrooms: 1 family share, 1 guest share, 1 private

Fienie and Stephen Clark

Experience a taste of early Dunedin. This heritage home was built on the High Street in 1908 to provide first class accommodation to its residents. Today it is still an impressive home with spectacular views of the city and harbour. The upstairs guest rooms and self-contained unit are carefully maintained to preserve their character for visitors, who delight in the many features in the home. Wireless internet is available and a courtesy vehicle can meet you at the bus or train if required.

- Doubles; queen, king, queen self-contained, twin singles
- Cooked breakfast extra
- Bathrooms: three
- Continental breakfast
- Pet-free home
- Children welcome
- Internet available

Just as we have variety of B&Bs
you will also be offered a variety of breakfasts,
and they will always be generous.

B&B

0.1 km N of Dunedin Central

770 George Street, Dunedin, 9016
(03) 477 2727 or 0800 441 441
albatross.inn@xtra.co.nz
www.albatross.inn.co.nz

Double: $120–$170
Single: $115–$130
Children: $15

VISA · MasterCard · Diners Club International · American Express · eftpos New Zealand Limited

8 Bedrooms: 1K 2KT 3Q 2D 5S
Bathrooms: 7 ensuite, 1 private

Glynis Rees

- Special breakfast
- Children welcome
- Internet available

Welcome to Dunedin and Albatross Inn! Our beautiful late Victorian house is ideally located on the main street close to the university, gardens, museum, shops and restaurants. Our attractive rooms have ensuite/private bathrooms, telephone, TV, radio, central heating, tea/coffee, warm duvets and electric blankets on modern beds. Firm beds upon request. Quiet rooms at rear of house. Several rooms have kitchenette and fridge. Enjoy our sumptious breakfast in our cosy breakfast room. We serve freshly baked bread and muffins, fresh fruit salad, yoghurt, juices, cereals, teas, freshly brewed coffee. We are happy to recommend and book tours for you. All wildlife tours pick up and drop off here. We can recommend many great places to eat, most just a short walk down George Street. Nearby laundry, non-smoking, cot and highchair. Some comments from our visitors Book! The right balance of everything location, breakfast and lovely room. Delightfully different. Absolutely fantastic as always. Home away from Home. A touch of Class, lovely home beautifully presented. Perfecto! Winter special $90 Double – special conditions apply. Complimentary e-mail and wireless internet.

Grant's Farm

B&B Farmstay • Apartmenst with Kitchen
8 km SW of Dunedin

151 Old Brighton Road, Fairfield R.D.1, Dunedin 9076
(03) 488 0336
info@bnb-dunedin.co.nz
www.bnb-dunedin.co.nz

Double: $130–$190   Single: $100–$120
Children: By arrangement

2 Bedrooms: 1Q 1D 1S
Bathrooms: 1 ensuite

Tom and Jeanette Grant

Our typical NZ woolshed on 20ha is now a unique home with fully self-contained guest accommodation with woodfire and free wireless internet. Situated on the Kaikorai Estuary we have heaps of bird life sheep cattle and also an airstrip with biplanes.

We are in a peaceful rural setting with wonderful views, only 15 minutes from Dunedin Airport and eight minutes to either Dunedin or Mosgiel.

Excellent restaurants and miles of beach walks are minutes away. Guests wish they could stay longer!

- Bathrooms: the ensuite is a private bathroom for the apartment and is share when required
- Dinner: not supplied
- Continental breakfast
- Pet-free home
- No smoking on property
- Internet available

Hazel House Boutique Bed & Breakfast

B&B
5 km SW of Octagon

50 Hazel Avenue, Hazelhurst, Dunedin, 9012
(03) 487 6550 or 021 631 642
info@hazelhouse.co.nz
www.hazelhouse.co.nz

Double: $125–$165

2 Bedrooms: 1K 1Q
Bathrooms: 1 ensuite, 1 private

Sandy and Brent Ward

A classic 1900's villa located only five minutes from Dunedin's City Centre. With the majestic rooms, ornate ceilings and lead light windows, it is an absolute delight to offer a peaceful and quiet location with warm inviting rooms, scrumptious breakfasts and southern hospitality. Spectacular quests lounge, king bedroom with private bathroom, or queen bedroom with ensuite, include top quality linen and facilities. Sky TV, wireless internet, tea and coffee, central heating, courtyard with spa pool, and warm welcome from hosts Sandy and Brent Ward.

- Bathrooms: king with private bathroom, queen with ensuite
- Full breakfast

Dunedin — Grandview Bed & Breakfast

Luxury B&B • Guest House
1 km NW of Dunedin

360 High Street, Dunedin 9016
(03) 474 9472 or 021 101 9857
nzgrandview@msn.com
www.grandview.co.nz

Double: $125–$250
Single: $100–$200
Children: $25 per extra person or child

VISA · MasterCard · AMERICAN EXPRESS · eftpos NEW ZEALAND LIMITED

5 Bedrooms: 2KT **4**Q
Bathrooms: 3 ensuite, 2 private

Steve Scott

- Dinner: By Arrangement
- Continental breakfast
- Children welcome
- No smoking on property
- Internet available

Welcome to GRANDVIEW one of Dunedin's oldest listed Mansions dating back to the 1860's. Open to guests for a lovely Bed and Breakfast experience with amazing views and the charm of Dunedin's heritage. Just a short stroll to the City Centre, Cafes, Restaurants and Bars, this makes Grandview a convenient location for guests. We have Bedrooms to suit all budgets, plus Kitchen and Laundry facilities, Sauna and FREE Wi-Fi available. Come experience Dunedin the GRANDVIEW way! Hope to see you soon.

Company Bay, Otago Peninsula — Arts Content Bed and Breakfast, Otago Peninsula

B&B • Cottage with Kitchen • Attached to house but completely self-contained
13 km N of Dunedin

1 Castlewood Road, Company Bay, Otago Peninsula, Dunedin 9014
(03) 476 0076
artscontent@hotmail.com
www.artscontentbnb.com

Double: $135–$160   Single: $130–$145
Children: under 12 free

VISA · MasterCard · eftpos NEW ZEALAND LIMITED

1 Bedroom: 1Q   **Bathrooms:** 1 ensuite

Alex and Cathy Shemansky

- One bedroom with ensuite downstairs
- One sofa bed suitable for a child upstairs
- Full breakfast provisions
- Children welcome
- No smoking on property
- Internet available

Absolute waterfront, self-contained, cottage style accommodation ideal for a couple. The B&B adjoins our home, has private entrances and off street parking. Upstairs is a lounge dining kitchen with comfortable seating including a sofa bed which can accommodate an extra person. French doors open to sweeping harbour views from the private deck. Downstairs the spacious bedroom with Queen bed and Ensuite opens into our beautiful garden. Heatpumps make both spaces warm and cosy. A generous basket breakfast is also provided.

Edgeley Bed & Breakfast

Luxury B&B
6 km SE of Information Centre

29 Spencer Street, Andersons Bay, 9013
(03) 454 5568 or 027 715 3635
edgeley@xtra.co.nz
www.edgeley@xtra.co.nz

Double: $180–$240
Single: $155–$180
Children: Under 2 free, otherwise adult rate

VISA MasterCard

2 Bedrooms: 2Q 1S
Bathrooms: 1 ensuite, 1 private

Janet and Alan Parker

In 1923 Edgeley was described as one of the finest of the old homes round about Dunedin's. With outstanding ocean views from all the guest rooms, we invite you to stay at the home of the Parker family and Penny our very friendly dog, in Anderson's Bay, the Gateway to the Peninsula.

We offer a superior class of accommodation with a sumptuous home-cooked or continental breakfast served in our guest's lounge. Enjoy staying in one of Dunedin's historic homes.

- Emery Room has queen bed, Paterson Room has queen and king single beds
- Full breakfast
- Children welcome
- No smoking on property
- Internet available

Arden St House Homestay Bed and Breakfast

B&B Homestay • Guest House • Hostel
2 km km N of Dunedin

36 Arden St, Dunedin, 9010
(03) 473 8860 or 800428689
joycelepperd@gmail.com
www.ardenstreethouse.co.nz

Double: $85–$130
Single: $65–$100

VISA MasterCard eftpos
NEW ZEALAND LIMITED

5 Bedrooms: 2Q 2D 2S
Bathrooms: 2 ensuite, 3 guest share

Joyce and Dave Carter

EDITORS CHOICE and highly recommended by the LONELY PLANET 2013 Guide Book. They say 'An organic garden and a very welcoming host. With a recurring leopard theme, crazy artworks and porthole in the bathroom. Several readers raved about fabulous dinners (NZ$12–15) with neighbors, artists, woofers and guests.' The house has large character spacious bedrooms with fabulous views. Only five minute walk to Knox College and Botanical 10-minute walk to the Forsyth Barr Stadium Your hosts Joyce and Dave love meeting guests from around the world and really make you at home. There are two very friendly cats on the property.

- Bathrooms: showers
- Dinner: 15–25
- Continental breakfast
- Pets welcome
- Children welcome
- Weddings and functions
- No smoking on property
- Internet available

Dunedin

Beach Haven B&B

B&B

55 Bedford Street, St Clair, DUNEDIN, 9012
34555388
mj.leach@xtra.co.nz
www.beachhavenbedandbreakfast.co.nz

Double: $140–$150

4 Bedrooms: 4K
Bathrooms: 4 ensuite

Joy and Murray Leach

- Continental breakfast
- Children welcome
- No smoking on property
- Internet available

Located just a minute's walk from the beautiful St Clair Beach, Beach Haven offers a high standard of accommodation, with a family atmosphere.

Beach Haven is a warm, modern home a few minutes' walk to six café/bar/restaurants. Enjoy a stroll on the golden sands of St Clair Beach, year-round surfing, a swim in the hot salt water pool (in season), and a drink or a meal at one of the restaurants.

An ideal base for many Dunedin attractions.

East Taieri, Dunedin

Marg's Manor

Homestay
2 km SW of Mosgiel

103 Main South Road, East Taieri, Mosgiel, Dunedin
(03) 489 2030
msscott@xtra.co.nz
www.bnb.co.nz/MargsManor.html

Double: $100
Single: $80

1 Bedroom: 1Q
Bathrooms: 1 ensuite

Margaret

- Full breakfast by arrangement
- Dinner: $30 – By arrangement
- Continental breakfast
- Not suitable for children

Haere Mai, welcome to my sunny cottage home, situated halfway between Dunedin Airport and Dunedin city. With rural views over the Taieri Plains. Enjoy your own entrance and outdoor table just beside your room, or relax up in the back garden spaces amongst the vegetables and herbs that I enjoy cooking with. Dinner and cooked breakfast by arrangement, off street parking available. Resident cat called Fluff.

B&B Homestay — Mosgiel, Dunedin

B&B Homestay
15 km S of Dunedin

46 Eden St, Mosgiel, Dunedin, 9024
(03) 489 4602 or 21435565
arrangements@arrangements.co.nz
www.bbhomestay.co.nz

Double: $130
Single: $110

2 Bedrooms: 2D
Bathrooms: 1 ensuite, 1 private

Brenda and Bill Botting

A warm welcome to B&B Homestay located in Mosgiel, Dunedin. Our bed and breakfast accommodation offers privacy, peaceful surroundings and charm, just 20 minutes from Dunedin city. Your hosts, Bill and Brenda invite you to stay in a boutique room with ensuite, detached from the main house. We hope you enjoy your time relaxing with a hot chocolate or glass of wine while looking around the garden or soaking in the spa.

A scrumptious continental breakfast and evening dinner can be provided with prior arrangement.

- One double bed in house, with separate bathroom
- Continental breakfast
- Pet-free home
- Not suitable for children
- Weddings and functions
- No smoking on property
- Internet available

Lesmahagow — Balclutha

Luxury B&B • Boutique
4 km N of Balclutha/Catlins

146 Benhar Road, Benhar, RD 2, Balclutha 9272
(03) 418 2507 or 0800 301 224 (NZ only)
lesmahagow@xtra.co.nz
www.lesmahagow.co.nz

Double: $190–$190

3 Bedrooms: 3Q 1S
Bathrooms: 3 private

Noel and Kate O'Malley

Lesmahagow offers excellent accommodation in an historic homestead and garden setting. Centrally situated, discerning travellers can make Lesmahagow their base to explore the Catlins region, Dunedin and the Otago Penninsula or the historic goldfields of Lawrence. Centrally heated, with delightful bedrooms and gorgeous bathrooms, you can be sure of wonderful hospitality and a truly memorable stay. Evening meals are our speciality and our breakfasts will satisfy all taste buds! Come and discover this hidden paradise! You will love the experience.

- We can use a 4th bedroom (with a queen bed) with a shared bathroom for 2 couples
- Lunches on request
- Dinner: $40
- Full breakfast
- Children welcome
- Weddings and functions
- Internet available

B&B

25 km SE of Balclutha

27 Main Road, Owaka
(03) 415 8300 or 027 433 4146
enquiries@catlinsretreat.co.nz
www.catlinsretreat.co.nz

Double: $100–$125
Single: $55–$125
Children: $45

VISA MasterCard

4 Bedrooms: 2Q **1**D **5**S
Bathrooms: 2 ensuite, 1 guest share

Robbie Hodge

- Queen ensuite $125, third person extra. 1 Double with shared bathroom $100
- Dinner: By Arrangement
- Continental breakfast
- Pet-free home
- Pets welcome
- Children welcome

Welcome to Catlins Retreat, your home away from home in the heart of Owaka village and the Catlins.

You're centrally located for visiting the Catlins Heritage Trail and Southern Scenic route, the incredible Catlins coastline including fur seal and sea lion colonies and the walks of the Catlins, Parukanui Fall, Catlins River walk and Cathedral Caves.

You'll receive a warm welcome from your host Robbie who is happy to provide you with local information and guidance.

If you would like dinner
most hosts require 24 hours notice.

Southland,
South Catlins &
Stewart Island
Gibbston
Earnscleugh
Kingston
Garston
Ettrick
Te Anau
94
Manapouri
Mossburn
99
Lumsden
96
6
Gore
99
1
Invercargill
92
Stewart Island
0   Kilometres   30
0   Miles   18

Te Anau — Shakespeare House

B&B • Separate Suite
1 km NE of Te Anau Centre

10 Dusky Street, PO Box 32, Te Anau
(03) 249 7349 or 0800 249 349
shakespearebnb@xtra.co.nz
www.shakespearehouse.co.nz

Double: $100–$135
Single: $90–$110
Children: $5–$15

VISA · MasterCard · eftpos

8 Bedrooms: 8K **3**T **4**S
Bathrooms: 8 ensuite

Marg, Jeff, Kylie and Ray

- Self-contained, 2 bedrooms – sleeps 5
- Bathrooms: no Baths
- Full breakfast
- Pet-free home
- Children welcome
- Internet available

Shakespeare House is a well established Bed and Breakfast, where we keep a home atmosphere with personal service. We are situated in a quiet residential area yet are within walking distance of shops, lake and restaurants. Our rooms are ground floor and have the choice of king, queen or twin beds. Each room has private facilities, TV, tea/coffee making. Tariff includes continental or delicious cooked breakfast. Guest laundry available, internet and payphone facilities on site. Winter rates May to September.

Te Anau — Cosy Kiwi B&B

B&B • Guest House
0.2 km SE of Te Anau Central

186 Milford Road, TE ANAU 9600
32497475 or 800249700
info@cosykiwi.com
www.cosykiwi.com

Double: $165–$185
Single: $150–$155

VISA · MasterCard · eftpos

7 Bedrooms: 4KT **3**Q
Bathrooms: 7 ensuite

Eleanor and Derek Cook

- Studio Rooms
- $45 extra person
- Special breakfast
- Children welcome
- Internet available
- Laundry (small charge)

Eleanor Derek and Mia and Jax (our miniture Schnauzers) welcome you to our Bed and Breakfast Guest House. Privacy with comfort, quiet spacious ensuited bedrooms, quality beds, individual heating and televison. Breakfast buffet of home-made breads, jams, fresh fruits, dessert fruits, yoghurt, brewed coffee, special teas, plus mouthwatering pancakes with maple syrup or ham and cheese. Two minute walk to shops and restaurants, bookings arranged for all tours, pick-up at gate. Guest lounge with free internet access to desk top computer, free wireless for personal laptops, ,free off-street parking and free luggage storage.

Rose 'n' Reel   **Te Anau**

B&B Farmstay • Cottage with Kitchen
2 km E of Te Anau

89 Ben Loch Lane, RD 2, Te Anau
(03) 249 7582 or 027 4545 723
rosenreel@xtra.co.nz
www.rosenreel.co.nz

Double: $0–$135
Single: $80–$120

VISA MasterCard

3 Bedrooms: 2Q **1**D **1**S
Bathrooms: 2 private

Lyn and Lex Lawrence

Genuine Kiwi hospitality in a magic setting five minutes from Te Anau. Hand feed tame fallow deer, meet our friendly cat Ben and dog Meg. Sit on the veranda of our fully self-contained cabin and enjoy watching deer with a lake and mountain view. The two room cabin has cooking facilities, fridge, microwave, TV, one queen, one double plus bathroom. Our two storey home is set in an extensive garden. Two guest bedrooms. Lex is a fishing guide, I love to garden. Directions: please phone.

- Continental breakfast
- Internet available

House of Wood   **Te Anau**

B&B Homestay
0.2 km N of central Te Anau

44 Moana Crescent, Te Anau, 9600
(03) 249 8404 or (021) 1586686
houseofwood@xtra.co.nz
www.houseofwood.co.nz

Double: $135–$160
Single: $115–$145
Children: Cost by arrangement

VISA MasterCard

4 Bedrooms: 1K **2**KT **3**Q
Bathrooms: 3 ensuite, 1 private

Merle and Cliff Buchanan 

A warm welcome is assured when you arrive at our home. We really enjoy meeting guests from overseas (and locals). Our house is a unique architecturally designed home of native and exotic timber. Sit at the outdoor tables and enjoy beautiful views. Our interests are boating, golf, fishing, rowing, gardening. We can help you plan your activities and book trips, with pick up at door. Two minutes walk from town, five minutes to Lake. Dinner by arrangement. Wireless internet available. Check-in after 2pm please.

- Dinner: 3 course dinner with drinks usually served (pre-booked)
- Full breakfast
- Pet-free home
- Children welcome
- No smoking on property
- Internet available

Manapouri — Cathedral Peaks B&B

B&B

44 Cathedral Drive, Manapouri, 9643
(03) 249 6640
cathedralpeaks@ihug.co.nz
www.cathedralpeaks.com

Double: $250
Single: $220

VISA   MasterCard

3 Bedrooms: 1K 1Q 1D
Bathrooms: 3 ensuite

Janice Duncan

- Full breakfast
- Pet-free home
- Not suitable for children
- No smoking on property
- Internet available

Janice and Neal, your friendly hosts warmly welcome you to share their recently built home. Take advantage of our lakefront view location and share with us the majestic and stunning scenery. Enjoy a continental and cooked breakfast in the guest shared lounge/dining room overlooking the lake to the Cathedral Peaks Mountain range.

All our rooms have lake and mountain views. Each room has tea/coffee making facilities, fruit basket, TV, DVD player plus DVDs, heater, refrigerator, hairdryer, bathrobs, free internet, electric blanket, iron and board.

Mossburn — Turner Farmstay

Farmstay
25 km S of Mossburn

RD 1, Otautau, Southland 9689
(03) 225 7602
murray.joyce@farmside.co.nz
www.innz.co.nz/host/e/etalcreek.html

Double: $120
Single: $80
Children: under 12 $30

3 Bedrooms: 1Q 4S
Bathrooms: 1 guest share, 1 private

Joyce and Murray Turner

- Dinner: $40 3 course with NZ wine
- Full breakfast
- Internet available

Our modern home on 301 hectares, farming sheep, is situated half-way between Invercargill and Te Anau, which can be reached in one hour. We enjoy meeting people, will provide quality accommodation, farm-fresh food in a welcoming friendly atmosphere. You can have a farm tour or just relax with our pet bichons Holly and Katie. The Aparima River is adjacent to the property. Murray is a keen fly fisherman. Guiding and advice available. Evening meal on request. Directions please phone 24 hours notice to avoid disappointment.

Hokonui Bed & Breakfast — Gore

Luxury B&B • Rural Lifestyle
3 km NW of Gore

258 Reaby Road R D 4, GORE, 9774
(03) 208 4890 or 0800 70 72 75
stay@hokonuibandb.co.nz
www.hokonuibandb.co.nz

Double: $120–$140
Single: $90–$100
Children: negotiable

VISA MasterCard

3 Bedrooms: 1K 1Q 1T
Bathrooms: 2 ensuite, 1 private

Brian and Shona McLennan

Brian and Shona welcome you to their private, spacious, and modern new home on a 12 acre lifestyle property with uninterrupted panoramic views. Private upstairs unit, underfloor heating and full size snooker table. Close to the Mataura River which is world famous for Trout Fishing, 18 hole Golf Course and Native Bush Walks. A perfect base for sightseeing Southland and attending the Gold Guitar Awards, Waimumu Fieldays and Hokonui Fashion Awards Interests – golf, fishing, snooker, horse riding and dog trialing, gardening, music and wine tasting. We have Horses, Sheepdogs and Sheep.

- All bedrooms have ensuites/bathrooms and great views.
- Dinner by arrangement
- Full breakfast
- Children welcome
- Internet available

Kowhai Place — Gore

B&B
0.5 km S of Gore

41 Huron Street, Gore, 9710
(03) 208 8022 or (027) 203 8734
kowhaiplace@xtra.co.nz
www.southland-homestays.co.nz

Double: $130–$150
Single: $75–$90

3 Bedrooms: 4KT 1Q
Bathrooms: 1 ensuite, 1 guest share

Helen and John Williams

We are right on the banks of the Mataura River, so famous for it's fly-fishing. Our place the ideal base if you wish to make day trips to many places including The Catlins, Invercargill, Bluff and Queenstown. Te Anau and the World Heritage Fiordland National Park are all within a two-hour drive from Gore.

We will be happy to advise you on places to visit and things to do during your stay here and we know you will enjoy our typical southern hospitality!

- Queen bedroom has ensuite, lounge sofa bed and kitchen.
- Dinner by arrangement $35
- Full breakfast
- Children welcome

Invercargill

Glenroy Park Homestay

B&B Homestay
5 km N of Invercargill city

23 Glenroy Park Drive, Invercargill
(03) 215 8464 or 027 376 2228
maggymae@xtra.co.nz
www.bnb.co.nz/glenroypark.html

Double: $120–$130
Single: $90–$100
Children: $12, up to 12 years

3 Bedrooms: 1Q 1T 1S
Bathrooms: 1 guest share, 1 private

Margaret and Alan Thomson

- 1Queen, twin, single
- Bathrooms: heated tile floors
- Dinner: $35 ,3 course
- Full breakfast
- Children welcome

Exclusively yours, in a quiet retreat near restaurants and parks. Be our special guests and share an evening of relaxation and friendship. Our interests are golfing, meeting people, travel and cooking. We look forward to your visit. Invercargill is the gateway to Queenstown, Fiordland, Catlins and Stewart Island. Directions: from Queenstown turn left second lights (Bainfield Road), take first left, third house on left. From Dunedin turn right second set of lights (Queens Drive), travel to end, turn left, first street right, third house left.

Invercargill

Bushy Point Fernbirds B&B

B&B
7 km SW of Invercargill

197 Grant Rd, Otatara Invercargill, 9879
32131302 or 027 491 3855
enquiries@fernbirds.co.nz
www.fernbirds.co.nz

Double: $150–$150
Single: $140–$140
Children: $20

3 Bedrooms: 2Q 1D
Bathrooms: 1 guest share

Ian and Jenny Gamble

- Extra adult $40
- Continental breakfast
- Children welcome
- Non-smokers only
- Internet available

Bushy Point Fernbirds provides a natural New Zealand experience for our guests. We are close to Invercargill but with a feeling of being in an isolated location. Perfect peace and quiet, night and day.

Our B&B is situated on a privately owned reserve with a track and boardwalk through forest and wetland. We work to protect the birdlife including Fernbirds with an extensive predator control network and revegetation.

Our tariff includes a guided walk on our property.

Lovett Lodge

B&B

31 Duke Street, Invercargill, 9810
(03) 21 86060 or 027 383 8206
lovettlodge@xtra.co.nz
www.lovettlodge.co.nz

Double: $80–$110
Single: $75–$90
Children: Welcome

VISA MasterCard eftpos

8 Bedrooms: 1K 1KT 2Q 1D 2T 1S
Bathrooms: 2 ensuite, 3 guest share

Maree and Kelvin

Lovett Lodge is an eight bedroom Accommodation venue, two with ensuites and three further shared bathrooms. All with wheelchair access. Situated in quiet suburban street, only five min drive to CBD. There is large guest lounge and conservatory area with Sky TV and DVD player and tea and coffee making facilities. Shared kitchen and laundry facilities available to guests. Ample off street parking; Wi-Fi internet access. Close to a golf course, park, museum and local restaurants.

Dinner is available by prior arrangement. Airport pick ups complimentary.

- Evening meal available by prior arrangement. From 20.00 pp
- Continental breakfast
- Children welcome
- No smoking on property
- Internet available

Glendaruel Bed & Breakfast

B&B
1 km S of Oban

38 Golden Bay Road, Oban, Stewart Island
(03) 219 1092 or 027 519 092
glendaruel@xtra.co.nz
www.glendaruel.co.nz

Double: $240–$240
Single: $120–$175
Children: By arrangement

VISA MasterCard

3 Bedrooms: 1KT 1Q 1S
Bathrooms: 3 ensuite

Raylene Waddell

Peaceful bush setting, ten minutes' walk from village, three minutes from Golden Bay, base for water taxis to Ulva Island Bird Sanctuary in beautiful Paterson Inlet. Large guest lounge and extensive decks with bush and sea views. Colourful garden alive with birdsong. Central Heating. Tea/Coffee Facilities in each room. Courtesy Transfers. Advice and assistance with local activities. I speak French and a little German and enjoy hosting guests from around the world. My Cairn Terrier, Macpherson, and I assure you of a warm welcome.

- 1 King/Twin 1 Queen 1 Single
- Dinner: Three course meal, local seafood if desired, $65 per person
- Full breakfast
- Children welcome
- No smoking on property
- Internet available

Notes

Notes

Notes

Notes

The New Zealand
Bed & Breakfast
Book

2014

Please help us to keep our standards high

To help maintain the high reputation of The New Zealand Bed & Breakfast Book we ask for your comments about your stay. You can simply stick a stamp on this form or save all your comment forms and return them in an envelope.

Alternatively, leave your comment at our website www.bnb.co.nz

Name of Host or B&B _______________________________________

Address _______________________________________

Considering things such as breakfast, meals, beds, cleanliness, hospitality and value for money, what is your overall satisfaction rating, with 1 being the lowest and 10 being the highest rating?

1   2   3   4   5   6   7   8   9   10

Do you have any comments?

____

____

____

We may display your comments on our website. The rating will be confidential and will be kept for administration purposes.

Fill in your details to go into our regular prize draws! Your details will not be passed on to anyone else. If you do not have email we suggest you use a friend's email address.

Your name: _______________________________________

Your town/city: _______________________________________

Country: _______________________________________

Email: _______________________________________

Please Post this form to:
**The New Zealand B&B Book,
PO Box 6843, Wellington, New Zealand**

The New Zealand
Bed & Breakfast Book

2014

Please help us to keep our standards high

To help maintain the high reputation of The New Zealand Bed & Breakfast Book we ask for your comments about your stay. You can simply stick a stamp on this form or save all your comment forms and return them in an envelope.

Alternatively, leave your comment at our website www.bnb.co.nz

Name of Host or B&B _______________________________________

Address _______________________________________

Considering things such as breakfast, meals, beds, cleanliness, hospitality and value for money, what is your overall satisfaction rating, with 1 being the lowest and 10 being the highest rating?

1   2   3   4   5   6   7   8   9   10

Do you have any comments?

____

____

____

We may display your comments on our website. The rating will be confidential and will be kept for administration purposes.

Fill in your details to go into our regular prize draws! Your details will not be passed on to anyone else. If you do not have email we suggest you use a friend's email address.

Your name: _______________________________________

Your town/city: _______________________________________

Country: _______________________________________

Email: _______________________________________

Please Post this form to:
**The New Zealand B&B Book,
PO Box 6843, Wellington, New Zealand**

The New Zealand
Bed & Breakfast Book

Freepost Authority 243850
The New Zealand Bed & Breakfast Book
PO Box 6843
Marion Square
Welllington 6141

The New Zealand
Bed & Breakfast Book

discount voucher

10%

Present this voucher to a participating B&B and receive a 10% discount. Can not be used in conjunction with any other promotion, discount or agent bookings. **Valid till 1/1/2015**

The New Zealand
Bed & Breakfast Book

discount voucher

10%

Present this voucher to a participating B&B and receive a 10% discount. Can not be used in conjunction with any other promotion, discount or agent bookings. **Valid till 1/1/2015**

The New Zealand
Bed & Breakfast Book

discount voucher

10%

Present this voucher to a participating B&B and receive a 10% discount. Can not be used in conjunction with any other promotion, discount or agent bookings. **Valid till 1/1/2015**

The New Zealand
Bed & Breakfast Book

discount voucher

10%

Present this voucher to a participating B&B and receive a 10% discount. Can not be used in conjunction with any other promotion, discount or agent bookings. **Valid till 1/1/2015**